Vanishing Cambridgeshire

Vanishing Cambridgeshire

MIKE PETTY MBE

Published in association
with the
Cambridge Antiquarian Society
and the
Cambridge Evening News

breedon **books**
PUBLISHING

First published in Great Britain in 2003 by
The Breedon Books Publishing Company Limited
Breedon House, 3 The Parker Centre,
Derby, DE21 4SZ.
Revised edition published 2006

ISBN 1 85983 532 5

Printed and bound by Cromwell Press, Trowbridge, Wiltshire.

CONTENTS

INTRODUCTION
THE SURVEY

IN 1904 the prestigious Cambridge Antiquarian Society embarked on an exciting new venture which was to see its members journey from the high chalklands of Ickleton to the fens of Whittlesey: *In view of the continual disappearance of interesting features in the country, through natural decay, accident, or wilful destruction, the Council have decided to undertake a photographic record of Cambridgeshire. A collection of permanent photographs of places and objects in Cambridgeshire will be formed and placed under suitable custody in a museum where it can be consulted for purposes of research, while a selection of the views will also be publicly exhibited from time to time.*

The Cambridge Antiquarian Society had been founded in 1840; its earliest purpose had been the study of the history and antiquities of the university, county and town of Cambridge and the collecting and printing of information relating thereto. But as Dr A.H. Lloyd recalled in his Presidential Address in October 1931: *It was soon found that the appetite of the community ranged beyond the local antiquarian and archaeological interests and the Society enlarged its declared objects to enable it to supply lectures upon those subjects relating to any part of the world.*

He explained: *Cambridge University at that time had no such lectures, but the Disney Professorship of Archaeology was founded in 1851 and Readership in Classical Archaeology in 1883 and the holders of these offices promoted lectures covering a world-wide range. After the First World War the creation of the Faculty of Archaeology and Ethnology and the establishment of a Tripos had largely relieved the*

Fenland near Whittlesey.

Society of the duty of bringing to Cambridge information regarding extraneous archaeology. The Society was free therefore to give increased attention to its more particular object of the study of local history and antiquities and it might well devote its energies intensively to the fulfilment of the ideals of its founders 90 years ago. [Cambridge Antiquarian Society Proceedings (PCAS), vol.33.]

The Photographic Survey owed its initial success to Dr Frank James Allen, a retired Professor of Physiology at Birmingham University, who became its first Secretary. He had a special interest in church towers and spires, contributing two papers on the subject in

High chalkland near Ickleton.

1909 and 1911, illustrating his lectures with lantern slides he had taken himself.

By 1906 the photographic record numbered 76 prints, 22 from Dr Allen, 20 from Scott and Wilkinson the commercial photographers and 17 presented by William Hayles, a carpenter who lived and worked in Union Road, New Town. Hayles was a member of the newly-formed Cambridge Photographic Club with whom the Antiquarian Society was co-operating. They sought prints of archival quality as the 1907 report commented: *Many of the amateur photographers have important negatives but since the owners do not use either of the permanent processes of photographic printing it has not been possible to obtain prints suitable for the record. Some hundreds exist and it would be worthwhile to ask owners to allow permanent prints to be made from them by a professional, the expense to be defrayed by a fund to which the Cambridge Antiquarian Society and the Cambridge Photographic Club might contribute.* The Record expanded its role, purchasing copies of some of the earliest street scenes of Cambridge taken by Arthur Nicholls in the 1860s.

Various displays were given to increase interest, but by 1909 Dr Allen was finding himself under pressure: *The Secretary, having been extremely busy during the past year had not been able to collect any new prints for the Record. He had however taken a number of negatives and several have been taken by other workers from which prints will be obtained in the near future. He hopes to arrange for an exhibition some time during the winter.* Others did not share his enthusiasm and many members of the Society met his appeals with indifference.

Photographic surveying, like much else, was severely disrupted by the outbreak of War in 1914 and Dr Allen took on the responsibility of Secretary to the Antiquarian Society itself, a post he held until 1931. Shortly afterwards he returned to his home town in Somerset leaving his photographs behind him in the Record he had established.

In 1925 the Cambridge Antiquarian Society revived the project, and determined to make a fresh attempt to obtain a representative photographic record of the county. An appeal was circulated to all members of the Society and to all people who were considered likely to be interested. It set forth the kind of pictures which it was proposed to collect, including buildings of every description, domestic and ecclesiastical, earthworks, bridges, industries both ancient and modern, ceremonies, flora & fauna.

They again sought the co-operation of the Cambridge Photographic Club, and a Joint Committee was appointed to set the work on foot. It comprised the Society's President (then Mr M.C. Burkitt), the Secretary, Mr J.H. Bullock, Dr Louis Cobbett, Dr William Mortlock Palmer & Dr H.P. Stokes while the Cambridge Photographic Club was represented by their President, Dr Robinson, and by Mr Parker Smith, Mr William Tams and one of the Secretaries, Mr R.T. Bellamy. Dr Palmer, who was a member of both bodies, was appointed Chairman, and Miss E.S. Fegan was subsequently elected as Secretary to the Committee.

At its first meeting the Committee outlined its objects:
(1) to create a permanent pictorial record of the Cambridge district.
(2) to draw up a list of subjects, representations of which should be included in such a regional survey.
(3) to collect, classify and store the collection.
(4) to house the collection in the University Museum of Archaeology and Ethnology, and to be accessible to members of both Societies.
(5) the Librarian of the Museum to be asked to be Curator of the collection.

There would be a card catalogue of the photographs with a duplicate catalogue at the Headquarters of the Photographic Club.

The active work of the Committee was to consist in taking, or causing to be taken, photographs; ascertaining the actual existence of

negatives and old prints, and causing photographs to be made from them. Both groups voted money to provide photographic paper. The prints were to be definitely only for record purposes, and copyright and right of reproduction could be reserved by the owners of negatives or prints.

They had soon collected 761 photographs and 75 negatives with many more promised. Half of them had been taken by one man, J.H. Bullock – *and how much more might be done with others of such calibre!* The Cambridge Photographic Club instituted a Photographic Record Class for its autumn exhibition, the photographs going automatically to swell the collection, and organised its summer excursions to promote the Record, photographing Duxford and Barrington one year, and targeting Balsham, Over, Swavesey, Toft and Whittlesford the next.

A selection of photographs was shown at Antiquarian Society meetings in the hope of making the aims of the Committee more generally realised and enlisting further support. Dr Palmer stimulated much interest in the work through lantern-lectures to the Cambridge Photographic Club and to the Cambridge Antiquarian Society and also addressed the Annual Meeting of the County Federation of Women's Institutes to appeal for their help in collecting material. He addressed the Summer meeting of the Royal Archaeological Institute in 1927, demonstrating how rich the county was in ancient and historic relics, a presentation interrupted with frequent applause.

Dr Palmer's ambition was to get a print of every cottage in Cambridgeshire worth looking at, or of interest for any reason. He appealed for members resident in the county to send in any prints they happened to possess. Pictures of past or present industries, such as those of the woad mill which had been donated by Sir R. Biffen, the flint-knapping industry, turf-cutting, and so on, should all find their place in such a collection as theirs ought to be.

A Sub-Committee was appointed to examine and select prints and negatives offered. By now the earlier insistence on top-quality photographs had been dropped; Palmer stressed that one need not be a great photographer in order to help on the photographic record and showed some of his own lantern slides, poor photographically, but important as records. They would accept any print, however bad, as long as it represented an object no longer in existence. They welcomed any size of print or negative, large or small, but preferred ½-plate or postcard size & he urged members to go to any village shop and buy as many different picture postcards of the village as they could – particularly those issued before the war.

Linton clapper stile.

It was one thing to take photographs, another to record what had been snapped. Care should be taken to be exact in the name of the village, street or place or to follow the example of Mr J.H. Bullock, who numbered his prints according to the number of the plot on which the building stood, as given in the large scale Ordnance Survey map. Sadly this example was seldom followed and many prints contain sketchy information as to where and when they were taken.

An appeal was made for volunteers to be responsible for whole villages and several were allocated. But the majority of the photographs were taken by a small core of enthusiasts who travelled out into the surrounding countryside on expeditions of exploration with their cameras and tripods. Dr Palmer and J.H. Bullock often travelled together, sometimes photographing one another at work and Douglas Reid's motor car, registration number EW 4131 finds its way into a number of the pictures. Together they journeyed from the high chalk lands of Ickleton to the fenland washes of Whittlesey and obtained pictures of virtually every village in Cambridgeshire.

The survey continued to expand; the report for 1936 acknowledging more than 700 prints from Mr J.H. Bullock, photographs and lantern slides from the late Dr A.H. Lloyd, photographs of Ely from Lady St John Hope, prints and negatives from Mr Brindley amongst others. It now contained over 5,400 prints, of which 907 had been given during the past year. Cambridge itself was now undergoing tremendous demolition and rebuilding but it was regretted they had no photographs of areas of Peas Hill, St Andrew's Hill and Petty Cury which would probably be redeveloped during the coming year.

Much of the work of accessioning had been undertaken by Dr Mary Scruby, who had tackled and cleared up difficult problems which had been shied at by her predecessors.

During 1938 the Record gained a further 404 prints, 7 watercolour sketches, 26 photostats and 117 negatives. A series of photographs of the old houses and yards on the west side of Bridge Street was given by Mr Bullock and many town and country views by Dr Cobbett. About 100 photographs of Great Chesterford were given by Mr G.H.S. Bushnell. The Society diversified by offering a prize for a water-colour sketch in the Borough of Cambridge; 12 entries were received and the prize went to Miss B. Pickering for a sketch of the junction of Fitzroy Street and Burleigh Street taken from the roof of Laurie and McConnal's Stores. The competition sketches and a series of 38 studies of the old Yards of Cambridge painted by Miss M.C. Greene were exhibited in the Museum of Archaeology and Ethnology and were visited by about 200 people.

The Record suffered a serious blow with the death of Dr William Mortlock Palmer in 1939. His energy had infused new life into the survey, and to his continued interest and exertions its success was mainly due, wrote CAS President Louis Cobbett, himself a major contributor to the survey.

The Report for 1942 shows that the Record grew steadily though slowly during wartime; prints, postcards and a watercolour sketch were received during the year. Mr G.H.S. Bushnell sent a series of prints of Ickleton and Hinxton churches and Miss K.M. Murray views of Oakington and Girton Churches. The total number of prints was now over 7,300 and new gifts were always welcomed.

But the appeal seems to have gone largely unanswered. Although a number of prints were submitted by Canon Bywaters in the 1950s the Photographic Record ceases to feature in the annual reports of the Cambridge Antiquarian Society until 1968–9 when the Librarian, J.G. Pollard noted that modest additions were still being made as the product of his own travels in the Shire. But wider coverage was desirable and he appealed for colour transparencies, the modern equivalent of the lantern slides of the start of the century.

Subsequently the Cambridge Antiquarian Society's Photographic Record was transferred from the Museum; the glass lantern slides were deposited at the County Record Office, Shire Hall. The prints were lodged in the Cambridgeshire Collection in the new Lion Yard Library, together with an extensive collection of negatives, many of which have never been printed. Both collections have been listed and indexed and have been scanned for this current selection of photographs.

Vanished shops in Bridge Street, Cambridge.

THE PHOTOGRAPHERS

MORE THAN 150 contributors are recorded in the annual reports of the Photographic Survey, including a number of ladies. Some people donated single postcards, others covered a group of parishes while Mrs F.L. Harlock bequeathed a large number of glass negatives of Ely dating back to the 1860s, one of several such donations of that city.

Frank James Allen

Frank Allen first came to Cambridge as an undergraduate at St John's College in 1875. The son of a cheese dealer from Shepton Mallet he obtained a First Class degree and went on to further training at St George's Hospital London before becoming Professor of Physiology at Birmingham University from 1887–99. He then returned to Cambridge and joined the Cambridge Antiquarian Society where in 1904 he became secretary to the new Photographic Record.

Allen was an expert on church towers and spires, contributing two papers on the subject in 1909 and 1911 illustrating his lectures with his own lantern slides. In 1914 he took on the responsibility of Secretary to the Cambridge Antiquarian Society itself, a post he held until 1931. Shortly afterwards he returned back to his hometown in Somerset leaving his photographs behind him in the Record he had established.

James Henry Bullock

James Henry Bullock was a Cambridge man, born in Wheeler Street in October 1862. He attended the Perse School and Trinity College before making a career as a printer and a reputation as a Town Councillor with special interest in education. He joined the Cambridge Antiquarian Society and served on its Council, acted as Excursions Secretary and gave much advice on the editing of the Society's 'Proceedings'.

He was one of the Executive Committee when in 1925 the Society decided to revive their Photographic Record. He became its most prolific contributor, taking care to annotate his pictures with details of date and place. On his death in 1949 his widow presented the Society with a large collection of prints and negatives which comprise the backbone of the survey.

J.H. Bullock at work, Stuntney.

Frederick James Bywaters

Canon F.J. Bywaters was a vicar who served the parishes of Haddenham, Sawston and Willingham between 1926 and 1964 when he retired to live in Trumpington until his death a few years later.

He contributed to the Photographic Record during the middle 1950s. Although most of his photographs show churches there are a number of mills and cottages that caught his eye. He also bequeathed a collection of historic photographs of Willingham.

Louis Cobbett (1862–1947)

Dr Louis Cobbett was a distinguished pathologist and bacteriologist. He attended Trinity College and became House Surgeon at St Thomas' Hospital in London. He returned to Cambridge in 1892 and became demonstrator of pathology for a year. In 1900 Cambridge was faced with a serious outbreak of diphtheria of which Cobbett produced detailed studies and in 1902 he was appointed scientific investigator to the Royal Commission on Tuberculosis. From 1906–7 he was Professor of Pathology in the University of Sheffield and in 1908 appointed Professor of Pathology at Cambridge University, a post he held until 1929.

Cobbett was an enthusiastic and prolific contributor to the Photographic Record, travelling throughout the county and around the town. He also found time to pursue his interest in the history of the Cambridge area with papers on Saxon grave stones, Ickleton church, Duxford and Ely. He served as President of the Cambridge Antiquarian Society in 1939.

Cambridge market by Louis Cobbett.

Charles Harold Evelyn-White (1850–1938)

Charles Harold Evelyn-White was appointed Rector of Rampton in 1893, a post he held for 37 years, during which he transformed the building. He was a noted antiquarian and a prolific writer – including one book on Cambridgeshire churches compiled when he was 61 years old which involved him in a great deal of cycling – and was editor of the 'East Anglian, or Notes and Queries'. However he fell out with the Cambridge Antiquarian Society in 1900 and set up another – the Cambs & Hunts Archaeological Society which he ran almost single handed for six years, although he still contributed various pictures to the Photographic Survey. In 1930 he retired to Felixstowe but was brought back to Rampton for burial eight years later.

Henry Castree Hughes

Henry C. Hughes was an architect with a passion for windmills, lecturing on the subject to the Cambridge Antiquarian Society in

November 1928. At that time the sight of numerous fen drainage mills were still fresh in people's memory. Two of them still stood, a small one at Wicken fen and a large mill at nearby Soham Mere. This latter was owned by Cambridgeshire County Council though Hughes' hope that this might be preserved for posterity were to be dashed when the 'dangerous structure' was subsequently destroyed by dynamite.

Other mills were disappearing year by year, the long periods of idleness caused by a lack of wind allied to developments in other forms of milling were making the antiquated machinery uneconomic to work and repair, though some were being preserved as museum pieces.

Hughes went on to survey the existing Cambridgeshire windmills, touring the county taking photographs of several of the surviving monuments of a bygone age which he added to the Antiquarian Society's Photographic Survey where they are filed in a separate sequence along with others taken by enthusiasts.

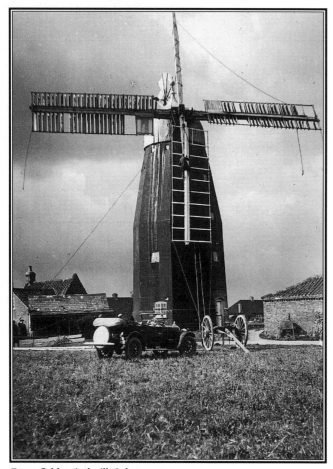

Downfields windmill, Soham.

Herbert Samuel Johnson 1881–1971

Herbert Johnson started his career as a craftsman with Bell and Son of Gloucester Street, setting up his own business just after the Great War in the loft of a two-storey wooden building in Emery Road, where he was joined by Mr C. Bailey to found 'Johnson & Bailey'. They moved to Norfolk Street and later Coldham's Lane becoming by his death in 1971 one of Cambridge's 'big five' building firms.

Herbert Johnson was also an enthusiastic photographer who amassed a copious library of Cambridge scenes which had changed during his lifetime. A few of these he contributed to the Cambridge Antiquarian Society's photographic record in 1930. They are in the form of stereoscopic prints, producing a 3-D effect when seen through a viewer. His subjects ranged widely from street scenes of Petty Cury, Market Hill and Sidney Street to derelict cottages at Cherry Hinton. He also photographed Midsummer Fair in 1929

including 'The world's fattest girl' where he snapped the shutter moments after the showman had exhibited to the crowd 'one of the lady's more intimate garments of enormous size'.

H.S. Johnson.

William Mortlock Palmer 1866–1939

William Mortlock Palmer was born in 1866 at Meldreth. In 1881 he was apprenticed to Alderman Campkin, chemist of Rose Crescent, working 13 hours a day making millions of sticky brown pills and selling penn'orths of hair oil before sneaking off to the Public Library in Wheeler Street to pursue other researches. Palmer entered Charing Cross Hospital as a student chemist and developed his knowledge of medicine before taking an appointment of ship's surgeon with the P & O Navigation Company. During the long days at sea he devoted himself to Cambridgeshire local history, compiling the first of his many publications. In 1900 he settled as the village doctor for Linton and the surrounding villages, journeying many miles on horse, dog cart, bicycle and later a somewhat erratic motor car, often taking antiques in payment for services rendered, until his retirement in 1925. Somehow he made time to continue his local history studies and lectures publishing numerous articles in a variety of magazines, newspapers and journals. He became an MD of Durham in 1907 and in 1935 was awarded an Honorary MA degree by the University of Cambridge.

Dr W.M. Palmer (left) at Burwell Castle excavation.

When the Cambridge Antiquarian Society relaunched its photographic record in 1925, Palmer's energy and drive was instrumental in ensuring its success. He commissioned Linton photographer Edgar Morley to accompany him on his travels around the county and bought his own camera with which he took many pictures of Linton, Melbourn, Meldreth, Shepreth, Kingston and other villages. His snaps may not match the technical quality of many of his contemporaries but nevertheless constitute a unique record of the area. He died in 1939 and the Photographic Survey ceased soon afterwards.

Douglas Gavin Reid 1881–1934

A distinguished graduate of Edinburgh University Douglas Reid spent over 30 years as a demonstrator at the Cambridge School of Anatomy. He was devoted to his work and the author of several authoritative medical books. But it is as a photographer of the fenland landscape that he is perhaps best remembered.

Amongst the photographs belonging to the Cambridge Antiquarian Society are a series of boxes of negatives taken between 1929 and 1934. They record areas of the fenland taken when he was resident at Grange Road, Cambridge and – apparently – driving a convertible motor car registration number EW 4131 which finds its way into some of the photographs. A reliable vehicle would have been essential to journey to many of the far-flung areas otherwise inaccessible. On one expedition he came across a group of gypsy caravans on Turf fen, between Chatteris and Doddington which provided him with some interesting snaps. On another occasion he came across flooding near Whittlesey with water right across the road with only pollarded willows and telegraph poles serving to mark the route. His fenland photographs are a unique record of the area.

Douglas Reid's car at Fleam Dyke.

Percy R. Salmon, 1872–1959

Percy R. Salmon was a photographic prodigy. The son of a Cambridge policeman he started photography as a hobby as a lad of 12 and in 1891 won the Cambridge Camera Club cup for the best set of five photographs taken in and around the town. Later he studied in Paris and travelled the world with his camera, contributing to nearly all the English and American newspapers and magazines. Many awards were to follow. He became a Fellow of the Royal Photographic Society in 1898 and an Honorary Member in 1947, 20 years after he had retired to live in Melbourn. There his interest in photography continued with many lantern lectures illustrated by his views, and his journalist skills were exercised as village correspondent for the 'Cambridge Independent Press'. Amongst his many writings was a contribution to the 1911 edition of *Country Home* in which he turned his attention to various Cambridgeshire cottages.

Percy Salmon died in August 1959 at the age of 87. As well as his contributions to the Photographic Survey many of his other lantern slides and negatives have been deposited in the Cambridgeshire Collection

Melbourn fruit cart by Percy Salmon

William Tams

William Tams played cricket on Parker's Piece with the famous Hayward Brothers, Tom and Dan; as a young man he became butler to the Master of St John's College. But he is remembered for the hobby that became his business – photography. About 1905 he published a series of postcard views of Cambridge that are as clear and crisp today as they were when first produced. By 1912 he had established himself as a professional photographer & became official photographer to the University of Cambridge, taking college pictures and photographs of documents. In 1916 he was elected President of the Cambridge Photographic Club to whom he lectured on technical subjects as well as regaling them with his account of a visit to a coal mine and by 1938 was producing colour transparencies. Tams represented the Club on the Photographic Survey committee and contributed some of his postcard views.

Rex Wailes 1901–1986

Rex Wailes started his lifetime's work in 1923 when as an engineering apprentice in Lincoln he was approached to undertake a survey of the county's windmills. Two years later he joined the Newcomen Society for the Study of the History of Engineering and Technology and was encouraged to collect and collate data and make photographic records of the interiors as well as the exteriors of mills. It was in that year that Wailes photographed Cambridgeshire windmills with views of Fulbourn, Willingham & Soham being his first to be added to the Cambridge Antiquarian Society's survey. More followed next year. In 1950 he contributed an article on the Cambridgeshire mills to the Newcomen Society's Transactions followed four years later by his best-known book *The English Windmill*. By then the Society for the Protection of Ancient Buildings had formed a Windmill section to which he became honorary technical adviser.

By his death in 1986 he was acclaimed as the most distinguished man of his time in the study of windmills and watermills, both nationally and internationally.

THE TOPICS

Cambridge Town 1904–1942

In February 1924 a committee of the Cambridge Antiquarian Society drew up a list of topics to be covered. Cambridge pictures were to be arranged in various categories.

River Cam: boathouses, boatyards, ferries and bridges

In 1904 some commercial river trade still plied to Cambridge, with timber and other products offloaded at Quayside until 1914, and deliveries to the Gas Works on Riverside continuing until 1933. The sporting and recreational use of the river increased with a rapid rise

Jesus Lock. c.1905.

in the number of College boathouses whilst the introduction of punts in 1906 was a great success, by 1907 every boatyard possessed a flotilla. Throughout the 1920s new footbridges were erected in place of the chain ferries that plied across the river to Chesterton. Increased motor traffic led to a new Fen Causeway Bridge, but plans for another crossing to Newmarket Road and a wider Magdalene Bridge did not materialise.

Churches

The survey includes a photograph of the spire of Holy Trinity Church, wreathed in scaffolding, which an intrepid photographer climbed up

Holy Trinity Church.

to survey central Cambridge. Elsewhere St Clement's Church lost its spire in 1928 and St Peter's Church had to be underpinned to stop it falling down in 1932. A number of nonconformist churches were erected, demolished or rebuilt. Those photographed include exterior and interior views of St Andrew's Street Baptist Chapel before its demolition in 1903 and the Hobson Street Methodist Chapel which was sold for a new County Hall in 1912.

Inns

Amongst the inns that were closed were the Three Tuns on Castle Hill and the True Blue which was demolished to provide a site for the new Dorothy Ballroom. The Jolly Millers at Newnham was rebuilt but the Eagle & Little Rose survived largely unchanged.

The Jolly Millers.

St Clement's Workhouse.

Interiors of houses, inns etc

The most interesting picture in this category was taken by H.P. Stokes in 1912 of the inside of St Clement's workhouse on Castle Hill. The decorated ceiling at 5 Market Hill and an ancient fireplace discovered during the demolition of an old house on the corner of Petty Cury were also recorded.

Celebrations – fairs etc

The thrills of the fairground attracted various photographers and earlier pictures show the Midsummer Horse Fair, but nobody seems to have covered the Stourbridge Fair before its abolition in 1934. There are various pictures of streets decorated for coronations, of Good Friday skipping on Parker's Piece, and of the bonfire erected on Midsummer Common to celebrate the Relief of Mafeking, which was taken in

Mafeking bonfire.

1900 by F.G. Binnie and printed by J. Johnson 31 years later.

Mills – wind and water

The Kings and Bishops Mill on Mill Pool was photographed before and after its demolition in 1928, and the survey includes photographs of the windmills on Milton Road and French's Road.

Streets, roads and lanes

Cambridge underwent a period of massive rebuilding throughout the period under review and this is by far the largest category of photographs. Members of the Society recorded many of the changes, with special emphasis on the Bridge Street and Castle Hill areas. There is also a survey of barber's shops by Louis Cobbett which includes one in King Street, 1939.

King Street barber.

Yards and courts

Cambridge had numerous small yards and courts which providing homes for townsfolk, including Trinity Place in King Street.

Cambridge University ceremonies, museums and laboratories

The Photographic Survey contains few photographs of University ceremonies, official occasions or laboratories.

Trinity Place.

Cambridge University colleges

Although there are a number of boxes of unprinted negatives there are comparatively few university or college views.

Cambridgeshire Subjects

Cambridgeshire pictures cover a number of subjects.

1 Churches and other places of worship
The survey includes photographs of most parish churches including the interior of West Wickham church before its restoration in 1898 and Croydon church before its extensive restoration in 1937. Some churches such as Great Abington and Heydon were damaged by bombs during World War Two. By 1947 Duxford St John was in such an advanced state of decay that the rector petitioned for its demolition whilst Wendy church was demolished in 1950. Ickleton was damaged by fire in 1979 when Cambridge Antiquarian Society photographs were used to aid the restoration. Nonconformist chapels at Cottenham and Kingston are featured.

St Wendreda's Church, March.

2 Monastic buildings
Amongst the monastic buildings surveyed were Duxford Priory Chapel, Swaffham Bulbeck Abbey, The Bishop's Palace, Little Downham and the buildings of St John's Hospital at Ely, whilst Isleham Priory was being used as a store for farm carts.

Priory barn, Isleham.

3 Houses
The survey includes photographs of a large number of significant buildings that have been lost including Lordship Manor, Cottenham, demolished 1937, Rookery House Hildersham – its bricks used for a barn in 1868, and Cardinal's Manor Horseheath which was derelict and demolished in 1924. Other properties have been restored including Nine Chimneys Balsham, Croxton Manor House, Elsworth Manor, Papworth St Agnes Manor and Fortrey Hall, Mepal.

Crumbling cottages, Conington.

Cottages and barns
Virtually every village surveyed includes photographs of thatched cottages and barns in a derelict state, an indication of the poverty of the inter-war years.

4 General views of streets
Although the majority of the photographs are of individual properties the survey also includes more general views of village streets.

High Street, Mepal.

5 Village greens
The greens at Ashley, Barrington, West Wickham and Wicken are included.

6 Watermills and windmills
There are numerous photographs in these categories; some watermills such as Grantchester, Shepreth and Sawston were

Topcliffe's Mill, Meldreth.

Haymakers at Hildersham.

destroyed by fire, others such as Lode have been restored from a derelict condition.

Windmills were the subject of a special survey which includes pictures of virtually every mill in the county. They are filed in a separate sequence, kept in the Cambridgeshire Collection in Lion Yard Library.

7 Dovecotes, sundials, stocks and pounds

This heading could be expanded to cover a wide range of structures, including fire engine houses, lockups, pumps and wells, milestones, mazes and memorials.

8 Ancient earthworks, Roman Roads and ancient trackways

The Proceedings of the Cambridge Antiquarian Society are the county's major record of archaeological excavations, with many photographs and drawings of artefacts and finds. The Photographic Survey however contains comparatively few photographs of digs or archaeological sites; my selection includes photographs of Aldreth causeway, Bartlow Hills and the Devils Dyke at Reach.

9 Old customs and ceremonies

Fairs and feasts were an important part of country life and those at Ely, Royston and Reach are illustrated; the traditional picking of peas at Sawston features as do the words of the Whaddon Whitsun song and a very rare photograph of Comberton Maze.

10 Rural occupations

The photographs depict a wealth of bakers, blacksmiths, builders, garages, pubs, shops, wheelwrights and farmers. It includes rod peeling (Willingham), peat digging (Wicken), watercress beds (Fowlmere), woad-making (Parson Drove) and the fruit carrier from Melbourn.

11 Characteristic landscapes

Members of the Society travelled from the high chalklands of Ickleton to the flooded fenland at Whittlesey – an area extensively covered by Douglas Gavin Reed.

12 Notable trees

Melbourn elm tree where in 1640 villagers gathered to oppose a new tax, and Stetchworth May Day Tree where villagers gathered for more peaceful purposes were amongst those recorded.

13 Fords and bridges

Hinxton ford was an attraction to children but for others crossing a river was a serious task. To cater for increasing motor traffic new bridges were built at Earith, Mepal, Stretham and Twentypence, where the ferry was replaced as part of a major new road linking Cottenham and Wilburton.

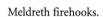

Meldreth firehooks.

THE CAPTIONS

MOST OF those who actually took the pictures recorded such details as they knew, or could remember, on the back of the photographs; but some did not. Their notes, together with any additional details in the card catalogue, or on the boxes of negatives, form part of my description. Some of the pictures were published in the Cambridge Antiquarian Society Proceedings or in newspaper articles, and in more recent times other local historians have incorporated copies of the photographs in their work. Members of the Cambridgeshire Local History Society have also repeated the Antiquarian's Survey for many villages, identifying the site and taking modern equivalent pictures. I have incorporated any such information in my descriptions.

I have also sought out reminiscences or village histories that give an insight into the community at that time, including many articles appearing in the *Cambridge Daily News*. The text in italics is based on the sources indicated, all of which are held in the Cambridgeshire Collection at Lion Yard Library, Cambridge. I have yet to meet anybody who can identify the location of every photograph taken by the photographers over 60 years ago. Inevitably there will be mistakes, for which I apologise, and I would be grateful for any assistance in correcting them. Please contact me via my website: www.cambridgeshirehistory.com/MikePetty

The current selection is only a fraction of what the Cambridge Antiquarian Society's survey compiled. For every one picture reproduced there will be at least a dozen more – pictures of your village or perhaps your house. I am grateful to Dr John Pickles, Librarian of the Cambridge Antiquarian Society, Dr Philip Saunders of the Cambridgeshire County Record Office and Christopher Jakes of the Cambridgeshire Collection for their help in the selection and identification of the pictures, and to my wife for her infinite patience and assistance in the many hours it has all taken.

The Society's collection of over 2,700 glass lantern slides may be consulted at the Cambridgeshire County Record Office at Shire Hall, Castle Hill, Cambridge. The files of photographs and thousands of unprinted negatives are housed in the Cambridgeshire Collection at the Central Library, 7 Lion Yard, Cambridge, who would welcome modern equivalent views.

For more information on the Cambridge Antiquarian Society please write to The Secretary, Cambridge University Museum of Archaeology and Anthropology, Downing Street, Cambridge, CB2 3DZ.

For this revised edition I have taken the opportunity to amend several of the original captions to incorporate additional information and to update some of the information.

I have also included two completely new sections to reflect the special surveys made of the Cambridgeshire and Lincolnshire fenland by Douglas Gavin Reid and of Cambridgeshire windmills by a group of enthusiasts including Rex Wailes and H.C. Hughes

Mike Petty
April 2006

INTRODUCTION TO THE REVISED EDITION

FOR THIS revised edition I have taken the opportunity to amend several of the original captions to incorporate additional information and to update some of the information.

I have also included two completely new sections to reflect the special surveys made of the Cambridgeshire and Lincolnshire fenland by Douglas Gavin Reid and of Cambridgeshire windmills by a group of enthusiasts including Rex Wailes and H.C. Hughes.

Boats on Wicken Lode – July 1929 (Photograph: D.G. Reid)

Market Hill – fountain, 1938. *Cambridge can show few livelier prospects than her Market-place as seen on some sunny Saturday in early summer. The spacious square and tall church tower, the wide array of canvas-covered booths, the blocked streets, and the gay and good-humoured throng crowding through every available space amidst shouting hawkers, heaped-up flower stalls, pyramids of country produce and the decrepit vans of village carriers, form a scene which for brilliance and vivacity recalls rather the air of a continental town than that of the seat of a sober English University. [A.B. Gray. Cambridge Revisited. 1921].* It was a scene that Louis Cobbett set out to capture for the Cambridge Antiquarian Society's Photographic Record in 1938. Dominating the centre of the Market Square was an ornate fountain that had replaced the old Hobson's Conduit in 1856 following a fire that had swept the area. Those buildings not razed to the ground had been removed to create the square market place we know today. The fountain proved a magnet for undergraduate climbers during numerous 'rags' and bonfires but by 1953 the stonework was in poor condition and the ornate canopy was removed. Some of the stone figures were placed in the Folk Museum, leaving the base of the fountain in situ. (Photograph: L. Cobbett)

Market Hill – David's Bookstall. David's Bookstall was a prominent feature of the Market Place. David himself became such a character that the University offered him an Honorary Degree and when he died in 1936 the University Press produced a little book of appreciation. The high-spot of the week was on Saturday morning when the new supply of books was put on display; Lord Keynes, as an undergraduate, was so keen on having a preview that he used to help David unpack the books on Friday night. In 1911 a quarter of the 250 stalls were removed and the roads around the square widened to cater for increased motor traffic.

Market Hill, north side – Rose Crescent, *c.*1930. Rose Crescent, formerly the Rose and Crown Yard, had been previously redeveloped in the 1820s. In 1935 S.C. Roberts lamented the changes to Bacon's Tobacconist's shop: *Apart from certain alterations to the frontage in 1894 Bacon's shop differed little from the days of its founder. It is therefore with a tinge of regret for things past that one looks upon the new premises, since although the inside of the store still contains many relicts of bygone days, the march of progress has precluded any serious attempt to reproduce the old style of the exterior. Nevertheless, consolation may be sought in the fact that this is now one of the finest tobacco stores of its kind in the kingdom.* Bacons closed in 1984. (Photograph: *Cambridge Chronicle*)

Market Hill, *c*.1890. Much of the north side of Market Hill was rebuilt by Gonville and Caius College in 1934, part of a massive redevelopment of central Cambridge that was transforming the town. Not everybody approved: *Everywhere the house-breakers are busy, College purses are swollen as old leases fall in. When the purse is full the rest is simple. Round comes the concrete-mixers, along come the steel girders, and up goes another white-faced box. Cambridge has seen Gonville and Caius pull down one side of the Market Square and watches the new buildings go up with some uneasiness.* [*Morning Post*, April 1935] (Photograph: W. Tams)

Market Hill – Macintosh's ironmonger's shop. William Macintosh began trading as a coppersmith in Market Street in 1816 and became an ironmonger in 1845. He moved to Market Hill in 1884 occupying premises that had been an ironmonger's shop since 1688. The front was set back and the whole shop refitted in 1901. They sold stoves, grates, cast-iron chimney pieces, wood mantel pieces, cast iron portable boilers and a range of other commodities. The business went into voluntary liquidation in 1962. [K. Alger, Cambridge iron founders, 1996]

Market Hill – south side, *c*.1901. The south side of Market Hill also underwent major redevelopment in the 1930s. The old Guildhall, its large hall catching the light, was used for a range of events from civic receptions and stately balls to political meetings, though those who attended an advertised lecture on spiritualism by Sir Arthur Conan Doyle were disappointed when he failed to materialise. Proposals to rebuild it had been rejected in 1897 but were revived in 1928. The tall buildings on the corner of Peas Hill were pulled down and the first stage of the new Guildhall completed; then the old Guildhall was demolished and rebuilt. The scheme was completed in 1939 but never formally opened due to the imminence of World War Two. (Photograph: H. Pain)

Peas Hill – east side, 1930. As the buildings on the east side of Peas Hill were pulled down they were discovered to be 18th-century timber-framed houses, and one had been the residence of a well-to-do Tudor merchant. R.C. Lambeth traced its history: *Number 17 was the oldest house and stood in front of the oldest part of the Guildhall from which it was divided by an old right of way. In Queen Anne's time its old timber frame was hidden behind a dummy front, dummy bricks were nailed on over the plaster frontage and the lower storey was carried out level with the upper. The bottom of the high-pitched roof was curved in the fashionable way and false eaves attached. It was a butcher's shop, then a booksellers and a club.* There were hopes that the building itself would be saved: *It will rise again for Mr Colin Clark, who lived there in its last days, is to have it re-erected on another site. The ancient oak timbers have been taken down, numbered and laid aside until they are ready to go to their new home. Most are as solid as when they were put up in the 15th or 16th century.* [*Cambridge Standard* 29 March 1935] (Photograph: F.G. Turner)

Peas Hill – east side, fire 1904. In 1904 fire destroyed Bell's large granary on the corner of Peas Hill and Wheeler Street and rats fled across the street. In 1915 two cottages in Wheeler Street were swept away and the corner premises set back making the Bell Inn protrude prominently. New offices were built for the Council Education Department and were later used by the public library. The fish stalls stood there every Saturday until the outbreak of war in 1939. (Photograph: T. Hayles)

Peas Hill – yard behind the Arts Theatre, 1937. John Saltmarsh traced the history of the buildings on Peas Hill: *The aristocrat of Peas Hill is undoubtedly No.6. Its modern front hides a tall old house and a wing at the back with a curious cruciform tiled roof and a picturesque gable with carved wooden ornaments. 'In this house', wrote Blomefield, 'I saw a picture of Samuel Spalding, town-clerk of Cambridge, and another of Francis, his daughter, in her winding sheet: this child being young went into a garret in a remote part of the house, and the door shutting upon it, it was there starved to death'. One of the attics in No.6 has an evil reputation still, and ghostly fingers are sometimes heard to tap on the window.* [J. Saltmarsh, Peas Hill – Cambridge Review, 7 June 1935] (Photograph: L. Cobbett)

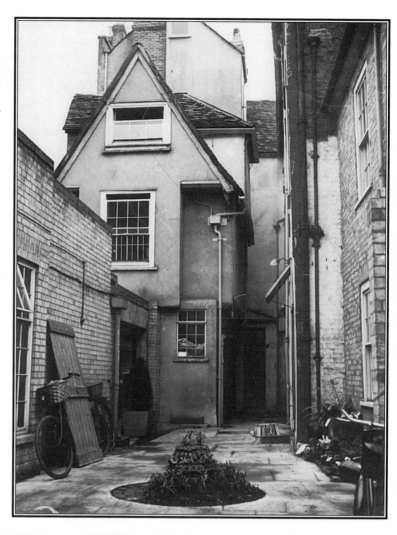

Peas Hill – west side 1935. Saltmarsh continued: *The buildings on the frontage were all ancient; No.2, lately Fletcher's the butcher's consisted of three floors of low mean rooms above the shop, arranged round a central winding staircase. All had been derelict for many years; their condition had to be seen to be believed, and the seeing was attended with some personal risk. No.3, lately Shrive's, was roomy and rambling; built around a massive chimneystack. It had been reconditioned in relatively recent times. The Sugar and Spice coffee house, one in appearance, is really two separate cottages, Nos.4 & 5; its low social status seems to have saved it from white brick, and its tiled roof and little dormer windows will remain permanent ornaments of the College hostel.* (Photograph: J. Baldwin)

Peas Hill – the Central Hotel, 1936. The Central Temperance Hotel on the north side of St Edward's Passage was demolished in 1959, despite widespread protest, to be replaced by a hostel for King's College. The Central Hotel was the last property to be operated by the Cambridge University and Town Coffee Palace Company set up on temperance lines to supply the needs of workmen, cabmen, market gardeners, artisans and others in an effort to attract custom from the gin palaces and public houses. They had also run the Norfolk Hotel, Hills Road, the George and Dragon, Newmarket Road, the White Ribbon, East Road and Mill Road Coffee Tavern. (Photograph: M. Murray)

Market Hill, east side – London & North-Eastern Railway office, c.1930. The oldest building on Market Hill is No.5, a timber-framed structure faced with modern tile-hanging which was probably built in the 17th century. It was occupied by the London and North Eastern Railway Company and later by Thomas Cook, the travel agents. On the first floor there is a magnificent plaster ceiling dating back to 1688, believed to be the work of Henry Doogood who was employed on Christopher Wren's London churches. In the white building alongside a cinema called the Electric Theatre opened in 1911; it was renamed the Victoria in 1915 and moved to a new site near the corner of Market Street in 1931.

Market Hill, east side – Coronation celebrations, 1902. The east side of Market Hill decorated for the coronation of King Edward VII in August 1902. The original Coronation date had to be postponed owing to the King's illness. The dominant building of Hallack and Bond's grocery shop at the corner of Petty Cury was erected in the 1890s. It replaced one of the oldest domestic properties in Cambridge, built about 1538 by a grocer named John Veysy. Hallack and Bond continued to trade until 1927. (Photograph: E.C. Hoppett)

Market Hill, east side – Veysy House fireplace. A number of stone fireplaces were discovered during the demolition of the Veysy house. One was incorporated in Hallack and Bond's shop during rebuilding and another was placed in the old Free Library, now the Tourist Information Bureau in Wheeler Street. (Photograph: Scott & Wilkinson)

Petty Cury decorated for the Coronation of King George VI 1937. Petty Cury was made a one-way street in 1925 *with the object of relieving congestion in these streets whose narrowness has ever been the subject of discussion.* [CDN 19 January 1925] But parking remained a problem: *Sir – When will something be done about the disgraceful state of the traffic in Petty Cury. On Saturday there were 15 large cars parked from Sidney Street to Guildhall Street, and as prams and mail carts can only use the sidewalks, pedestrians who venture on the street are taking serious risks of getting knocked down. Truly a street only fit for the quick or the dead – W.M.F.* [CDN 30 July 1947] It was here that closed-circuit television made its world debut: *Traffic scenes on Market Hill were televised to the Accident Prevention Exhibition in the Corn Exchange. 'Closed-circuit' as it is called is the latest development of the Cambridge firm of Pye Ltd. Two cameras were operated, one fixed to the balcony of the Guildhall and the other on top of a van at the corner of Petty Cury. Along this narrow, one-way street, between 8am and 6pm approximately 7,000 bicycles and 2,000 other vehicles pass each weekday.* [CDN 26 November 1948] It was to be 1972 before pedestrianisation came. (Photograph: J. Baldwin)

Petty Cury demolition on the corner of Sidney Street, 1938. Much of the south side of Petty Cury had been redeveloped by the Victorians, the changes lamented by historians such as W.B. Redfarn in his *Old Cambridge* published in 1876. But fewer people recorded the large-scale redevelopment of the north side that took place in the 1930s for a new Boots the Chemist store. Boots has traded in Petty Cury for over a century: *A stroll through Petty Cury, Cambridge and a glance at the shop windows of Boots Limited gives a good idea of the effort which this firm has made to cater for all tastes and all classes. Those desirous of purchasing suitable presents for their cousins, their aunts, and sweethearts should pay a visit to Boots, in the Cury* [CDN 17 December 1898] (Photograph: J. Johnson)

Petty Cury, south side – Heffer's Bookshop. William Heffer opened his bookshop in Petty Cury in 1896 having bought out a chemist whose stock he sold off, but the giant bottles were to remain in the windows up till 1922. *On the day that war broke out, 1914, the Oak-Room-and-Gallery was opened, stretching backwards where the Lion's stables had stood. As the shop expanded upstairs into the rest of the building it retained mementoes: the wallpaper was that of the university lodgings, while bedroom 40, renamed The Science Room, still sported a chandelier. In 1928 the shop expanded into adjacent premises and a new frontage, designed by Arthur Heffer was installed.* [H. Bosanquet, Walks round vanished Cambridge: Petty Cury, 1974] The firm moved to Trinity Street in 1970 and the building was demolished as part of the Lion Yard redevelopment that saw the clearance of the south side of Petty Cury and the lanes and alleys beyond. Had the Antiquarian Society photographers realised the extent of the demolition that was to occur they may have devoted more of their plates to the area.

Lion Hotel yard, 1935. The back entrance to the yard of the Lion Hotel with St Tibbs Row on the right. A reporter commented: *On market days its spacious yard resounded to the echo of hundreds of hooves and of the wheels of carts and carriages. Today its yards are now filled with cars, and the stables are no longer required.* The former courtyard was roofed over and became the hotel lounge: *Omnibuses used to drive over what is now the floor of the court; in fact it was used by traffic up to 1907.* For more than 80 years, up to its sale in 1938, the Lion Hotel had been in the Moyes family. Mrs A.A. Moyes had built up its reputation: *Her charming, pleasant nature was well-known by countless visitors. Many commercial travellers remembered how, even if they only visited the hotel twice a year in the course of their rounds, Mrs Moyes could take up a conversation practically where it had been left off and could recall the details they had told her of their family life. Undergraduates had a great respect for her; even during the liveliest of moments she was able to quell impending trouble; her appeals to the lively ones not to put her out of business invariably resulted in quietness being restored.* [CDN, 1936] She died in 1922, leaving the hotel to her daughters. The hotel closed in 1963 and was demolished for the Lion Yard redevelopment. (Photograph: L. Cobbett)

St Andrew's Hill – St Andrew the Great workhouse, 1911. Amongst the jumble of buildings south of Petty Cury was the old parish workhouse of St Andrew the Great in St Tibbs Row. It was erected about 1829 and after Poor Law reform in 1836 was used for the reception of about 30 married couples and aged women. It was sold two years later when it was bought by a shoeing smith and, with some alterations, was still standing in 1911. [H.P. Stokes, Cambridge parish workhouses, 1911 – PCAS vol.15] (Photograph: H.P. Stokes)

St Andrew's Hill, 1937. As the number of cars increased a garage was established at the junction of Corn Exchange Street in a building that had originally been the Corn Exchange and then become the Arcade music hall; its name has been revived in the Grand Arcade shopping development. The rear of the old Arcade can be seen on the right looking across to houses at the corner of St Tibbs Row. A jumble of streets and yards, the properties were gradually swept away. (Photograph: J. Baldwin)

Pembroke Street, 1937. University laboratories were opened on the south side of Downing Street by King Edward VII in 1904, after which there was a student rag of such exuberance that Metropolitan Police had to be brought in to control the situation. Zoological laboratories on the New Museums site, north of Downing Street were erected in the 1930s. Amongst the traders in Pembroke Street 1937 were a print seller, tobacconist, tailor, boot maker and typewriter agent, but there was also a saddler and motor engineer, one of many catering for an increasing number of cars. (Photograph: L. Cobbett)

Pembroke Street, *c*.1904. Pembroke Street had been home to cars at the beginning of the century. The Humber Cycle Supply Company, which had its main premises in Regent Street, was one of four motor companies in 1904. The first motor car in Cambridge had been owned by an undergraduate, the Honourable C.S. Rolls in 1897; it was a 4-seater Peugeot that had to be preceded by a man with a red flag. After the abolition of the Red Flag Act Rolls imported a De Dion tricycle complete with a French mechanic. When it broke down he sought assistance from Mr King and Mr Harper who specialised in making bicycles, and they repaired it. King and Harper then built their own tricycle, which they converted to a four-wheeler to allow passengers to be carried. It was exhibited at the 1902 Crystal Palace Motor Show where it won a Gold Medal. The number of cars increased from 27 in January 1904 to 42 that April, when there were 202 licensed drivers. All this caused difficulties in Cambridge streets: *A few years ago the problem was bikes, now the real terror is the motor car & motor bike scorching by at 30-40 mph.* [CDN 25 June 1904] By 1905 it was considered *Doubtful if any town of similar size has as many motors and motorcycles running about the streets as Cambridge in term time* and the problem was exacerbated by speeding undergraduates, one crashed into a cow in Victoria Avenue [CDN 20 May 1905]. Cambridge had truly entered the motoring age.

Trumpington Street – snow 26 December 1906. The Fitzwilliam Museum dominates a largely unchanged scene. World War Two presented the Museum with particular problems: *The collections had to be packed and removed in 1939 to places of safety as remote as Wales and Cornwall where they remained until they could be gradually brought back to Cambridge six years later. The Museum itself and those of its possessions too frail to be moved had meanwhile to be protected. By the Spring of 1940 the museum reopened with the first of more than 40 exhibitions arranged during the war, although deprived of all the fit younger members of staff. By 1944 the Museum had more visitors than in 1937 or 1938. The Museum had finally to be restored to order before members of the staff away on National Service had returned.* [Fitzwilliam Museum, Report, 1947] (Photograph: H.A. Chapman)

Trumpington Street – Addenbrooke's Hospital, *c.*1890. Fire damaged Addenbrooke's Hospital in September 1902: *A fire broke out in the women's ward at the top of the left wing of Addenbrooke's Hospital. In a very short time the flames secured a firm hold and the unfortunate patients had to be removed. Flames burst through the roof and worked towards the centre of the building. Nurses and probationers heroically entered the wards and brought their patients to a place of safety. Many scenes, tragically distressing, were witnessed. To such proportions did the fire assume that it was deemed advisable to remove other patients and several afflicted old men were brought to the lawn. The news of the outbreak spread quickly throughout Cambridge and some thousands of people gathered in front of the Hospital.* [CDN 1 October 1902] The Duke and Duchess of York opened new wards in 1932, including an X-Ray clinic, the result of an anonymous bequest. With the opening of a New Addenbrooke's Hospital various departments were transferred and the old Hospital finally closed in October 1984. The building was redeveloped to house the Judge Institute but retains much of the character of a century ago.

Trumpington Street – The Little Rose, 1938. A 16th-century inn, mentioned by Pepys, the Little Rose was a stopping place for country carriers. It was in the 1930's the meeting place for two undergraduate clubs. *The 'Little Rose Club' is exclusively for Saloon Bar Undergraduates, the 'Bluffers' being open to anyone who drinks in the Public Bar. The activities are trivial enough, but the ideal is spreading friendship around the world. Members wear a special tie and before the war any undergraduate coming into the Saloon not wearing the tie was either asked to join, by standing a pint all round, or else to go into the Public Bar.* [Varsity cutting] (Photograph: L. Cobbett)

Mill Lane – No.12. Ellis Minns recorded his feelings of Mill Lane in 1950: *On the South side we have most self-conscious 'building' in Cambridge, the most perfect reproduction of exquisite Georgian, incongruously named Stuart House. Beyond we have Messrs. Eaden Lilley's Bedding Factory and Hearsery, the delightful Queen Anne front of the University Women's Club, once the Miller's house. But the jewel of the Lane is being taken from us. No.4 on the South side was the printing-house owned by Mr. Hall the bookseller, who also called himself a publisher. It was about 16 feet across and half the height of its neighbour, but very sensibly designed with the great window extending absolutely the whole width of the building to give light to the compositors. The University wanted the site to display the elegancies of Stuart House and to make better access to the Lecture Rooms. But Mr. Hall, sturdily replied that he would be damned if he would walk an extra step to go and look after his printing. After his business came to an end the little shop was occupied by the English Instrument Company. A sketch of it will be preserved in the Antiquarian Society's 'Photographic Record' to which pictures of all threatened buildings should be sent.* [E.H. Minns, Hall's printing house in Mill Lane – The Cambridge Review, 4 November 1950]

Mill Lane – Scudamore's Boatyard. Scudamore who had their premises in Mill Lane were one of the early punt-hirers along with Dolby, Strange, Mathie, Bullen, Banham & Reynolds. In 1939–40 Reynolds bought out a number of the others after three years of bad business and poor weather, but retained the name of Scudamore for his boat-hiring business. [R.T. Rivington, Punts and punting, 1982] This led to protest in 1947: *Sir – May I protest against the excessive charges now being asked for the hire of a punt on the river. It is within easy memory that it was possible to hire a punt out for an afternoon and evening for five or six persons and still have 10s change from a pound note. I can see nothing which warrants the present-day prices. Is it that the ordinary townsfolk are being slowly squeezed from the river in order to allow the Varsity men and the more wealthy visitors to the town to enjoy 'our' river? The Borough Council should either consider setting up a municipal boatyard for the hire of punts or investigate the charges with a view to softening the blow to the everyday working-class family of Cambridge – 'Constant User'.* [CDN 20 August 1947]

King's and Bishops Mill, 1924. Three watermills had stood on Mill Pool for 900 years, their story was related by Dr H.P. Stokes in 1910. [H.P. Stokes. The Old Mills of Cambridge – PCAS vol.14] Two shared the same roof, one called the Bishop's Mill had belonged to the Abbot of Ely at the time of the Domesday survey, the second, known as the King's Mill had been erected shortly after. Both were acquired by Ebeneezer Bird Foster in 1842 but with the coming of the railway he erected new mills in Station Road. By 1911 motorists were urging a better link to Newnham and a new bridge across the Mill Pool was proposed. It would mean demolishing the old mills and the Corporation bought out Foster's interests. But the scheme collapsed and the premises which were old and dilapidated could not be relet and became derelict. Gwen Raverat described the scene: *We used to spend many hours watching the fat corn-sacks being hauled up a pulley into the overhanging gable, sometimes from a barge, but more often from the great yellow, four-horse wagons, which stood beneath the trapdoor. The sacks butted the trapdoors open with their own noses, and the doors fell to with a loud clap behind them. I find it hard to believe that the boys, who now sit fishing on the parapet, have no idea that there once was a great mill behind them.* [G. Raverat, *Period Piece*, 1952] (Photograph: Scott & Wilkinson)

King's & Bishop's Mill site clearance, 1928. The mills were cleared in 1928 and the University expressed an interest in acquiring the site: *Cambridge councillors debated whether part of the King's and Bishop's Mill site should be sold to the University to erect new lecture rooms. The Corporation should not sell its property in this way; it should do so on the public market. They might get a higher offer from a firm who would like to put up a Woolworth building but they wanted an appropriate end to the Backs & such improvements would give an almost Venetian effect to the whole of the Backs river. They should pull down the remains of the mill so that everyone could see what the site looked like. It would expose some quite ugly buildings which would not be hidden by any plans before them.* [CDN 8 April 1927] The Council decided not to sell but to reconstruct the sluices and slipway and construct a weir and footbridge. The cottages in the background were replaced by the University Centre in 1967. (Photograph: J. Palmer Clarke)

Newnham Mill before 1902. Newnham Mill stands on the other side of the Mill Pool, alongside the Jolly Millers public house owned by the Star Brewery, whose sign is visible above the door. The pub was demolished in 1903 and replaced by another in a Mock-Tudor style. [J.A. Gray, Newnham, 1977] Road widening on the corner of Barton Road in 1902 saw the demolition of the front of a 17th-century brewery and two of the outhouses. In May 1912 the remains of the malting, formerly used to store grain, were converted into a small hall with two galleries and a stage. Many concerts and meetings were held there, including a lecture by Albert Schweitzer. (Photograph: Harold Smith)

Silver Street bridge, *c*.1890. A cast-iron bridge at Silver Street was constructed in 1843 replacing the last of a series of wooden bridges. In 1913 a survey revealed that it was unsafe for heavy loads. It was further weakened by the floods of 1947 and replaced in 1957 by a bridge designed by Sir Edward Lutyens. Hidden beneath the trees to the left of the bridge were picturesque old cottages used by college servants; they were demolished in 1935 to make way for the Fisher Building of Queens' College.

Queens' Lane – almshouses. Almshouses in Queens Lane were founded by Andrew Dockett, President of Queens' College in 1484. By 1850 inmates received a pound of meat and 2s weekly, together with a chaldron of coals yearly. They also had £1 in September and 2s 6d on Christmas Eve. In 1911 the College sold one of the almshouses to King's College and demolished the rest for its Friar's Court. (Photograph: E. Hilton)

Trumpington Street – Corpus Christi cellar, 1939. Excavations for Air Raid trenches in the front court of Corpus Christi College in Autumn 1939 revealed an unexpected cellar. It was thought to be 18th century and probably belonged to the Dolphin Inn. The College had enjoyed a similar discovery in the early 1800s when during excavations in the floor of an old cellar in Bene't Street workmen had found an earthenware jar, full of silver coins. (Photograph: G.H.S. Bushnell)

Bene't Street – St Bene't's Church, 1892. St Bene't's Church seen from a window at Corpus Christi College with the Eagle Inn in the background. An extensive renovation took place at this time: *St Bene't's church reopened for public service with an improved organ and organ chamber. Archdeacon Emery said that the condition of the Church in 1849, when he was ordained Deacon, with its organ Gallery at the West End, high pews in the nave, and green baized pews in the Chancel was then far different to what it was now. Since that time the South aisle had been erected, the West End and Tower opened and restored, & the Chancel and church generally restored.* [CDN 9 May 1898] (Photograph: F.J. Allen)

Bene't Street – The Eagle, 1937. The courtyard of the Eagle Inn. During World War Two it became a meeting place for British and American air crew, many of whom wrote their squadron numbers on the ceiling of the bar. It was a favourite lunching place for researchers at the Cavendish Laboratory. (Photograph: J. Baldwin)

Free School Lane, 1939. The Cavendish Laboratory was established in Free School Lane in 1874. In 1919 a Royal Commission reported that *The growth of science at Cambridge has been perhaps the greatest fact in the history of the University since its foundation.* In that year Ernest Rutherford succeeded J.J. Thomson to the Chair of Experimental Physics and numerous scientists flocked to the Cavendish, including a Russian physicist, Peter Kapitza for whom a new Mond Laboratory was constructed. After Kapitza was not allowed to return to Cambridge from a visit to Russia, Rutherford arranged for the equipment to be sent to him there so that he could continue his researches. After Rutherford died in 1937 his room was locked and remained so until 1977 when it was thoroughly cleaned for fear of contamination from radiation. (Photograph: Miss K. Cooke)

Bene't Street, looking towards Peas Hill, 1937. Bene't Street had been widened in 1908 and was made a one-way street in 1936. The name of the Friar House Restaurant on the corner of Free School Lane commemorates an Augustinian Friary that once occupied the south side of the street. [H.P. Stokes, The Augustinian Friary in Cambridge and the history of the site, 1918] (Photograph: J. Baldwin)

Kings Parade, January 1928. Heavy railings in front of King's College were removed in 1927 as part of a scheme to improve the street. But the College was worried: *It will interest many people to know that the authorities of King's College propose pulling down the railings in front of the college on King's Parade but are a little timid about what might follow this step and have consulted the Town Council. The Watch Committee was asked to enter into an agreement not to take any portion of the land between the railings and the college buildings for a parking place. They have reassured the college that they have no power to establish parking places on private property.* [CDN 16 July 1927] Temporary railings were erected before the building of the present low wall in 1932. In 1936 it was reported that repairs would have to be undertaken to the chapel buildings due to chemical pollution but more immediate dangers were faced in 1939 and the glass was removed from the chapel windows for fear of damage during air raids. (Photograph: J.H. Bullock)

Above: **Kings Parade** Coronation Day procession, 1902. The band march past a shop run by Mr Greef; others were occupied by Mr Pain and Mr Sadd. The latter moved his antiques business to St Edward's Passage in April 1914 but fell from the roof of Kings College chapel that September. He left a note in verse which ended:
Then trade was bad –
Not much to be had
And he getting old.
Now isn't that SADD.

Right: **Trinity Lane** – Old Schools, before 1889. The old gateway of King's College, which had been begun in 1444, was left unfinished until 1889. The University underwent considerable change throughout the period covered, but little of it features in the Cambridge Antiquarian Society's survey and their photographs of college buildings are equally scarce. (Photograph: Scott & Wilkinson)

Next page: **Trinity Street** – Matthew's café, 1937. Some town buildings remain largely unchanged; when the Antiquarian Society visited in 1907 they noted: *No. 12 Trinity Street, formerly Messrs Foster's Bank, and now the Oriental Café. The woodwork, of this old house, especially a mantelpiece in a room on the ground floor, is good.* [CAS, Excursions round old Cambridge, November 1907 – PCAS vol.12] In 1927: *The fascinating experience of lunching in Cambridge in the atmosphere of our Elizabethan forefathers is made possible by the opening of new rooms at Messrs Matthew's Café in Trinity Street. They have acquired the two upper storeys of the building & turned rooms which were formerly part of a lodging house into a charming medieval retreat. The original beams and window frames remain as well as some beautiful old carvings and the rooms have been furnished in the style of the period, pains having been taken to secure faithful reproductions even down to lamps and pewter pots.* [CDN 29 October 1927] (Photograph: J. Baldwin)

Trinity Street – west side. Arthur Shepherd opened his first shop in Oxford in 1877 and his son, Ernest, set up in Cambridge in 1902. There have been huge changes in the clothes men have worn over the years: at the time of the Photographic Survey undergraduates wore college blazers and club ties under their college gown, all professional men wore suits and, in cold weather, most people wore overcoats. By the 1960s tailors were lamenting the trend to jeans and duffel coats, sloppy-joes and 17in trouser bottoms, which led to a demise in their trade. *Thirty years ago students were proud of their dress and bought four suits at a time. Now they shuffle around in jeans and sweaters and do not have two halfpennies to rub together,* said a spokesmaan for Pratt, Manning and Company, Cambridge's oldest bespoke tailor, when it closed in 1962.

Trinity Street – St John's Street, *c.*1860. The Antiquarian Society's photographic collection includes a number of older photographs which were taken by Arthur Nicholls and donated by J. Palmer Clarke. This picture of Trinity Street in the 1860s, is one of the earliest in the survey. The tower of All Saint's Church had projected into the street following realignment of the footpath in 1821 but was demolished and replaced by a new church in Jesus Lane at about the same time that St John's College was constructing a new chapel across the street. (Photograph: A. Nicholls)

St John's College – front 1912. Colleges have a constant problem maintaining their old buildings: *Last year, when the front of the college was restored the two gateway turrets facing St John's Street were demolished and rebuilt; now the turrets within the court are being renovated. Restoration work has disclosed old oak panelling. The discovery was made after repairs to the roof on the east side of the first court had revealed damage by the death-watch beetle, necessitating the removal of a number of the original oak beams. On the other side of the court the parapet over the offices and the dining hall has been rebuilt and the brickwork re-pointed and replaced where necessary. Hand made bricks of the 16th century were obtained to match the original work. The entire face of the building has been washed down by hand, only hard brushes and softened water being used.* [*Cambridge Standard*, 13 September 1935] (Photograph: H. Skelton)

Trinity Street – St John's Street, *c.*1890. Comparison with the picture opposite illustrates the impact of the Victorian changes. Trinity College's Whewell's Court commands the corner of All Saints' Passage, the Selwyn Divinity School, built in 1878–9, occupies the background whilst the tower of the new St John's College chapel dominates all Cambridge. Railings in front of Trinity College were removed in 1937 and St John's Street widened in 1946. (Photograph: Hills & Saunders)

Bridge Street west side – rear of properties, 1938. Throughout the 1920s and 1930s colleges were undertaking new schemes. A number of houses in Bridge Street had been cleared for St John's College's new Master's Lodge in 1863 and more demolition followed in 1937; the college needed extra accommodation and the corporation wanted to widen the street to improve access for the growing number of motor cars. Members of the Cambridge Antiquarian Society compiled a photographic record of the demolition: the back of Nos.59–61 Bridge Street seen from the north wall of St John's College Chapel, 1938. W.F. Turner pointed out a window: *This was once kept as a butcher's shop. At the side overlooking the front garden of St John's College was a small window, which must be the most expensive window that ever existed. The story ran that the butcher had a lease of the property from the college and thought he had a right to brick the window up. The college got an injunction against him. He fought this in the court and lost the day. Not satisfied with that he took it to a higher court and lost again. He took it to the House of Lords and again he lost, and subsequently went bankrupt* [W.F. Turner, Old Cambridge – *Cambridge Chronicle*, 19 November 1929] (Photograph: J.H. Bullock)

Bridge Street west side, 1938. J.H. Bullock commented on Nos.48–45 Bridge Street: *Antiquarians may regret the disappearance of some of the older buildings, in particular the picturesque dormers at St John's Street corner. No.48 is quite a good one. It is notable for the rings under the eaves of the roof. Before the Co-operative Society, Percy Frohock had it as a shop. The buildings beyond formed the front of the Old Red Lion with the entrance in the yard between. Of late years only a small part of the premises was used as a tavern. Dick Turpin is said to have frequented the Old Red Lion. We shall be sorry to see these picturesque gables disappear* [J.H. Bullock, Bridge Street – Cambridge Public Library Record, 1939] (Photograph: L. Cobbett)

Bridge Street west side – The Old Red Lion Yard. This section of the street was honeycombed by a number of yards and passages. One property in Sussums Yard included a very fine carved oak mantel-piece dated 1594 which was removed to the Combination Room of St John's College. In the Old Red Lion Yard *Alderman Nutting carried on his business about 1750 as a coal merchant and dealer in corn, deals, iron, timber and salt. He may also have kept the inn. But he always lived like a gentleman while in trade, the late Earl of Oxford, Sir John Hind Cotton and the chief gentry of the county visiting him and lying frequently at his house.* [J.H. Bullock, Bridge Street, 1939] (Photograph: L. Cobbett)

Bridge Street west side – Magdalene Bridge, from Fisher's Lane, 1931. Magdalene Bridge was built in 1823, replacing a stone bridge constructed in 1754 by James Essex, the architect famed for his 'Mathematical Bridge' at Queens' College. But although the wooden bridge is a triumph, his Magdalene Bridge was a disaster. It was criticised for being too narrow and by 1798 was 'in decay and ruinous'. In 1822 the decision was taken to pull it down. The replacement cast-iron bridge was of an extremely revolutionary design for its time and included ornamental railings cast by the Finch foundry in Cambridge. Their strength was tested in 1929 when a motor car crashed through them and hung over the river. By then the whole bridge was carrying far more traffic than ever intended and planners were talking about widening the road on either side to make a new thoroughfare straight into the heart of the town. In 1953 a weight restriction was imposed but by 1967 there was a two-inch dip in the centre. Buses and lorries were banned and the Government announced plans to replace it by 1971. However opposition prompted a change of heart and the bridge was remodelled, retaining its original appearance. (Photograph: L. Cobbett)

Fisher's Lane seen from Magdalene Bridge showing Bullen's boat yard. The buildings were cleared in 1932 but the proposed quadrangle that was to replace them was never built W.F. Turner recalled earlier times when barges unloaded coal here: *The wharf down Fisher's Lane was at one time a very busy place when barges came filled with merchandise and in the cottages lived the bargees. At the Pickerel Inn there still existed a room called the Cock Pit where the men who plied the ferry which existed before the first bridge was built used to spend their spare time in cock fighting. He was given to understand that at one time the Binn Brook was a waterway up which coal and merchandise was taken to Barton and Coton. One of the old inhabitants well remembered the state of affairs when there were very elementary sanitary arrangements, and the river was the source of water supply. When he was a boy, the old man said, there lived an old woman who used to get her water every evening in a bucket attached to a pole with a metal clip at the end. One evening when she was filling her bucket he noticed a dead dog in the water near the bucket and called to her, "Oh! look there's a dead dog" to which she calmly replied, "I always boils my water before I drinks it".* [W.F. Turner, Old Cambridge – *Cambridge Chronicle*, 19 November 1929] (Photograph: F.J. Allen)

Magdalene Street, west side 1937. Listed buildings on the west side of Magdalene Street, including The Cross Keys, once the largest of the five inns in the Street. It is a fine example of 16th-century work, the interior contains some good oak panelling, and a beautiful carved oak mantelpiece. Magdalene College plans commissioned in 1927 envisaged the demolition of these old properties to allow the road width to be doubled, but were not implemented. When in the 1950s there were further suggestions that the street should be widened to improve traffic flow and that the old buildings be swept away Magdalene voiced its opposition. *Sir. Twenty-five years ago Magdalene College started a scheme which might have involved the widening of Magdalene Street and the removal of buildings opposite the college. But it does not now contemplate the completion of the scheme and is now strongly opposed to the widening of the street and the demolition of the buildings on the west side. The College would be strongly prejudiced if it should be divided by a street similar in character to the widened part of Bridge Street and would strongly object to such a change of character and loss of amenity in the neighbourhood – Henry Willink, Master.* [CDN 14 January 1952] The street fronts remain largely unchanged, though the advertisements for dog food have been removed. (Photograph: J. Baldwin)

Magdalene Street, west side – Cross Keys Yard, *c*.1920. Until 1915 the Cross Keys Yard housed a malt vinegar brewers and mustard and potted meat manufacturer. *After an existence of 108 years the vinegar works of Messrs W.K. Bird and Son of Magdalene Street is closing down. This is not in consequence of the war or of loss of trade, for the firm have conducted a highly successful business up to the very last. The premises have been sold to Magdalene College, who have long been anxious to obtain them, and the proprietors are retiring to private life. As the step has been in contemplation for some time there will be practically no displacement of labour; most of the men employed have already secured other work.* [CDN 21 August 1915] Nearby Tan Yard or Rowley's Yard was entered from a passage near the corner with Northampton Street and included a circular drying house used by tanners for curing skins.

Northampton Street, *c*.1890. Northampton Street looking towards Magdalene Street showing Cory House, two separate 16th-century structures linked by a narrow 18th-century building, filling a former carriageway. The tranquillity of the street is deceptive; it was a busy traffic thoroughfare and was the first junction in Cambridge to gain traffic lights in September 1929. It has experienced numerous accidents: *The eccentricity of a horse at Chesterton last night caused its driver and a fare some alarm. It bolted along Chesterton lane at a furious rate, resisting all the efforts of the driver to get it under control. At this point the driver came to the conclusion it was quite useless trying to hold the horse in any longer and advised the gentleman inside the cab to 'quit'. He took a flying leap into the darkness and grazed his face somewhat severely. The driver fell off the box and the off wheel passed over his legs. Continuing his career the horse came into collision with a gatepost at Northampton Street which knocked it on its hindquarters.* [CDN 14 October 1898]

Northampton Street corner 1904. Northampton Street was widened in 1908 with the removal of William Collin's timber and coal merchants yard: *The improvement makes a fine approach to the town from the Madingley Road, but one sincerely hopes that now the obvious danger of the corner has been removed, cyclists and others will not forget that the narrowness of the street remains none the less real. The larger portion of the traffic comes from Chesterton Lane and until the opposite corner has received the attention of the road-layer the improvement can hardly be regarded as complete. The great activity sadly disturbed the 'work-shys' who are wont to congregate at the corner for the purpose of holding up the wall. It was a delightful sight to see these groups huddling together, trying to snatch a snooze in the midst of all the clanging clamour of swinging hammers and picks. Now the road is to some extent open the human house-props are found at their usual haunts, though considerable indignation prevails among the more energetic.* [CDN 29 August 1908] (Photograph: F.J. Allen)

Northampton Street – The School of Pythagoras. Hidden behind the Northampton Street frontages is the oldest secular building in Cambridge, the School of Pythagoras. T.D. Atkinson explained: *The principal room was on the upper floor, with the kitchen offices below. It was entered by a doorway, now blocked, at the north end. It was probably used for store-rooms only, for the original windows are mere loopholes; there seems to be no evidence as to the position of the kitchen. The upper floor was reached by an outside staircase at the north end. The original door is still used, and one or two windows of the original work remain. The roof is entirely modern.* [T.D. Atkinson, Old houses in Cambridge, 1908 – PCAS vol.13] In 1910 its gardens became a major attraction: *Much to the regret of the Proprietors of the Cambridge University and Town Roller Skating Rink, who have taken a lease of the beautiful Pythagoras Gardens, and to the disappointment of the public generally, it has been found necessary, owing to complications arising as a result of a misunderstanding between themselves, the lessees and Merton College, Oxford, the owners, to discontinue the use of the gardens for public entertainment. For some time past, hundreds of visitors have spent an enjoyable hour upon the open-air rink and splendid lawns.* [CIP 8 July 1910]

Northampton Street – St Giles' workhouse, 1911. Almost next door to the opulence of the School of Pythagoras was a building representing the other side of Cambridge life – St Giles' workhouse. *It consisted of six cottages, three in the front, later altered to a public house known as the Borough Boy, and three in a court at the rear with a large room where the paupers dined together. There is an old lady living near who has vividly described the condition of affairs just before the reforms; the men, women and children huddled together, and loafing in the court and streets; there was one man, mad and raving, 'like a wild beast', who lay on straw in a barred room. Two open privies were not a pleasant feature of the situation. After the poor law reforms of 1836 the buildings were let to Mr Benjamin Clark for £20 a year, the tenants of the cottages in the street being allowed the use of the pump and privy. The yard was sometimes called 'Gentle's Yard' from the name of the chief tenant, a tradesman who was coffin maker to the Mill Road Workhouse.* [H.P. Stokes, Cambridge parish workhouses, 1911 – PCAS vol.15] (Photograph: H.P. Stokes)

Kettles Yard from Northampton Street, 1941. By 1941 a shop had opened but the Spotted Cow and several properties had been removed in a slum clearance programme. But as old properties were replaced by new houses the landlords demanded higher rents, driving out former residents and reducing the trade of pubs and shopkeepers. Four small cottages at the Castle Street end considered by Cambridge Preservation Society to be capable of conversion were allowed to remain standing. They were bought by Jim Ede in 1957 and form the nucleus of the Kettle's Yard gallery. The rest were demolished for old folk's flats which opened in 1956 and won a Civic Trust Award. St Peter's Church had to be underpinned in 1932 to stop it falling down. It was declared redundant in 1958 and is now cared for by The Churches Conservation Trust. (Photograph: G. Strickland)

Kettles Yard from Northampton Street, 1904. Kettles Yard ran from Northampton Street through to Castle Street and was a tightly-packed area of working-class houses. Spalding's Directory for 1904 lists the occupants as Frederick Hammond, carpenter, Mrs Mortimer, William Clark, labourer, Charles Conner and Benjamin Pilsworth but there were a number of empty properties with only half the tenements in the Spotted Cow Yard occupied. One local resident in the area was George Randall: *He was the blind man who sold matches at the street corners, and he always had with him his faithful little dog, which guided him from place to place and kept a watchful eye to see that those who took his master's matches dropped a coin in the old man's tin mug. Randall throve chiefly in Term time, when pitying undergraduates would give him helpful contributions. They would offer him as much as half a crown to go home out of the cold weather, but he always insisted on sticking to his post. But it was at best a very precarious livelihood.* [CDN 10 July 1910] (Photograph: F.J. Allen)

Mount Pleasant, 1937. St Peter's vicarage, Mount Pleasant was amongst the properties visited by the Cambridge Antiquarian Society in 1908: *This is a house of, perhaps, some 130 to 150 years old. It is now divided into three cottages, the middle and the eastern ones containing features of interest. The lower front room of the centre cottage is of panelled oak, with pictures painted on the frame-like panels. This room has been covered entirely with wall-paper, though, fortunately, in such a manner as to preserve the paintings beneath. In the easternmost cottage some panelling and two good fireplaces of late 18th-century date still remain. One of the most interesting features of this building is the site upon which it stands and which it helps to preserve. It has been erected on the edge of the sloping bank which formed the defence, on the western side, of the enclosure of the Norman Castle. The road outside runs along the bottom of the ancient fosse.* [T.D. Atkinson, Old houses in Cambridge, 1908 – PCAS vol.13] (Photograph: J. Baldwin)

Shelley Row, 1937. Clearance continued in Shelley Row, where the cottage on the left was condemned in October 1936. Nearby on the corner of Albion Row the Old Nags Head played a prominent position in the Cambridge cattle market which covered the Pound Hill area until its transfer to Hills Road in 1885. Much business was discussed over its excellent 'market dinner', a regular Saturday feature for which a shilling was charged. It was demolished about 1910 and two houses erected on site, one of six inns in the neighbourhood, all of which with the exception of the Cow and Calf had vanished. A major redevelopment of the area was announced in 1962, prompting Erica Dimock to comment: *It is unlikely to retain its present appearance for very much longer and in years to come will be quite unrecognisable as the rural type street it is today.* [CN 10 March 1963] (Photograph: L. Cobbett)

Shelley Row – barn, *c.*1909. Amongst the properties cleared was a former gaol: *Antiquaries will regret to hear that this week workmen are engaged in removing an interesting building in Castle End. It is an old barn, situated in Shelley Row and in it rested the French prisoners who were captured in the Peninsular War (1809–1814), on their march from the South of England to the great prison at Norman Cross. For a number of years the barn, which is a lofty building with a thatched roof, was occupied by a Mr Henry Herring Smith who carried on a blacksmith's business. He sold it to a Mr White and said that he clearly remembered the French prisoners using the barn as a resting-place. He could remember them making dominoes and dice out of bones, which they sold through the bars to people as curios.* [CIP 31 October 1909]

Castle Street – Three Tuns Inn, *c.*1907. In 1907 members of the Antiquarian Society were told: *A bedroom at the back of the house where Dick Turpin used to sleep was so dilapidated it had been demolished a fortnight before their visit; they saw a letter of 1739 said to be from the landlord re his effects. This was the inn from which Elizabeth Woodcock started her journey home to Impington in 1799 when buried in snow for eight days. In 1659-60 the site was Corporation waste; it was probably built about Christmas 1685 when it was leased to William Sell. It was known as Three Tuns for the first time in 1754 and by 1855 was occupied by John Whyman in whose family it remained for several years, gaining the name of Whyman's Inn.* [CAS, Excursion round old Cambridge, November 1907 – PCAS vol.12] (Photograph: E.C. Hoppett)

Castle Street – Three Tuns Inn, 1936. The pub was renovated but magistrates still refused to renew its licence on grounds of structural defects. The County Arms was built as a replacement to which the licence was transferred and the Three Tuns was demolished in August 1936. (Photograph: Miss E. Rolleston)

Castle Hill – County Gaol, exterior 1930. The County Gaol on Castle Hill had been built in 1802 on the site of the castle bailey and enlarged in 1868 and 1870. In 1878 it became a State prison and several additions were made; it continued to hold prisoners until 1916 after which it was used to store documents until it passed to the County Council in 1928. Two years later some 8,000 people took the opportunity for a tour of inspection before the building was demolished for a new Shire Hall. (Photograph: H.S. Johnson)

Castle Street – County Gaol, interior 1930. Johnson also recorded the interior of the former gaol, including the corridor on the first floor, the condemned cell and gallows. The final person to be hanged was a murderer in 1913. Nearby stood the Assize Court: *The Court House built of brick and stone in the Italian style has a portico supported on columns and comprises two courts and a magistrates' room from which three prisoners recently escaped by removing an iron grill over a window. The whole of the structure of the 112-year-old courts of assize is unsafe and liable to collapse at any time. Dry rot has been attacking the floors and has now spread up the walls and plaster and into the roof. The damage is said to be irreparable and it is virtually certain that the County Council will have to write off the building as a total loss.* [CDN 28 July 1952] It was demolished, unphotographed by the Survey, in 1953. (Photograph: H.S. Johnson)

Castle End, from Castle Mound, 1937. Cambridge Antiquarian Society organised a relay of observers during the excavations for the new Shire Hall, during which many interesting discoveries were made. When Dr W.M. Palmer researched the history of Cambridge Castle he lamented: *The immediate surroundings of the Hill are shameful. For the site of this castle, which is intimately connected with three of our greatest rulers, William the Conqueror, Edward the First and our own great rebel, Oliver Cromwell, is allowed to lie desolate, and worse than desolate, encumbered with an unwanted prison, mean tenements, bushes and rubbish.* [W.M. Palmer, Cambridge castle, 1928] The castle mound is now well kept and open to all providing a view across Cambridge. (Photograph: J. Baldwin)

Castle Street, 1937. The White Horse Inn on the corner of Castle Street dated from the 16th century and contained many original features, although an overhanging upper storey was removed in 1932 as it had been clipped numerous times by passing buses and lorries. The pub closed in 1934 and was threatened with demolition for road widening. It reopened as a Folk Museum in 1936 with the support of the Cambridge Rotary Club and the patronage of many influential people including Alderman E. Saville Peck. *Very early in its history the Museum was fortunate in securing the services of Mr Reginald Lambeth as Curator. Walking past a demolition site one day he saw a complete Georgian shopfront. Thinking it would be a useful addition to the Museum he asked permission to take it away, but was refused. Nothing daunted he made numerous nocturnal visits on his bicycle, until eventually the whole shopfront was rebuilt in the yard adjoining the Museum – where it can be seen today.* [E.S. Peck, The Cambridge and county folk museum 'early days' – Cambridge Magazine, Spring 1947] (Photograph: J. Baldwin)

Magdalene Street east – corner with Chesterton Lane, demolished 1912. The east side of Magdalene Street saw major change with the demolition of old properties at the corner of Chesterton Lane and the erection of Benson Hall. W.F. Turner reported: *Chesterton Lane Corner house was at one time called the Three Swans and kept by Albert Pointer, it was afterwards a saddler's shop kept by Mr Bennett. The inn next door was the King's Head and here the Cambridge Boxing Club was first formed. The road then was about half its present width.* [W.F. Turner, Old Cambridge – *Cambridge Chronicle*, 19 November 1929]

Quayside, 1910. Quayside stretches for about 250ft alongside the River. J.H. Bullock recollected: *There were quays and warehouses on both banks of the river and on both sides of the bridge. To these quays came everything needed for the life of the district by barge. By far the greater part of the goods were landed at Quay Side. When I was a boy I used to hear tales of the pre-railway days when the 'bridge-porters' used to prop up the bridge while waiting for a job. Facing the street, but standing some yard back, with an open market frequently held in front of it, stood an ancient inn called the Half Moon, demolished about 1875. The date of the beam of its entrance yard was 1552. Lower down, in the palmy days of the Quay, were a sequence of inns, the Checkers, the Griffin, the Ship, the New Ship and the Union. On the site of the Ship was afterwards the Anchor Brewery which was in the hands of the Potts family till recent years. Near the Anchor Brewery was an ancient building, the Sedge Hall. Said to have been for a time a Hostel, for some centuries it was a storehouse for sedge, an important fuel for heating homes and colleges. The Hall was pulled down in 1924 being too ruinous to preserve. Near it stood the Weighing Machine; it belonged to the Corporation and so late as 1852 was let for £30 a year.* [J.H. Bullock, Bridge Street, 1939 – Cambridge Public Library Record] The background is dominated by the chimney of the electricity generating station which was established in Thompson's Lane, in 1892, the site being chosen for its proximity of river water for cooling. The plant closed in 1966. These and various industrial buildings have now been demolished to provide flats, bars and offices. (Photograph: J.E. Foster)

Thompson's Lane. Thompson's Lane also housed a brewery, an ironfoundry, and the Cambridge Tapestry Works. This was originally founded at Ickleford, near Hitchin by Walter Witter and built up a great reputation for the quality of their repair work to valuable old tapestries. By 1924 they were employing about 160 girls. In 1934 Lord Fairhaven commissioned a tapestry for Anglesey Abbey which was admired by Queen Mary. The firm was commissioned to design and weave a tapestry of Windsor Castle for presentation to their majesties as a Jubilee gift. The Tapestry Works closed in 1941. [CEN 21 April 2000]

Thompson's Lane – Ninepin or Ellis Court, 1935. Ellis' Court, Thompson's Lane proved difficult to photograph, as W.F. Turner, one of those who contributed to the survey explained: *In some cases yards were so narrow that he had been cramped for room, and perhaps some door, lamp post or ventilating shaft had come in the direct line of the camera and he had been obliged to include them in order to get a record. Even to do this had meant his visiting some places several times to find when the sun would be at the right angle to light the subject.* [*Cambridge Chronicle* 19 November 1929] (Photograph: A.J. Winship)

Bridge Street, east side – Blackamoor Head Yard, 1932. This house, once occupied by Alderman Nutting, a coal merchant and Mayor of Cambridge in 1723 and 1743, was one of the better properties in Blackamoor Head Yard which contained 12 houses, four of which were rebuilt in 1884. The Yard was situated between the Mitre and the Baron of Beef, an area swept by fire in 1933: *Near midnight one of the fiercest fires in Cambridge for years partially destroyed the Baron of Beef, a modernised public house in Bridge Street. The premises were rebuilt only last year at a cost of between £4,000 and £5,000. The scheme involved the demolition of four old cottages and three others were destroyed to make room for the new garages.* [CIP 6 October 1933] (Photograph: W.M. Palmer)

Bridge Street looking north from the Round Church, 1937. The buildings on the left-hand side of Bridge Street were demolished for the St John's college development and those on the right seemed destined to suffer the same fate in the 1960s. They were in a poor state of repair and in danger of collapse. Plans were announced for their demolition and replacement but, following protests, the frontages were restored with new shops and offices behind opening in 1977. Bullock described them in 1939: *With numbers 10 and 11 – now claimed by the motor industry – begins a series of interesting old houses, many of which were inns. At no.12 formerly stood a licensed house with stabling, known as the 'George' or 'Old George'. A large part of these extensive premises was occupied for many years by Felton's oil and colour warehouse. It, too, is now devoted to motor cars. No.13 is a quaint little house. Cruse, a stationer, and Butcher, a photographer were here for years.* [J.H. Bullock, Bridge Street, 1939] (Photograph: L. Cobbett)

Bridge Street, east side – Jordan's Yard, before 1934. Jordan was a livery stable-keeper during the first half of the 19th century. *When the property was up for sale in 1861 it included five houses in the yard, a farriery, a smithy, a farmyard and a garden, in addition to stabling for 50 horses. The fifth house down is a quaint double-fronted one with some fine oak panelling. The learned Professor Mayor, President of St John's College, had it, and the house, like his rooms at St John's, was lined with books from floor to ceiling. Other rather airless houses have been built lower down.* [J.H. Bullock, Bridge Street, 1939 – Cambridge Public Library Record] Mayor's neighbours in 1904 included a bedmaker, blacksmith and painter. (Photograph: L.J. Jarman)

Ram Yard looking to Bridge Street, 1937. Suggestions for the demolition of this narrow thoroughfare were made in November 1900. *Sir. Among the many urgent improvements needed in Cambridge stands that of abolishing the old, worn-out buildings and improving the thoroughfares of the town. Disease is prevalent to a large extent and is to be found in districts with narrow thoroughfares and tumble-down houses. In any other towns these buildings would have been demolished long since but here, in the very heart of an important University town, we have a thoroughfare which would be a disgrace to any village, and should not be tolerated even in conservative Cambridge. I refer to the buildings situated between Round Church Street on the one side, and Ram Yard, looking into Park Street on the other. Here a collection of bricks and wood in the shape of miserable cottages, bar the way to what might be a worthy continuation of Trinity and St John's Streets to Park Street, bringing into touch one of the busiest parts of the town. It is only a matter of a few hundred pounds to buy these cottages and I am sure that were the owners approached they would have sufficient patriotism to let their property go for a consideration – W.* [CDN 19 November 1900] The buildings continued to provide much-needed homes in the centre of the city until the spring of 1961, although many of them had been condemned. They were finally swept away to widen Round Church Street and provide access to a new Park Street car park that opened in October 1963. Shortly afterwards an extension saw the demolition of Cambridge's last thatched cottage in nearby Clement Place. (Photograph: J. Baldwin)

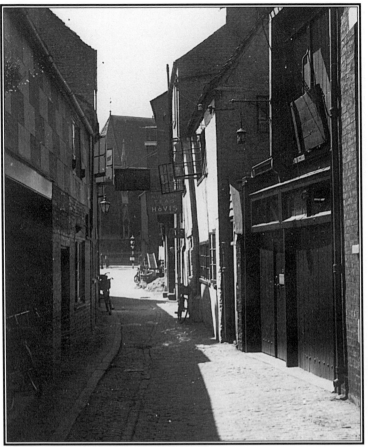

Bridge Street – looking south *c.*1880. The Hoop Hotel, near the corner of Jesus Lane closed in 1910 and was the scene of a dramatic discovery: *A gruesome relict has been discovered in the course of the renovating operations in progress at the Hoop Hotel. Concealed beneath the wall of the wine cellar was found a human skeleton, ghastly remains, grimly suggestive of a crime committed in days gone by. For hundreds of years Cambridge residents have passed along Bridge Street recking nothing of the horrible trophy which lay some ten feet beneath the pavement. A workman made the gruesome find while engaged in excavating operations in the wine cellar of the hotel. As soon as an attempt was made to remove the skeleton it fell to pieces. The skeleton must have been placed there after the house was built as it is just below the wall and floor and above the foundations.* [CDN 17 December 1910] (Photograph: Simpson Bros)

Sidney Street – Fuller's café and confectioners at the corner of Green Street. In 1934 the premises were taken by Bodgers, one of a range of bespoke tailors who catered for fashion-conscious undergraduates between the wars: *A young man, fashionably attired in a brand new plus-four suit paused at the cigarette machine outside the New Theatre, Cambridge, and inserting a sixpence drew forth a packet of cigarettes. Instead of shutting the drawer in the orthodox manner he turned his back on the machine and applied pressure by a retrograde movement. 'Snap' went the drawer, taking with it about six inches of the seat of the young man's voluminous 'bags'. Finding himself held captive he appealed for sixpences to release the drawer but none would do the trick. 'Debagging' was out of the question and the prisoner would not hear of being 'cut away'. After twenty minutes one bright person tried the very obvious idea of pulling the handle of the drawer and he was released amid loud cheers.* [CDN 30 July 1927] The more-relaxed style of dress of the 1960s undergraduate contributed to the closure of many such firms, Bodger's being sold in 1985.

Sussex Street during redevelopment, 1931. Sussex Street was redeveloped in two stages in the 1930s, to universal acclaim: *Amongst the many improvements in Cambridge during the past few years there is none more striking that that which has been effected in Sussex Street. Those who recall the dark narrow lane of bygone days, with its overhanging roofs on either side, and its small, ill-lit shops, will hardly recognise the imposing street that has emerged from the builders' hands. When the first part of the scheme was completed it gave promise of a really worth-while improvement, and now that the other side of the street has been given a new face, with its line of modern shops and shop-fronts, the full effect is visible.* [CDN 22 July 1938] (Photograph: E.F. Watson)

Hobson Street, west side 1921. Hobson Street was transformed from a quiet backwater with the erection of County Hall in 1914, to be followed by a new Central Cinema. It opened in 1921 and was rebuilt in 1930; nine years later the interior was gutted by fire, only the walls,

the fire-proof operating box, the foyer, crush hall and some rows of the back stalls remained intact. Nearby damage estimated at £2,000 was caused by a fire which broke out at the Cambridge Motor Service Company in 1927, among vehicles burned were a Bugatti racing car, an Austin Seven, a Trojan van and a number of motorcycles and bicycles. (Photograph: J. Johnson)

Holy Trinity Church spire, *c.*1901. Scaffolding erected during the rebuilding of the spire of Holy Trinity Church, Sidney Street. One photographer took his camera in his hand and climbed up the scaffolding to take a series of panoramic views over central Cambridge which were added to the Cambridge Antiquarian Society's Photographic Survey in 1946. This picture was taken from a window in Sidney Street and the negatives presented by the Revd H. Pain whose family ran an optician's shop. Arthur B. Gray gives a clue: *High on the spire of Trinity Church may be detected a thermometer! It was placed there by a parishioner when the spire was re-erected in 1901 in order that he might test the magnifying power of his telescopes by reading the figures on the little instrument.* [A.B. Gray, Cambridge re-visited, 1921]

Sidney Street – from Holy Trinity spire, *c.*1901. The changing face of Sidney Street was described by the *Cambridge Chronicle* in August 1933: *Probably no Cambridge street in the centre of the town has undergone so many changes during the present century as that part of Sidney Street which lies between Petty Cury and Market Street. Here many townspeople have established businesses whose names became bywords among residents, and although there still remain a few premises which date back far into the last century, the past 80 years is one of almost constant change, a reflection of virile trade. Where Woolworth's now stand was the small shop of Mr Thompson, gentleman's outfitters and over the gateway which gave access to the old County Court offices and those of Messrs Eaden, Spearing and Raynes, solicitors, was a curious coat of arms. Further along was the Leeds and Leicester Boot Company, while Heffers handsome building has risen where Mr Swann, upholsterer, occupied a fine old Georgian house.* [*Cambridge Chronicle* 9 August 1933] (Photograph: H. Pain)

Sidney Street – The True Blue Inn, before 1930. Part of the redevelopment saw the demolition of the Lord Nelson or True Blue Inn, a favourite meeting place for carriers. Probably erected towards the end of the 16th or beginning of the 17th century, it contained a good deal of carving of Jacobean date. On its site was opened in 1931 the Dorothy Café-Restaurant: *A modern caravanserie to match the modern splendours of Oxford Street & Regent Street, where a thousand people may dine & dance too if they are so minded; a place of dignity & comfort & of surpassing resource.* It remained a major entertainment centre until its closure in August 1972. (Photograph: F.P. Layburn-Yorker)

Sidney Street – west side, 1930. More changes took place on the west side of the street where many old properties were demolished for a new Boots store in 1930. Other frontages were set back as part of a road widening scheme introduced with the intention of *creating a thoroughfare of handsome dimensions from what was once a narrow cobbled lane in which carts could be left unattended by horse or man.* [*Cambridge Chronicle* 9 August 1933] Even graveyards had to comply: *A Consistory court heard a petition by the vicar of St Andrew the Great, Cambridge, for permission to sell to the corporation a strip of land in the church grounds required for street widening purposes. They all knew that the streets were hopelessly inadequate to deal with the volume of traffic which passed through. The only possible alternative would be to pull down the front of Christ's College.* [CDN 25 April 1924] (Photograph: H.S. Johnson)

Christ's Lane, *c.*1904. Christ's Lane provided a link to a new Drummer Street bus station which opened in 1925. It was not always well maintained: *Sir: Christ's Lane is a thoroughfare that is as much used as any in Cambridge, and is owned by a college. During the last two years it has been a veritable quagmire, I came through last evening and the mud was several inches thick through the lane. When is Christ's Lane to be paved in such a manner that it shall be as pleasant to walk through as it is walking across Christ's Pieces? – B.L.* [CDN 29 November 1897] The properties were rebuilt but it closed after the opening of Bradwell's Court in 1960. (Photograph: Scott & Wilkinson)

Emmanuel Street, 1938. Emmanuel Street was the centre of controversy after the Cambridge Borough Council agreed to exchange it for land owned by Emmanuel College that could be used to make a new road. But in 1911 the council changed its mind and instead constructed a subway under the street to new college property on the other side: *For some time housebreakers have been busily engaged in demolishing Southgate Lodge & the house adjoining to make room for the new wing of Emmanuel College. It is curious to note that the houses that are being demolished were the only really modern houses in Emmanuel Street. On either side are picturesque old buildings of considerable antiquity, and these the hand of the housebreaker has spared, for the present.* [CDN 27 July 1911] Demolition continued and rebuilding was finally completed in 1959. (Photograph: L. Cobbett)

Emmanuel Street corner, 1915. Troops of the Royal Welch Fusiliers leaving Emmanuel Street en route to St Neots on 4 May 1915. The war had a great impact on Cambridge colleges who, with a shortage of undergraduates, accommodated Officer Cadet Battalions. A military hospital was opened in the cloisters under the Wren Library at Trinity College and a prefabricated hospital erected on land off Burrell's Walk, the site later developed for a new University Library. The first phase of the Cambridge Antiquarian Society's photographic survey ceased, to be revived 10 years later. (Photograph: F.P. Layburn-Yorker)

St Andrew's Street, 1928. Buildings on the west side of St Andrew's Street were demolished in 1931 for a new Post Office. At Robert Sayle many of the employees lived in a hostel, complete with a reading room, in the upper storeys of the building. In the 1920s senior saleswomen wore long silk or satin gowns and men black suits, stiff white collars and cuffs to their shirts and black ties, with frock coats for seniors. Directors, shop-walkers and senior buyers used to wear shining top hats as they moved around the store. (Photograph: J. Johnson)

St Andrew's Street – the Spinning House, *c.*1875. The Spinning House where the University imprisoned suspected prostitutes was demolished in 1899: *The days of the Cambridge Spinning House are numbered. It is to be pulled down in order that a house of detention after the best approved modern ideas may arise on its site. There is no more stirring chapter in the history of modern Cambridge than that which this forbidding looking building in St Andrews Street recalls. It is an ugly monument of an ugly feud between the authorities of the University and town. The feud is dead: would that the razing to the ground of the Spinning House were sufficient to efface all memory of it.* [CDN 19 April 1899] A new police and fire station opened on the site in 1901. The old St Andrew's Street Baptist Chapel, on the right was replaced in 1903 completing the radical transformation of this stretch of the Street. (Photograph: Simpson Bros)

Regent Street, 1935. Regent Street, looking north from Downing College gateway during coronation week, 1935, saw great changes in the inter-war years. In 1924 Herbert Robinson opened a new garage: *There is room for the display of 15 cars at a time, and those at present on view include such well known makes as Vauxhall, Fiat, Hillman, Citroen, Daimler and Calthorpe, all of the latest type.* [CDN 26 April 1924] This was in turn rebuilt in 1936 when Llandaff House, once the first dwelling on the Linton-Cambridge Road with a porch jutting out into the street was pulled down. In 1934 the nearby Castle Inn caught fire and on its site arose a new Regal Cinema. (Photograph: J. Baldwin)

Regent Street – advertising hoarding and petrol station at the corner of Gonville Place. *Advertising hoardings have been long regarded as one of the most detrimental types of development,* planners stated in 1934. [W.R. Davidge, Cambridgeshire regional planning report, 1934] Under the Advertising Regulation Act in 1907 authorities had been given power to regulate hoardings more than 12ft high and a second Act in 1925 allowed councils to make byelaws for restricting advertisements. *Cambridge council considered the erection of advertising boards by the Empire Marketing Committee at Corn Exchange Street, Market Hill, Drummer Street, Butts Green, Northampton Street and the Cattle Market. But the path in Corn Exchange Street was only five feet wide and it would be dangerous if people stopped there to look at it. They would have to put up another sign, 'Safety first. Passengers must not stop to look at this advertisement'. (Laughter).* [CDN 26 July 1927] But advertisers had more than councils to fear: *The Rendezvous placard trolley, which has so many times gone its rounds of the streets of Cambridge advertising 'thrillers' and 'heart appeal' stories at this cinema met with an ignominious fate at the hands of undergraduates. It was seized by a party of merry gownsmen and pulled in triumph down Hertford Street and Magdalene Street where they sought to dispose of it by pushing it into the river. It fell on to the landing stage moored at this point but with undamped ardour the undergraduates endeavoured by their united efforts to confine this 'publicity agent on wheels' to the cold depths of the Cam. Then, the last rites having been performed, the revellers went on their way rejoicing.* [CDN 1 February 1927]

Parker's Piece – Good Friday skipping, 1937. *Why does skipping always take place on Parker's Piece, Cambridge on Good Friday and Easter Monday? An old man of 83 remembers skipping there as a boy of five or six and his father apparently did so before him. It seems that Good Friday used to be the publican's 'day out' and they used to repair to the Piece for a game of bat and trap, while their youngsters amused themselves with a skipping rope. We don't hear much about Bat and Trap nowadays but the skipping goes on as of yore.* [CDN 26 March 1937] (Photograph: R.H. Brindley)

Parkside – stalls, 1936. Stalls selling refreshments and knick-knacks were erected along Parkside: *Good Friday dawned damp and dismal. Parker's Piece was the great gathering place of the merry makers. In accordance with custom many people produced skipping ropes and skipped away to their hearts' content. Old men & maidens, young men & children – likewise grand dames – jumped up and down to 'Salt, mustard, vinegar, pepper' and similar meaningless jingles. Hawkers of balloons, ices, fruit and sweets had secured 'pitches' at the East Road corner and did good business.* [CDN 11 April 1925]. The tradition died out at the start of World War Two. (Photograph: R.H. Brindley)

New Square, 1930. In 1930 houses in New Square overlooked cows grazing on a meadow. With the growth of the motor car came the demand for somewhere to park them. In 1925 proposals to take a small piece of Christ's Pieces for a combined bus station and car park at Drummer Street met opposition: *The protest meeting against the taking of part of Christ's Pieces for parking motor vehicles attracted a crowd of over 2,000 people to Drummer Street & was marked by a remarkable climax. After a resolution of protest had been passed the crowd voted a desire to take it to the Mayor that night. Speeches had been delivered from a four-wheeled waggon and the shafts were quickly manned and the waggon containing councillors who had spoken was dragged at a good pace to the Mayor's house in Newton Road. Something like a 1,000 people followed in its wake.* [CDN 12 August 1925] Nevertheless the scheme went ahead. Within a few years the car parking problem was again acute and eyes turned towards the large grassy area of New Square; this time there was less protest and it was converted to a car park in 1932. By 1950 over 43,000 vehicles a year were using it. New Square reverted to grass following the redevelopment of the Kite area and the construction of the Grafton Centre car parks. (Photograph: K. Cooke)

Fitzroy Street near the junction with Gold Street, 1939. This was an area of homes for working-class families, together with a range of services: *The tripe season is now in full swing and the noted house for this commodity is E.J. Edward's, 36 Fitzroy St, Cambridge. Tripe is a valuable edible for dyspeptics and others suffering from impaired digestion and as such there should be a good demand for it during the ensuing festive season. Mr Edward's name has been before the public for the past 50 years as a tripe dresser and glaze manufacturer and there is no doubt the stock he has laid in for Christmas will be more than equal to the increased demand.* [CDN 3 May 1899] New shops moved into the area at the turn of the century including the Cambridge Co-operative Society and Laurie and McConnal who rebuilt their shop in Fitzroy Street following a disastrous fire in 1903. After World War Two slum properties were cleared and various proposals for major redevelopment were discussed. In October 1977 Laurie and McConnal announced their closure blaming indecision over plans for the Kite area. Despite opposition much of the area was cleared for the Grafton Centre, which was opened by the Queen in 1984. (Photograph: L. Cobbett)

Fitzroy Street, 1939. Morley's pawnbroker's shop at the corner of Fitzroy Street and James Street, 1939. Monday was the busiest day for pawnbrokers as people returned the suits they had retrieved to wear for church on Sunday. But not all transactions were legitimate: *At Bottisham police court a woman was charged with stealing four pairs of woollen stockings, two flannel vests and one shawl to the value of £1 the property of the Mental Hospital Fulbourn. She went in the shop of Messrs Morley & Co and offered two flannel vests and a shawl for pawn. The assistant noticed there were two pieces torn out of the vest. The mental Superintendent said it had a pink mark under a seam with some wool stitched over it. She was bound over in the sum of £10.* [CDN 15 January 1924] (Photograph: L. Cobbett)

Staffordshire Street, 1911. St Andrew the Less parish workhouse, 8-9 Staffordshire Gardens. Dr Stokes spoke to the occupier in 1911: *When the central Union was formed in 1836, this Workhouse was altered to a certain extent, and used for the reception of girls and boys (to the number of about 46). The interesting house is now inhabited by a venerable and intelligent old lady, who carries her 94 years with much vivacity. She knew the place well in her childhood, and she laughingly remarks that she has come to die in 'the Workhouse'. She remembers Mr and Mrs Arnold, the former master and mistress of the institution, who used to allow her and a few children living in Covent Garden to play with the pauper boys and girls after they had finished 'their work'. She asserts that the building was erected 'for the purpose', and that it was larger than other workhouses (some of which were only altered cottages). She thinks that it was used 'for several parishes'. An old inmate of the Albert Almshouses remembers that services were at one time held in this Workhouse by various clergy; he himself often attended these gatherings.* [H.P. Stokes, Cambridge parish workhouses, 1911 – PCAS vol.15] (Photograph: H.P. Stokes)

Newmarket Road, 1928. Newmarket Road looking west, with the corner of East Road on the left. *Considered some years ago to accommodate some of the most squalid and unsightly houses in Cambridge, various efforts have been made to clear the local slums. It has several terraces of 19th-century cottages, several large-scale business developments and a lot of small shops of considerable antiquity. The people living in these houses or running these shops are frequently members of families which have been on Newmarket Road for as long and they can remember and would never want to live elsewhere. However much people may grumble about the amount of traffic it has to carry and however much they complain that it is not the most attractive of approach roads, without it Cambridge wouldn't have any gas, any local newspaper, any fire service, or any airport.* [CDN 11 July 1963] It was also the entertainment centre of Cambridge with a Circus of Varieties in Auckland Road and the Festival Theatre opening in 1926. The scene was transformed by the building of a large roundabout leading to Elizabeth Bridge, which opened in 1971. (Photograph: J.S. Moore)

Walnut Tree Avenue from Newmarket Road, 1929. Walnut Tree Avenue was demolished to make the approach to Elizabeth Bridge. The Brunswick School in Walnut Tree Avenue was the first Council School when it opened in 1905. But by 1922 the building was found to be subsiding: *The Borough surveyor drew attention to the giving way of the building, and they first of all had to pull down the Boys' School because it was dragging the other part down, and eventually they pulled down the Girls' School. The girls were in temporary premises at Paradise Street School and the boys in Fitzroy Street. They had to bear in mind that a new bridge was going to be built at Walnut Tree Avenue some time – (laughter) – and when that was done they would have to accommodate some children from old Chesterton.* [CDN 5 June 1925] (Photograph: J.S. Moore)

Newmarket Road – Coldham's Lane, 1929. Cottages at the Junction of Newmarket Road and Coldham's Lane, photographed shortly before they were pulled down for road widening. *For the purpose of demonstrating the beauty and usefulness of modern Cambridge tiles, both hand-made and machine-made, the Cambridge Brick Company have renovated a block of old cottages which stand at the corner of Coldham's Lane. About 85 years ago the cottages were built from their own demolished materials. There are seven varieties of tiles, the colours ranging from red, mottled, dun to white.* [CIP 17 February 1932] (Photograph: J.S. Moore)

Newmarket Road – brickworks, 1938. Newmarket Road was dominated by brickworks, as Hilda Swann recalled: *The sizeable lake along the edge of Coldham's Common, near Barnwell Bridge, was once a clay pit. Until about 1916 huts connected with the works were still visible at the bottom, sticking out of the water. There were four brickyards making hand-made bricks up to the 1930s. Watts and Co stood opposite Stanley Road & the Cambridge Brick Company was on the same side of the road. During World War Two the pit was filled up by Mr Duce with old cars and the Coral Trading Estate stands on some of the site. The Stourbridge Brick Company was approached from Cheddar's Lane, on the opposite site of Newmarket Road. This brickyard faded out rather earlier than the other three. Near Barnwell Bridge stood Swann's Brickyard. The land extended to Garlic Row in one direction, Stourbridge Common formed another boundary and, years later, the pit was getting very close to the edge in one part. The other boundary was formed by the railway. All this land was bought by Cambridge Corporation, the pit was filled in with household rubbish and the buildings and house where we lived was bull-dozed down.* [H.S. Swann, The brickmaking industry of Cambridge, 1977] Cement works were established at the start of the 20th century: *The extensive Portland Cement Works which are being erected in the neighbourhood of Coldham's Lane and Mill Road are now assuming enormous dimensions. In fact the buildings already completed are ample evidence that one of the largest and most modern cement works in England will be situated near Cambridge.* [CDN 14 May 1900] Reminders of Cambridge's industrial past are preserved in the Museum of Technology in Cheddar's Lane. (Photograph: L. Cobbett)

Beche Road – The Cellarer's Chequer, Barnwell Priory, 1900. In 1908 members of the Antiquarian Society visited Newmarket Road to view one of the oldest buildings in Cambridge, once part of Barnwell Priory. T.D. Atkinson explained: *The checkers of a religious house were the exchequers or offices in which the heads of departments kept their accounts and administered their affairs. This building is thought to be the office of the Cellarer, to whom was entrusted the entertainment of guests, and who was consequently one of the most important of the obedientiaries of the house. The room is in the earliest Gothic style, and may therefore be said to date from the end of the 12th century or from the beginning of the thirteenth. In its original state it must have been singularly beautiful. It was lighted by two lancet windows on the west side; some of the original iron bars to keep out intruders still remain. The fire-place, now blocked, had formerly a sloping hood springing from a stone lintel which was carried on corbels. From this description it will be seen that the room was well warmed, well lighted and well ventilated, in fact, that it was one in which comfort and privacy were carefully considered.* [T.D. Atkinson, Old houses in Cambridge, 1908, PCAS vol.13] (Photograph: F.G. Binnie)

Midsummer Common – Horse Fair, 1898. Stourbridge Fair was held on the common beside Newmarket Road. It was once an important trading fair but by 1917 only the horse fair remained and in 1934 it was abolished by order of the Secretary of State. Horses were also sold at Midsummer Fair: *Business transactions at Midsummer Horse Fair were carried out under uncomfortable conditions. Horses of all sizes were put through their paces on the sodden grass. Business however was brisk, cart horses and nags forming the major portion of the stock. Buyers from many parts of the country were at the fair and quite an average amount of buying and selling was done.* [CDN 22 June 1900] Sometimes other forms of transport were sold: Some *half-score useful horses were offered for sale at Cambridge's Midsummer Horse Fair. Included in the vehicles offered for sale was one Ford touring car – this strikes a progressive note – an attractive living waggon with rubber-tyred wheels, a pair-horse brake, a dog-cart and a governess cart were also offered, good prices being obtained for the majority.* [CDN 25rd June 1924] (Photograph: E.C. Hoppett)

Midsummer Fair – Death Riders, *c.*1925. People flocked to witness other attractions: *The old cry of 'Biggest fair I've seen for years' suggests that the Fair is still growing. Thurston's roundabouts are again present and number about six in all. They include their famous golden dragons, gondolas and motor scenic railways. Three circuses and numerous 'laugh and grow fat' shows make up a good square mile of pleasure ground. There are the usual crockery and sweet stalls, rock kings, cheap jacks, fortune tellers and the like in unusual profusion. An objectionable feature this year is a diabolical engine that emits a banshee-like wail at frequent intervals. It ought to be smothered.* [CDN 22 June 1922] The fair continues.

Midsummer Common – Callabys, 1935. Callaby's sign lasted long after his death. *Callaby was a familiar character at the turn of the century; with a long-backed fancy mongrel under his arm he greeted undergraduates: 'Want a little dawg, sir? Buy this one sir?' At his home beside the Fort St George public house on Midsummer Common he also offered stables for University boat horses at 3/- and dogs at 2/6.* [A.E. Reeve] Louis Cobbett annotated his photograph: *The last of Callaby's; the picturesque roofed gate through which we used to ride the coaching horses back to their temporary stable at Callaby's was at the right end of the wall.* (Photograph: L. Cobbett)

Fort St George ferry, September 1926. Ferries crossed the river, but this posed problems: *The Cam Conservators got the Fort St George ferry up, but it sank again. It was impossible to do anything with the boat and impossible to get another one. At lunchtime too many people crowded on to the boat and a man could not order them off. The Conservators had carried on the ferry at a loss for years.* [CDN 8 April 1927] People agitated for bridges but were not satisfied when they got them: *There was a good deal of grousing before the inhabitants of Chesterton had a footbridge over the Cam at Dant's Ferry. Now they have got one they have found something else to grouse about. At five minutes to eight every morning the instrument workers at Pye's are hurrying to work from the other side of the river. They curse and groan, trip and stagger under the burden of carrying their bicycles up and down a steep double flight of steps. Sooner or later some panting person carrying a bicycle will fall backwards or pitch into the river. The bridge was not made for cyclists who should get up earlier and ride up Victoria Avenue.* [CDN 23 July 1927] On the other bank was Chesterton, not part of Cambridge until 1912 and treated in the Survey like any other village. (Photograph: H.D. Latter)

CAMBRIDGESHIRE

Abington, Great – cottage, *c.*1935. Picturesque thatched cottages at Great Abington, now the Old Guild House, 88 High Street. By 1957 the thatch had collapsed and the four cottages were converted into two. The well has been filled in. Many cottages relied on pumps, water butts or wells for their water supply. In 1889 one man described his village's water as: *Covered with a green, slimy substance and full of living creatures; and to add to its high flavour most of the liquid from the adjoining farmyard closets and pig sties are drained into it.* People with indifferent or unsatisfactory supplies would like nothing better than a pure supply of water, but did not like the idea of paying for it. An official survey in 1945 found that only 48 percent of rural homes had piped water and one in five householders had to walk over 100 yards to get to a pump. (Photograph: R. Bellamy)

Abington, Great – St Mary's Church, *c.*1910. The interior of Great Abington church; its tranquillity was shattered in 1941: *With the glorious sun shining down on it, and the sheep quietly grazing in the surrounding meadow, the lovely old church at Great Abington was on Sunday re-opened after having been closed for nearly two years. It was in 1941 when a bomb fell on the bridge, which is at the present moment undergoing repairs, that the church suffered its first shock. Then one was dropped on the Land Settlement, an aircraft also crashed in the vicinity, and there were one or two other explosions nearby which finally necessitated the closing of the church in November 1946, as it was considered unsafe for public worship. The work of restoration was begun in that year, but then had to be stopped for a time until a few months ago when Messrs Rattee and Kett Ltd, of Cambridge, were able to re-start and complete it.* [CDN 16 March 1948] (Photograph: W. Tams)

Abington, Little – Church Lane, 1924. William Mortlock Palmer was the Linton doctor, an enthusiastic local historian and the man responsible for reviving the Cambridge Antiquarian Society's Photographic Record in 1925. He gave lectures illustrated by lantern slides to various groups including the Abington Women's Institute in March 1924. His notes were published in the *Cambridge Chronicle* and subsequently reprinted. Of this picture he commented: *Considering the small number of houses in the two parishes, there are a large number of old ones. The house in which William Ison lives has a chimney stack with the shafts set diagonally, and was built about 1650 as a small farmhouse. Perhaps you would like to know how a house like William Ison's was furnished in the year 1661…* and Palmer went on to give an inventory. [W.M. Palmer, The neighbourhood of Hildersham and Abington, 1924] Ison's cottage, in Church Lane, was demolished and replaced by bungalows built by South Cambridgeshire RDC in the early 1960s. [J. Hirsh, Little Abington village history trail, 2002] (Photograph: W.M. Palmer)

Abington Pigotts – Downhall Manor gatehouse, 1936. The bell-capped lantern on top of the old gatehouse was used as a guide for the benefit of travellers. *As you turn up to the church you pass a large inn, extraordinary large for so small a village, called the 'Darby and Joan'. But the most interesting thing is the massive wooden gatehouse of Downhall Manor, several hundred years old, which now leads into the farmyard but probably once led into the courtyard of the manor.* [W.M. Palmer, The Neighbourhood of Melbourn and Meldreth, 1923] (Photograph: J.H. Bullock)

Arrington Hill, before 1922. A scene of tranquillity at Arrington where, in September 1898 even lawbreakers could appreciate nature: *Just now the grounds surrounding the Arrington police station present a pleasing aspect. The flowerbeds are looking their best, crowned as they are with all the colours of the rainbow. The beds on the lawn, which are composed of two shades of asters, look lovely, whilst the borders and windowsills are one mass of flowers. Superintendent Wilderspin spares neither time nor labour in making the building and its surroundings presentable; and the remarks that are bestowed upon the worthy police officer by passers-by are certainly deserved.* [CDN 8 September 1898] But things were not so rosy later: *Between the two wars the land fell into a derelict condition; it was bought by a speculator at £3 per acre and sold piecemeal to purchasers, some of whom came from London. Dwellings – little more than shacks – had been erected.* [CDN 4 August 1951] (Photograph: R.H. Clark)

Ashley – Silverley church ruined tower. *Ashley-cum-Silverley have been formerly two distinct towns, but are now united. We have the ruins of both churches, but both so dilapidated that they are wholly out of use* the rector reported at the start of the 18th century. In 1752 William Cole commented: *There is but one church remaining in this depopulated village, and nothing of the church but the tower, which was formerly a very noble one. It had one of the largest west doors into it I almost ever saw for a parish church.* By 1984 the tower had crumbled to a height of 12.5 metres. [R. Halliday, The churches of Ashley and Silverley, 1984 – PCAS vol.73] (Photograph: R.H. Sherborn)

Ashley – green, 1930. Ashley green showing a small timber-framed building successively used as the parochial chapel, the village school – described as wretched, squalid and neglected – and subsequently as a barn and garage, when it was photographed for the survey. By 1952 it was in danger of collapse and was demolished shortly afterwards. [R. Halliday, The churches of Ashley and Silverley, 1984 – PCAS vol.73] (Photograph: J.H. Bullock)

Babraham – George Inn, 1936. The George Inn, Babraham, painted by the Sawston historian T.F. Teversham, was one of a number of pubs acquired by the Cambridgeshire Public House Trust Association set up in 1903. *The movement is a commercial undertaking with a philanthropic end. They want to raise the tone of the public house and promote temperance. The managers obtain no benefit from the sale of alcoholic liquors but make a profit on non-intoxicants; hot soup is supplied and villagers seem to appreciate the change as more and more public houses are ready to supply non-alcoholic refreshments.* [CDN 13 February 1904]. The exterior remained largely unchanged until devastated by fire; it has since been restored. (Painting by T.F. Teversham)

Balsham – Nine Chimneys house was probably built in 1583. Only the south or parlour wing of the original E-shaped building survives with six of its nine chimneys. Restoration in 1930 exposed the beams and added an extension at the rear. The importance of preserving old cottages was stressed by the Davidge report on regional planning published in 1934: *It is of great consequence to the future of the region that the old cottages and farm buildings still surviving should be protected and maintained. In many villages the decay of the old cottages is noticeable and many are far-gone in a state of disrepair, but demolition should not be considered until the possibilities of restoration and adaptation have been explored.* [W.R. Davidge, Cambridgeshire regional planning report, 1934] (Photograph: W.M. Palmer)

Barrington – Royal Oak, 1953. The Royal Oak during restoration in 1954: a photograph taken by the County Planning Department. The development of cement works promised new employment in 1927: *The Prime Minister is expected to visit Barrington to open the new cement works. The new works are already turning out great quantities of cement and when the second kiln is complete will be one of the largest cement works north of the Thames. About 200 men will be employed there permanently and it is expected that from a country village Barrington soon will be transformed into something like a small industrial town.* [CDN 11 October 1927] But not everybody agreed that the benefits would be universal: *Sir – I see that Mr Baldwin is so delighted to find an undertaking which is employing more men rather than turning them off, that he is coming to open the new cement works in Barrington. I wonder if he will ask where the 200 men who are going to be employed are to be housed. I doubt if 20 houses have been built in neighbouring villages since the war and there is a long waiting list of people not connected with the works. A large proportion of the men at present employed are being lodged in houses where there is no proper accommodation for them, and if another hundred men are to be taken on shortly the congestion will be appalling – G.T. Garratt, Barrington.* [CDN 13 October 1927] Mr Baldwin did not visit the village, but the cement works has become part of the landscape. (Photograph: Cambs County Council)

Bartlow Hills, *c.*1905. Bartlow Hills stand just over the county border, in Essex. There were originally six or seven conical mounds in two parallel lines close to Bartlow church, of which only four survive. Excavations revealed that each contained one cremated body in a glass vessel within a large wooden chest, together with various bronze, glass and pottery objects, some of which held wine mixed with honey and blood and milk. Antiquarians expressed concern about their preservation in 1903: *Sir – the famous barrows known as the Bartlow Hills will soon be no more. It matters nothing that they were reared in Roman times or are the private property of a possessor bent on preserving these splendid relics. The railway company that would have destroyed them 50 years ago but for determined opposition at the time, has set its mind on their removal. They have elected to run their lines through the barrows instead of around them. So the picks of English navvies, backed by compulsory powers, will soon be at work 'dinging doon' these works of our Romano British forefathers, since they stand in the way of their company's dividends. It is nothing short of a national scandal – A.R. Goddard* [CDN 16 September 1903]. (Photograph: F.J. Allen)

Barton – Hagger's Farm barns, 1928. The photographs show many of the old thatched farmyard barns, such as these at Hagger's Farm off the Coton Road, were in a poor state of repair. In the inter-war years farming was in depression and undergoing a revolution as horses gave way to tractors. Robin Page described the scene at Barton: *The greatest adventure of all was a visit to the farm. There were animals to watch or chase, puddles in which to splash or fall and if we were lucky we would get a ride in grandfather's pony and trap. Dolly and Diamond were housed in the stable, two fine carthorses. They were not only able and willing workers but also valuable companions in the never-ending struggle with the elements. But sadly as they stood at their manger, snorting and stamping, proud and content, they were unaware of the significance of the blue tractor standing silently in the shed nearby. Soon two tractors stood in the shed and the stable was empty, save for memories and the smell of the past. The harsh facts of farming life meant they had to go.*[R.Page, The decline of an English village, 1974] (Photograph: J.H. Bullock)

Barway – drainage mill, before 1917. In the fens wind pumps were being replaced by more modern engines: Harrimere drainage mill at the junction of Soham Lode and the River Ouse, Barway. *The windmills that drained the fens for close on 250 years were finely constructed and made to last. This beautiful example was demolished in 1917 and its successor today is a characterless house of brick. The overseer of Harrimere lived in a bungalow nearby. His mill, he knew, was made strong and he knew too when maintenance was due. When the mill was needed cloths, or sweeps, were attached to the sails, the brake was released and away it went – sometimes too fast when the wind was strong. The cap was adjusted to the wind by hand. Great stress was put on the scoopwheel slapping the water upwards for hours on end, but they were made to withstand it.* [A. Day, Times of flood, 1997] (Photograph: F.L. Harlock)

Bassingbourn – High Street, 1924. Hagger's shop with its advertisements for Sheffield cutlery and Shell petroleum; villages were self-sufficient with tradesmen often having more than one job. Alfred Wing was a baker at the 'Crown' public house in the High Street and composed a poem that was printed on the bags in which his bread was wrapped:
Bassingbourn Bread by all 'tis said
Remains the best, for getting fed.
Easy digesting, within your reach;
And Alf Wing's cart your friends please teach
Delivers these loaves at twopence each
[Bassingbourn Local History Group, A chronicle of two villages: Bassingbourn and Kneesworth, 1894-1994, 1994] (Photograph: W.M. Palmer)

Benwick – drainage mill, *c.*1920. Fen drainage mill at Turf Fen, Benwick. Photographs show many drainage mills in need of repair. *Often the drainage commissioners and farmers put off repairs to their mills until the consequences of sudden structural failure was apparent. The most exposed parts of the mills were covered by weatherboards. These, like the scoopwheel hoods which prevented splashing, and the cap which needed regular maintenance to keep the inside of the mill dry, were tarred, or sometimes painted to keep them waterproof and the work was often done by*

one of the fen millers. [P. Filby, The fen millwrights – Proceedings of Mills Research Conference, 1996] One Benwick miller was forced to take action against a competitor in 1899: *Herbert Varlow, an agricultural and general engineer, residing and carrying on business at Benwick claimed £500 from an engineer and wheelwright of West Fen engine, March. He stated the defendant wrote and published an advertisement in the Peterborough Advertiser intending to convey the meaning that his business was for sale and he had become insolvent. As a consequence two customers had broken off business. After the advertisement had appeared his creditors 'well rounded on him', several pressed him and one issued a writ. The defendant was a trade rival of his. The jury awarded him £150 damages.* [CDN 19 January 1899] (Photograph: D.G. Reid)

Bottisham – Holy Trinity Church, *c.*1900. Bottisham church tower was probably intended to have a wooden spire. *Over the centuries the tower has suffered from the weight and vibration of the bells. A drawing made by Richard Relhan about 1800 clearly shows cracks on the south wall as well as features now missing, such as a sundial and images in the recesses. The five church bells were rehung in a new oak frame in 1929 and joined by another on loan from Kirtling to complete a ring of six. The church clock was erected in 1870 and renovated in the 1920s.* [H. Rogers, A history of Holy Trinity church, Bottisham, 2002] Relhan's remarkable paintings of many Cambridgeshire villages are part of the Cambridge Antiquarian Society's library available to researchers in the Cambridge University Library map room. (Photograph: L. Cobbett)

Bourn – windmill, 1928. H.C. Hughes undertook a survey of Cambridgeshire windmills in 1928 and reported his findings to a meeting of the Cambridge Antiquarian Society: *Bourn post mill is probably the oldest surviving in Cambridgeshire & thought to date from about 1636. Though one pair of sails was renewed with patent shutters, and a fantail has taken the place of the old tail beam, the mill itself is old. The roof kept the old straight sides, instead of being curved like a boat to fit down over the brake wheel. The sails were smashed in a gale in 1925, finishing its working life.* [H.C. Hughes, Windmills in Cambridgeshire and the Isle of Ely, 1928, revised 1931 – PCAS vol.31] It was photographed during repair in 1928 by C.S. Smith who noted: *The tenant will not let the owner pull it down.* In 1932 the mill was restored by Cambridge Preservation Society. It has needed constant care, in 1977: *Bourn windmill is expected to be in working order again in the Spring following the battering it received in last winter's gales. One pair of sails were torn off in a storm, but all four are being renewed, for it was discovered that the remaining pair were in such a bad state that a thorough restoration was needed. When the Cambridge Preservation Society embarked on the restoration work it was estimated that it would cost around £4,000. But the state of the remaining sails and their replacement has now boosted the costs to more than £7,000.* [CEN 10 January 1977] (Photograph: C.S. Smith)

Boxworth – Golden Ball, 1928. The Golden Ball, licensee George Brown, and adjacent cottages, 1928; the scene was largely unchanged by 2002. In 1990 Basil Thornhill recalled his early life at Boxworth Manor in the early 1900s: *A special treat was to be taken with his brother, by Nanny, for a walk to the Huntingdon Road. The road was made of rough granite chips – very muddy and slippery in winter and dry and dusty in the spring and summer. If they were lucky they saw a cloud of dust which indicated the impending arrival of a motor car. One day Dr Grove from St Ives stopped in his car and asked Nanny if the boys would like a ride. Overcome with horror at riding on the noisy machine the boys began to cry and, to their eternal shame, refused the offer.* [T. Doig, Conversation: Basil Thornhill, 1990] (Photograph: J.H. Bullock)

Brinkley – smithy. *Frederick Howard, Bill Howard and Harry Taylor at the smithy which moved to a new site opposite the turning to Hall Lane where William Howard continued as a farrier and blacksmith until his death in 1948. The smithy was demolished for new houses but the stable remains and was converted into a bus shelter.* [R.H. Cory, Historical notes on Brinkley, 1973] As the number of horses used on the farm declined so blacksmiths had to diversify. For example at Meldreth: *The owner had taken up the making of motor bodies, caravans, trailers etc, using modern machinery. In spite of this up-to-dateness, however, the old works retain their old-world picturesque appearance, and in the shops may yet be seen relics of bygone days.* [CIP 25 December 1936]

Burrough Green – washing day, 1929. Washing on the line outside Walnut Tree cottages on the north-east side of the green at Burrough Green, now replaced by modern cottages which retain the original name. It was a constant chore as Alice Hulyer, who lived at Six Mile Bottom recalled: *Bill's mother took all day to do the washing. It was very hard work, with having to draw all the water from the well.* Irene O'Brien remembered: *When I was younger we had to do most jobs by hand: washing clothes, lighting fires for heating, beating carpets, sweeping floors, making beds with endless blankets and sheets, cooking from scratch and grinding down vegetables for babies to eat.* [T. Minter, Millennium child, 2000.] (Photograph: J.H. Bullock)

Burwell – castle site. Burwell castle had been erected by King Stephen to defend against the ravages of Geoffrey de Mandeville about 1142. During an attack on the unfinished castle Geoffrey was wounded by an arrow shot by a 'low foot-soldier' and died at Mildenhall. [T.C. Lethbridge, Excavations at Burwell castle, 1936 – PCAS vol.36] By 1952 the site had a different use, being: *The finest scramble course for many miles. Situated on the site of an old Norman castle and incorporating several crossings of the now dry moats, the course included a number of very steep ascents from which most of the riders made spectacular leaps. Spectators were able to see most of the racing from the high ground in the centre of the track upon which the castle had stood.* [CDN 6 August 1952] (Photograph: D.G. Reid)

Burwell – tollgate on Fordham Road, before 1905. In 1899 a cyclist received an unpleasant surprise: *Sir – I was cycling from Cambridge to Soham and between Burwell and Fordham I came suddenly upon a closed and barred gate, which I was kindly permitted to pass through on paying a toll of twopence. I learned that the gate is called the Ness Gate, that the roadway at this point is Crown property. In its present position this gate is a danger to cyclists but its very existence is a ridiculous and monstrous anomaly with its toll of 1d for every vehicle hailing from Burwell and 4d for every vehicle coming from less favoured districts. It is a very unfortunate circumstance that this piece of road is rented by the vice-chairman of the County Council – A.J. Wyatt* [CDN 2 August 1899] The toll was removed in December 1905. (Photograph: J.H. Bullock)

Caldecote – Rectory Farm, 1928. Rectory Farm, now called Christ's College Farm. In the early 1900s a new settlement, Highfields, was set up at Caldecote on land bought by a speculative builder. He divided it into plots for smallholders who were intended to grow produce for local markets, but the houses were also well-placed for commuters who treated the plots as large gardens. [A. Taylor, Archaeology, vol.1 1997] *About 1941 a new water pipeline was laid to supply water to Bourn aerodrome. The chairman of Caldecote parish council persuaded Chesterton Rural District Council to obtain consent from the Air Ministry to allow standposts to be erected from this pipe at advantageous points in the village in order that water was made available to residents. This consent was granted the standposts erected, each ratepayer having a key to turn the water on, at a cost of 2/6 per year.* [P. Bays, Twentieth century Caldecote – Caldecote Parish Council newsletter, March 1974] (Photograph: J.H. Bullock)

Carlton – Rawlingson's Farm, 1926. Railway carriage at Rawlingson's Farm, Willingham Green. By 1900 living conditions in many villages were unacceptable; Linton Rural District Council became the first in the area to adopt powers under the Housing of the Working Classes Act of 1890. Having started in Linton by 1926 they applied for permission to borrow money for the erection of 12 cottages in the parishes of Carlton, West Wickham and Hildersham. Other councils used old railway carriages as makeshift homes. [F & I. Jeffery, Housing in Linton, 2001] (Photograph: W.M. Palmer)

Castle Camps – Parkin's Farm. Charleswood Farm, Castle Camps, when farmed by Charles Parkin. Given the pressure on agriculture visiting politicians could expect a warm welcome: *Sir W. Cuthbert-Quilter MP was announced to speak at Castle Camps and, a noisy meeting being anticipated, a policeman was stationed at the entrance so as to allow only electors into the building. On arrival he was received with loud hissing and booing. He said: "I have come 100 miles today to see you". (Hissing and "Go back another hundred"). He attempted to address the meeting, but being frequently interrupted asked "Will you hear me?" A voice: "We have heard such a lot of rubbish, we want to hear some plain truth now". "You will get that from me". "You will be the first one who has told the truth then".* [CDN 12 October 1900] A few years later political and other discussions were interrupted when the Cock Inn, said to be at least 300 years old, was practically destroyed by a fire. [CIP 27 January 1933] (Photograph: W.M. Palmer)

Caxton – Crossroads, an aerial view, 1936. In July 1934 the Duke of Gloucester landed near Caxton Gibbet on his way to inaugurate Papworth Hospital. Visible in the background is Caxton gibbet, which made news in 1939: *The famous Caxton Gibbet is no more. The famous hanging post, which stood on the side of the Old North Road as a reminder of olden days' justice, was cut down by someone unknown on Sunday. "Neatly sawn off" was the way the manager of the Caxton Gibbet Hotel described what she found early on Monday morning when only a stump of about six inches was standing. It was not knocked down by anything but carefully sawn through. It took eight men to carry the famous oaken sentinel to the hotel yard, where it now lies. Everyone is very indignant about it. Holidaymakers passing through called and wanted to know where the gibbet had gone. It was actually a replica of the one which stood at the spot years ago and had only been standing about five years.* [CIP 14 April 1939] The gibbet was replaced. (Photograph: E. Albone)

Caxton – George Inn, 1939. The George Inn at Caxton was once an important coaching inn; Elihu Burritt recorded his impressions in 1864: *Caxton, a small, rambling village which looked as if it had not shaved and washed its face, and put on a clean shirt for a shocking length of time. There was only one old coaching inn in the town, but it had contracted itself into the fag-end of a large, dark, seedy-looking building, where it lived by selling beer and other sharp and cheap drinks to the villagers; nineteen-twentieths of whom appeared to be agricultural labourers. The entertainment proffered on the signboard over the door was evidently limited to the taproom. Indeed, this and the great, low-jointed and brick-floored kitchen opening into to it, seemed to constitute all the living or inhabited space in the building. I saw, at a glance, that the chance for a bed was faint and small; and I asked Landlord Rufus for one doubtingly, as one would ask for a ready-made pulpit or piano at a common cabinet-maker's.* [E Burritt, A walk from London to John O'Groats, 1864] (Photograph: Miss E. Rolleston)

Caxton – George Inn fireplace. To his suprise Burritt obtained a room: *So I followed 'the missus' into that great kitchen, and sat down in one corner of the huge fire-place while she made the tea. It was a capacious museum of culinary curiosities of the olden times, all arranged in picturesque groups, yet without any aim at effect. Pots, kettles, pans, spits, covers, hooks and trammels of the Elizabethan period, showed in the fire-light like a work of artistry.* [E. Burritt, A walk from London to John O'Groats, 1864]

Chatteris – ferry tollgate, 1926. Joan Robinson recalled the Chatteris turnpike: *"I remember an uncle and aunt of mine used to go to Bedford quite often from Chatteris and they come to the Somersham Toll when it was 6d. It was 6d each way if you were not local and didn't live in Chatteris. The people that had the Toll, they were brother and sister Dyson, and he was very keen on his six pen'orth you know! He used to sit up and wait for uncle – the rogue – to go back in the evening, and uncle would deliberately stay as late as he could, you know, so he wouldn't have to pay anything, because half the time he used to leave the gate open. He was very keen and I remember one Sunday they came, and I went out to them and there on the running board (they had running boards, didn't they, for cars all those years ago), and there on the running board was the 6d and they must have passed it out of the window and Dyson missed it, and it had dropped on the running board – so he didn't get that one!"* [S. Oosthuizen, We're the characters now, 1992] (Photograph: O.H.H. Jermy)

Chatteris – Gipsy caravans at Turf Fen. Douglas Reid came across travellers of a different sort at Turf Fen, between Chatteris and Doddington. Gipsies were welcome at fairs – most of the time: *'Daisy Lee' was summoned for professing to tell fortunes to the wife of Police Sergeant Hillier of Ely constabulary. She made a picturesque figure in court and said she was a member of the old and well-known family of Gipsy Lee. She was born in a caravan and called a gipsy. She carried on a business as a 'character reader' and had stood in Ely Market Place often on market days without any complaint being made. Mrs Hillier said she had visited Lee's caravan at St John's Farm, Ely, had handed over a half-crown and been told to make a lucky wish. The gipsy then told her she had had a lot of worry and trouble – which was not true – and that she had a very good husband. The Bench fined Lee £10 and 10s costs and said she must consider herself lucky they had not given her three month's hard labour. The money was paid forthwith.* [CDN 17 December 1926] But the question of what to do with them has exercised minds throughout the centuries: *At Cambridgeshire County Council a report was submitted with reference to the conditions that obtain among gipsies and dwellers in vans and tents. These people lead an insanitary life, they are the frequent carriers of disease, often disturb the peace of the localities in which they pitch their camps, and their children contrive to evade the provision of the Education Act and are brought up in the most gross ignorance. It is clear that something ought to be done. How is school attendance to be enforced on children who never acquired a local habitation. The evils that call for remedies are so real that it is eminently desirable that as far as possible to do so, the gipsy should be brought within the pale of the ordinary law.* [CDN 5 November 1898]

Cherry Hinton – The Five Bells, 1930. The Five Bells was one of eight public houses in a village which became part of Cambridge in 1935. In 1927 Chester Jones considered how Cherry Hinton might be improved by regional planning: *Although the village is close to Cambridge it possesses a feature which is prized by the town-planner; this is a surrounding belt of agriculture and park land, isolating the village from neighbouring inhabited areas. The greatest care should be taken to protect this area from building.* Some of the agricultural land became Marshall's airfield and in 2002 there were plans for additional housing on what has become known as the Green Belt. *There is something highly delightful in strolling through a village looking for attractive houses and cottages which may remain. The straggling and untidy appearance of Cherry Hinton is partly due to the yellow brick erections of the last century, but a great deal could be done to improve it. A group of ghostly cottages near the railway crossing are now in a sad state of ruin and after every high wind look less and less like human habitation. To repair them now is beyond the realms of possibility.* [C.H. Jones, Cherry Hinton and regional planning – *Cambridge Chronicle*, 9 March 1927] (Photograph: J.H. Bullock)

Cherry Hinton – cottages in Church End, 1929. Chester Jones continued: *On the other side of the railway, at Church End, are rural thatched cottages, and one with a pleasant mansard roof.* In 1993 Mafeking Cottage on the left was still standing, though the cottages in the background had been replaced. One thing never changes – the love of gossip: *The village of Cherry Hinton has been agog with excitement with rumours regarding the wealth of a sexagenarian spinster, who was removed to Chesterton workhouse infirmary. The woman has been living in a little two-roomed whitewashed thatched cottage in the Chequers Yard under conditions of poverty. The amount of her wealth has been subject to considerable exaggeration and the latest rumours place the figure at about £1,000. A search revealed £140 in coin of the realm, including £15 in gold, a large number of half-crowns and many smaller coins, secreted in several places in each of the rooms of the cottage, a fact that points to her having hoarded small sums for many years.* [CDN 19 March 1924] (Photograph: J.H. Bullock)

Chesterton – Water Street, 1930. Thatched stables in Water Street Chesterton on the corner of High Street were destroyed by fire in the early 1950s; the site was cleared and is now occupied by council flats. During times of hardship chickens and ducks were a tempting source of food: *Thomas R—. of Cave's Yard, Old Chesterton was charged with having stolen a drake. Detective Marsh said he saw the prisoner with a sack on his back. He opened it and found a large brown and white drake which Thomas said he had bought yesterday from a man named Pope of Upware for 2s.6d. (12p). The bird was quite warm – prisoner replied it had been in his house by a blazing fire all day. Then he said: "I knocked it over down the fen against the sewage farm. It came out of a ditch and I gave it a crump. I ain't going to starve as long as there is anything about. You can do what you like: hang me if you like".* He was remanded for a week. [CDN 22 June 1901] (Photograph: J.H. Bullock)

Chettisham – St Michael's Church. Chettisham was not a lucky place for James Tuck of Ely who was twice struck by lightning. *In 1914 he was putting hay into an elevator at Chettisham when there was a vivid flash of lightning. The fork he was holding was torn from his hands. The lightning scorched his face and left red marks on his arm of a zig-zag shape. When he recovered doctors were astonished.* Then in August 1923: *On Saturday he was driving some pigs. Suddenly there was a vivid flash of lightning and he was stuck to the ground in a dazed condition. With the exception of still having a headache he is now little worse for his experience.* [CDN 21 August 1923]

Cheveley – almshouses at Little Green, 1930. *A row of four cottages, evidently intended as almshouses, was built by Lord Dover in 1692. But he failed to endow them and after his death they were taken over by the vestry and used as a parish poorhouse until 1835, when the Poor Law Amendment Act meant that they were no longer needed for that purpose. They were let to labourers whose refusal to pay rents led to their sale in 1864.* [VCH vol.10. 2002] (Photograph: J.H. Bullock)

Childerley – Manor, 1928. The Cambridge Standard newspaper, published from 1935 to 1936, carried a number of articles on local history topics, many by Dr W.M. Palmer. One was on Childerley Manor: *Along the road between Cambridge and Caxton Gibbet the stranger passes in ignorance of the existence of the mansion, for there are one-and-a-quarter miles of farm road if you would enjoy the dignity and charm of Childerley. After his capture in 1647 King Charles I was taken under escort to Childerley Manor where he remained virtually a prisoner for several days, attending divine service in the chapel on the Sunday. One of the two churches in the parish was demolished in 1489, and Sir John Cutts pulled down the remaining church and depopulated the village to enlarge his deer park. Through the following years services were held in the private chapel of the Hall but at last the parish was deprived of this last place of worship. About 1730 it was being used as a tool house and granary and the Bishop was unable to enter it since it was full of corn and implements. Later it was used by the inmates of the Hall as a smoking room and then divided into two, one part being adapted as a cottage. Today the other half is happily being used for its intended purpose. Mr Francis Brooke is the present owner and frequently entertains the County Hunt, for the estate provides some of the best of sport and in the hall of the house a fine mask and brush are a memento of 'fifty-five minutes of the best', a run which ended in the gardens. And each morning the postman wheels his bicycle through the fields from Dry Drayton to deliver letters to the hall.* [*Cambridge Standard* 27 September 1935] (Photograph: L. Cobbett)

Chippenham – New Road cottages, 1930. Although picturesque, such cottages could be unhygienic: *Newmarket Rural Council considered a report on the epidemic of fever at Chippenham during which five people have died. Dr Gellatly wrote: "As to sanitary defects, the worst is the cottages in New-row where a large number of cases have occurred, the absence of ventilation rendering them practically 'back to back' dwellings. The people will not keep out of each other's homes and in many cases do all they can to conceal the facts in regard to suspected cases. It is true that very many defects of sanitation exist in Chippenham, but in no case can it be said that the health of the inhabitants has been directly affected by these defects"* [CDN 31 August 1922] (Photograph: J.H. Bullock)

Chishill, Great – windmill, 1936. Great Chishill windmill carries an inscription dated 1726 inside but was substantially rebuilt in 1819. It was owned by the Andrews family until sold to John Pegram in 1903. Its last miller was Joseph Pegram, who worked it until the early 1950s by which time it was in poor condition. Cambridgeshire County Council acquired the mill in 1964 and the millwrights Thompson and Son of Alford, Lincolnshire replaced the trestle, repaired the stocks and sails and changed the corrugated iron which covered the roof for weatherboarding. [R.D. Stevens, Cambridgeshire windmills and watermills, 1985] (Photograph: L. Cobbett)

Chishill, Little – St Nicholas' Church, *c.*1956. This little church has a very low tower and a short pyramidal spire; it was largely unchanged by 2002. *In 1934 a survey by the Medical Officer of Health found the Manor House had a private supply of water obtained from a deep well, which was pumped up into a tank and made available to local inhabitants. In Great Chishill villagers fetched water from pumps, some of which had warning notices stating either that the water was not for drinking or that it should be boiled. Those villagers who did not own a water cart fetched their drinking water in two buckets suspended from a yoke across the shoulders or used the services of a village character known as 'Owd Lew'. He had a large water cart which he trundled round the village and sold water to the aged and infirm at ha'penny a bucket.* ['Chishillite', Water – water; Cambs Local History Society Review, 1999] (Photograph: F.J. Bywaters)

Christchurch – church, *c.*1920. Christchurch, formerly called Brimstone Hill, is a hamlet of Upwell. The church dates from 1862 and formerly had a tower on the north side, but this was demolished shortly before 1883 owing to the insecurity of its foundations. Major renovations were undertaken in the 1990s, with significant work being devoted to replacing the floor and repairing the roof. It was the home of Dorothy L. Sayers whose father was Rector and features in her novel *The Nine Tailors* published in 1934. [R. Horton, Christchurch village appraisal, 1999] (Photograph: J.H. Bullock)

Coldham – church, before 1913. Formerly known as 'Pear Tree Hill', Coldham was constituted a separate parish in 1874. The church of St Ethedreda's was completed in 1876 at a cost of £2,700 with a small western turret containing two bells, which had been removed by 2002. The church played a full part in the life of the community, with the Harvest Festival one of the highlights of the year: *The proceedings commenced with a Public Tea in the School Room. So popular was the entertainment that the room was more than twice filled, and all seemed to do full justice to the homely fare. Everybody seemed in high good humour and it was most gratifying to notice how perfectly all classes seemed with each other. We were only sorry to think that, owing to the habit which some labourers have to change their situations at Michaelmas, some of those present would soon be gone from among us. Upon entering the sacred building for the Thanksgiving Service we were struck with the exquisite beauty of the decorations, reflecting the greatest credit upon the ladies who performed this work of love for God's House. The Church was filled from end to end and the service was most hearty, especially the singing of the well-known harvest hymns.* [Parish Magazine, October 1883] (Photograph: J.H. Bullock)

Comberton – maze, *c*.1900. A turf maze known as 'The Mazles' was cut at Comberton some time after 1660, probably as a copy of a surviving maze at Hilton. It was located close to a crossroads and in 1846 was enclosed in the playground of the village school. The foundation deeds of the school stipulated that the maze should be kept and maintained, which it was for a number of years. But by 1892 J.S. Clarke commented: *In the days of its prime, when its serpentine paths were well and carefully kept it naturally excited much attention and attracted many visitors to the village. Though its grassy embankments are so worn down it still ranks as a local curiosity of considerable note* [Cambridge Express, 12 December 1892]. A new maze was cut in 1909 by the Revd F.G. Walker and members of the Cambridge Antiquarian Society, but on a different site and to a different design. This was destroyed in the autumn of 1928 when the school was extended and the playground resurfaced. [N. Pennick, Mazes and labyrinths, 1990] (Photograph: W.H. Hayles)

Conington – Marshall's Farm, 1933. Grass fields at Conington were used as an airfield in 1929; David Garnett left his Hilton home for a stroll with his wife across the fields to Conington. *The peace of the countryside was disturbed by the buzz of an engine as an aeroplane climbed, dived and landed in the farmer's field. They pushed through the hedge and strolled to the little shed where a group of young men were standing beside a light car and a couple of motorcycles. Did they give joy-rides – yes, come back in twenty minutes. They walked around the small village, past the*

church and back to the field. Soon the plane was down again and David picked up his courage and climbed awkwardly into the cockpit, hitting his head as he did so. He gripped the side of the cockpit as the machine bumped across the grass, then suddenly they were above the hedges, above the trees and above the thin, narrow-gutted building that was his own house, looking down one of the chimneys as the pilot turned. Then they were down and it was his wife's turn for her five-minute flip. But by March 1930 the Cambridge Aero Club was losing money, the telephone was disconnected, the machines dispersed. It was inconvenient to undergraduates who had to drive nine miles through twisty by-roads for a twenty-minute lesson. And there was an alternative for in April 1929 an aerodrome had opened on Cambridge's Newmarket Road and in October they too had started giving flying lessons. [D.Garnett, A rabbit in the air, 1932] (Photograph: J.H. Bullock)

Coton – Row of cottages opposite the rectory, 1928. Old cottages in the rear of the John Barleycorn public house, nearly opposite the church, which were likely to be demolished in 1928. Dottie Pitt recalled her childhood in Coton: *By the time the Great War started Dottie Pitt was in service at the Rectory. She was paid two shillings for three hours' work and still got some change after buying a pot of cream, a loaf of bread and some bananas. When Dottie was small Grantchester Road used to go round by Manor Farm but during World War One they made the new road to make it easier for convoys etc to negotiate. In 1921 she was married to Arthur George Pitt in Coton Church. The house in Cambridge Road (then known as the High Road), where they moved, was not completed until 1922 and so George and Dottie lived for 11 months in a house in the High Street. Dottie remembers how she used to enjoy watching Mr Blows Wilson, the village blacksmith, at work. He lived in the old house opposite St. Catharine's Farm, which was also occupied by three other families.* [K. Fowle, Coton through the ages, 1992] (Photograph: J.H. Bullock)

Cottenham – Lordship Manor. In 1937 Cottenham lost one of its oldest properties: *A link with the historic past is being broken with the demolition of the 500-years-old Lordship House – Lordship Manor as it was called in the days of Samuel Pepys, the diarist. It has monastic associations and remains of fishponds can be seen in the vicinity. The last person of any importance to occupy the old Manor was a wealthy French lady, who used to live there periodically with her retinue, and during her stay she re-stocked the old fish ponds. Her ghost is supposed to haunt the house.* [CIP 8 October 1937] In 1801 the Lordship Estate had been sold in plots and the house, yard and all the land fronting Lambs Lane was bought by Ellis Munsey, a Cottenham builder. He pulled down part of Lordship House and built several small cottages and the remaining part of the house was divided into three tenements but gradually fell into disrepair. [L. Milway, ed, Cottenham in focus, 2002]

Cottenham – Baptist Chapel, *c.*1900. Cottenham Baptist Chapel was used for wounded troops during World War One when it became the Cambridge Voluntary Aid Detachment Hospital Number 36, mobilised in May 1915. *Twenty patients were received in the chapel schoolroom. A bathroom containing a bath with hot and cold water was added in December 1916 at a time when few houses in the village had such facilities. The Chapel deacons asked the Red Cross to leave in October 1917 after occupants were discovered dancing and playing cards on the premises. The patients were subsequently accommodated at the Rectory.* [L. Milway, ed, Cottenham in focus, 2002] (Photograph: W.M. Palmer)

Coveney churchyard, *c.*1929. Coveney churchyard was the scene of a dispute after a parishioner sought to erect a memorial to his wife. *Sir: A beautiful white marble monument, standing some ten feet high was taken to be erected in Coveney churchyard. The rector refused to admit it, as he said its shape, an obelisk, was heathen and that the words 'Peace, perfect peace' were not suitable. However he allowed the mason to place it in the enclosure and after it had laid there some 100 days some good friends of the deceased assisted in erecting it in the early hours of the morning. There it remained for twelve weeks, when the rector, with the assistance of another, hurled it down. He was caught in the act by two women. In his sermon he said he would like to put his arms round that wretched monument and carry it out of the churchyard, only it was too massive.* [CDN 13 October 1899] The matter was taken to the Ely County Court and resolved: *The Coveney obelisk has been re-erected in the parish churchyard at the spot where it stood before being overthrown by order of the rector. Amid the peacefulness of the notorious little burial ground it is hard to imagine the controversy and ill-feelings which for some time raged and which culminated in litigation. On Monday the monument was erected in its proper position whilst the Rector watched the operations without raising any objections.* [CDN 7 June 1900]

Coveney – cottage at Wardy Hill, 1930. Thatched cottage at Wardy Hill, near Coveney, now restored. It was at one time home to David Cox who, according to a local poem, had four wives:
But David's first, with all her tricks,
Lived till he was seventy-six.
But then a fair one crossed his path,
Said he "My dear, you'll grace my hearth".
At Coveney church the folks all stared,
When the Parson had declared,
That David Cox at ninety-one,
With matrimony had not done
[H. Painter, Sutton-in-the-Isle, 1980] (Photograph: W.M. Palmer)

Croxton – Manor House, 1938. *Croxton Hall and the tiny village that nestles nearby is falling into disrepair. But the owner is embarking on a project that will restore the village to a thriving community.* [*Hunts Post*, 3 December 1981] The scheme did not materialise but in 1989 new proposals to restore and preserve the village were announced by Christopher Curry, formerly of Acorn Computers, and William Sindall. Many of the cottages were by then completely derelict but others were saved and restored and 14 new houses built. [CEN 10 August 1989] *By 1906 the Manor House was divided into three homes for estate workers, including the tractor driver and milkman. Ernest Saywell, chauffeur at Croxton Park in the early part of the century kept a shop in the centre part, selling sweets, groceries and cigarettes. It later became two homes: Miss Bowie, Lord and Lady Eltisley's personal secretary, occupied the eastern and centre part with Alf and Ada Jakes remaining on the west side until their death. Mr C. Grain bought the house from Mr Curry, and after extensive restoration it once again became one dwelling. Repairs were needed to the roof after a fire caused considerable damage in February 1992, soon after the two-year restoration had been completed.* [R. Riley, Croxton: chronicle of a village, 1996] (Photograph: E. Rolleston)

Croydon – church, 1927. Croydon church was in poor condition in 1932: *The main walls of the church have been pushed outwards, the new buttress has pulled the old buttress off the tower and the south wall of the nave with its arcade leans outward to a serious extent, while the walls of the tower are cracked at the centre of each side from the ground upwards. Probably there is no church in the diocese in more perilous condition.* [*Cambridge Chronicle* July 1932] An appeal had its effect, by July 1937: *The south transept has been practically rebuilt, the tower, which had cracked, had been 'grouted' and strengthened, the inside base of the tower almost rebuilt and the chancel roof renewed. But the church still needed restoration of the north side of the nave, the repair of the plaster of the interior, the rebuilding of the porch and the interior re-decoration.* [CIP 9 July 1937] (Photograph: L. Cobbett)

Croydon – Croydon Wilds, 1928. Croydon Wilds, a 17th-century moated house with a brick tower in the middle was demolished in the 1950s. It featured in an advertisement in 1897: *Croydon Wilds, aptly so called, is one of the most remote parts of England. Its few inhabitants are housed in a couple of roomy cottages and it was to one of these cottages that a representative of the 'Cambridge Independent Press' penetrated, and had a talk with the most respected and intelligent of the inhabitants, Mr Smith, who has lived there for thirty-four years. His daughter, as the reporter passed through the cottage garden, stood bright and blooming beneath the lintel. But she had not always been so fit: "I was weakly and unwell since childhood … a doctor said I was in a consumption and I should never get better … I went into the Hospital in Cambridge, but I had given myself up".* Then came the miracle cure: *"I happened to read of 'Dr Williams Pink Pills for Pale People' … I had taken nearly one box when I began to feel better. Now I can walk easily, am strong and well, and quite able to get through my work without the slightest fatigue".* [CDN 14 July 1897] (Photograph: E.S. Palmer)

Doddington – High Street, 1932. A mass of advertising outside Doddington shops in 1932. Fifty years ago Alan Bloom wrote: *The road to Doddington runs along the lowly ridge of the second largest island in Fenland. It is only on the islands that real meadows are seen, for these fens are too profitable as arable to have much down to grass. Along the road are houses: some old and squat of cottage proportions; some newer and a little larger box-like structures of those who planned not for beauty, nor with regard to any consideration save that of having walls with which to support a roof under which to live. But a few quite modern houses have been built with taste, and with ample gardens. I suspect that March business folk live in some of these, not because the Fenman – worker, smallholder or farmer – is quite devoid of taste, but because generally speaking he bothers little about appearances. Passing through Fen villages, one doesn't see many gay cottage gardens. So often the house is built so close to the road that no front garden is possible. That makes the plain front of the house even plainer. Slate roof, dull yellow or mottled red brick, built quite often with windows only back and front even when detached, is the kind of house most frequently seen. But even where a garden patch exists, whether at front, side or back of the house, flowers are mostly less conspicuous than Brussels sprouts and potato tops.* [A. Bloom, The fens, 1953] (Photograph: E.B. Haddon)

Downham – Bishop's Palace, 1914. The refectory of the Bishop's Palace, Little Downham, used as a barn in 1914. The Palace was constructed by Bishop Alcock at the end of the 15th century. In 1611 Isaac Casaubon, accompanied Bishop Andrewes from his London residence to the Manor of Downham. He had bitter memories of the East Anglian climate. *"At Downham we never know what heat is! There are few houses, yet it has more than 400 bulls and cows besides flocks of sheep. I was amazed when I saw one man on stilts alone with one little son tend 400 cattle".* He described how huge stiltwalkers on very high stilts ran very swiftly and had their hands free all of the time. The longevity of the villagers greatly impressed him: *"It is quite common to see here men who are over 100 years old and 120 years old. I myself saw men over 80 and 85 years strong in body and able to work in the fields".* [M. Hughes, Downham in the Isle, 1998] (Photograph: J.H. Bullock)

Downham – pound, 1930. The village pound on the corner of Tower Road, by 1994 it was the site of an electricity sub-station. The remains of a street light recall a dispute of 1925: *Little Downham parish council are hoping to brighten the main parts of their village by means of acetylene gas lamps but they want the money to do it. In expectation of support for such a project they arranged for a public meeting, but scarcely a dozen ratepayers put in an appearance. The idea is to revive a custom started in 1911 when acetylene gas was generated at the Pound, Town End, and voluntary subscriptions met the financial obligations. Since the war the gas plant has been lying idle and the lampposts have served only for supports for the weary.* [CDN 21 October 1925]. (Photograph: J.H. Bullock)

Dry Drayton – the Old Bakehouse, 1929. John Hacker and Sid Martin recalled: *Old thatched cottages were small, damp cold and dark. Many large families had only one room upstairs and one room downstairs. Two bedrooms were a luxury and should there be two ground floor rooms, the chances were that one of them would be the best or front room, containing a few precious and treasured pieces of furniture. It was out of bounds for the family except for weddings, funerals and christenings, all of which happened much more frequently than they do today. One often had to step down into the kitchen-living room, but even then the low beams were a hazard. In the poorest homes the ceilings were frequently only the undersides of the floor beams above, and I remember some with sacking nailed to the joists to check the dust from filtering through from the room above. The rooms were usually dark with only one poky little window hidden behind curtains so that the family lived in semi-darkness. Doors and windows did not always fit; draughts were accepted as a part of life, but the worst cracks were stuffed with paper or rag. Brick and tile floors were uneven and worn, stairs were not a routine fitment; sometimes there was simply a ladder up the hatch and even this might be external. Before going to bed the children might be sent out for a brisk walk or jog so they might be warm and glowing before getting into a cold bed in a cold room. When there were insufficient covers coats were used as extra blankets unless someone had thoughtfully placed a warmed brick wrapped in a cloth in the bed.* [Dry Drayton 2000, Gallows piece to bee garden, 2000] (Photograph: L. Cobbett)

Dullingham –The Kings Head, 1931. It could be dangerous to cycle at Dullingham in the 1920s: *W.G. Fullick complained of the dangerous state of Gypsy Lane, Dullingham; hardly a day passed without someone falling from a bicycle. He supposed the Council would rather pay out compensation than put a little gravel down and noticed that the Councillors all had good roads to their residences. He hoped the Council would soon wake up and do something.* [CDN 13 December 1928]. (Photograph: T.S. Moore)

Duxford – cottages and lock-up on the village green. The Cambridge Antiquarian Society became involved in a mystery in 1935: *Duxford have lost their ancient stocks. They stood in front of the old lock-up on the village green. But now they have disappeared. The unfortunate loss, together with the deplorable state of the lock-up itself – which during the last few months has been stripped of everything of value – has prompted Mr F. Slipper to write to the Cambridge Antiquarian Society. What the Society can do at the moment is difficult to see, since nobody is anxious to claim ownership of the unfortunate building.* [CIP 31 May 1935] The article brought a response from a local resident, Mr C. Sheldrick: *I and others who have known this ancient building for over 60 years have always known it as the lock-up or the cage. It was supposed to be a place to lock up wicked or unruly people while someone fetched the police, but we have only heard of one drunken man being detained there during our lifetime. For many years it was kept locked up, and during the war the village lamps were taken down and placed in there for safety. By some means the building became unlocked the lamps got broken -the frames were smashed to pieces- and by rough usage the roof of the building fell in. Now the four old flint walls stand derelict. Boys and girls climb on top of the walls and old tins and rubbish are scattered about inside and out. Altogether the scene is an eyesore. As the building stands on the village green, it would appear to belong to the Parish Council. Unless the Cambridge Antiquarian Society decides to take it under their care, it should be demolished as it is a disgrace to our old-world village. Visitors have commented to me about it many time, so 1 hope something will now be done to improve its appearance or clear it away.* [CIP 21 June 1935]

Duxford – Priory Chapel, Whittlesford Bridge, 1903. The chapel was founded about 1200 as a small hospital run by a prior and monks. It was intended to give medical help to the poor but its position by the bridge on a major route of the Icknield Way also involved it in providing hospitality to travellers. In the 14th century it was rebuilt as a chapel and was in use until the Dissolution. [C.E. Sayle, The chapel of the hospital of St John Duxford, 1903 – PCAS vol.10] It was visited by William Home in 1849: *The basement of the building is partly composed of pebbles and stone: the roof is thatched, and now used as a barn; and through a gable or porch near the west end is the entrance for waggons and carts. It was just then filled with corn from the field, and we expressed disappointment at not being able to see much of the interior, but our host of the Red Lion said with a smile, "it was never filled better". The west end is bricked up entirely, and appears of no very ancient date; and, from a foundation which was discovered some years ago, it may be presumed the chapel once joined the house, which was probably the refectory. The north and south side have each three corresponding windows; at the east end was a large window vaulted with stone, but the spandrels and mullions are destroyed, and the whole is blocked up. A little paddock at the east end of the chapel, now used as a drove for cattle, is supposed to have been the ancient burial place, as many human bones have from time to time been there dug up.* [W. Hone, Year Book, 1849] It was taken over by the Ministry of Works in 1954 in a ruinous condition, especially the thatched roof and woodwork. A new floor was laid and the pebbled walls repaired inside and out. The ruinous east window was boarded up and a substantial tiled roof replaced the old thatch. In 1960 the road was bypassed. [T.F. Teversham, History of the hospice and priory chapel... Whittlesford Bridge, 1968] (Photograph: F.J. Allen)

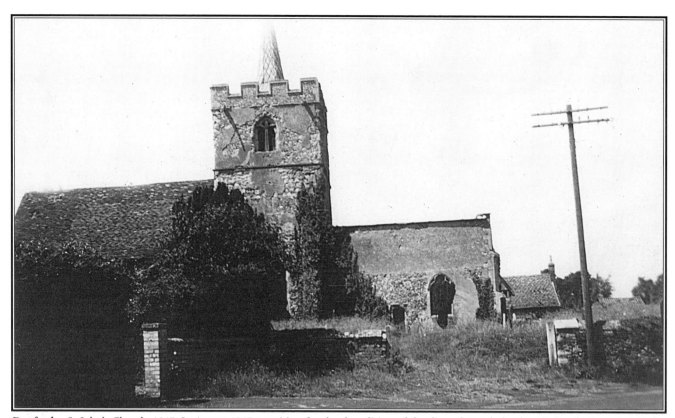

Duxford – St John's Church, 1947. In August 1947 a petition for the demolition of the disused St John's Church, Duxford was heard at a Consistory Court at Ely Cathedral. *The rector reported that it was in a very advanced state of decay and there was a possibility of serious accidents happening; it had been broken into, defiled and misused in a great many and scandalous ways and in a state of considerable dilapidation. The walls were opening up and breaking away from the roof, and tiles were coming off. The rain had already destroyed a great deal of the medieval contents and irreparable damage had been done to 'really good stuff'. Efforts had been made to persuade the R.A.F. to take over the church as a chapel in memory of the American pilots who fell in the Battle of Britain, but that scheme ended in failure.* [CDN 29 August 1947] The church was closed but repaired by the Churches Conservation Trust. (Photograph: G.H.S. Bushnell)

Elm – village and church, *c.*1920. The now peaceful village of Elm was the centre of uproar in 1881: *There was great parochial unrest when proposals were made to lay a tramline through the village, even a petition sent to Parliament. The tramway was laid from Wisbech to Upwell alongside the canal. Alas neither has survived, the tramway was a victim of Dr Beeching and the canal was filled in when the Anglian Water Authority re-routed the drainage in the fens. Many of the villagers remember the tramway and the canal, which was well used in the past, particularly on Saturday nights when revellers came home from Wisbech by barge, singing all the way! There are of course more houses now, a change from the last century when the scattered cottages all had their own small-holding or at least a large cottage garden. It is still an agricultural area with fruit, vegetables, flowers and grain being harvested throughout the year, but most of the newcomers go further afield to work. Social life centres round the church, church house, four public houses and the three village shops. In the 1920s there were five bakers in the village and the smell of new bread was wonderful!* [Cambridgeshire Federation of Women's Institutes, The Cambridgeshire village book, 1989]

Elsworth – Manor House, 1938. The Manor House at Elsworth, built by Samuel Disbrowe in the 17th century, was in danger of being pulled down in 1937: *It is the only house in Elsworth of any size, and it and the church are consequently the principal architectural features of the village. The house is, moreover, of considerable beauty and historic interest.* [CIP 8 October 1937] The house survived and by 1995 had been converted into three dwellings with a porch over the middle section. Other residents of Smith Street houses were waiting for basic facilities in 1976: *The continuing problem of some Elsworth council house tenants who have to use buckets for lavatories has prompted their parish council to back their demands for improvements. Most of the pre-war homes in Brockley Road and Smith Street have no lavatories and no hot water. There are about 16 houses altogether occupied by more than 50 people. The tenants have been campaigning for improvements for years and when sewerage mains work was completed recently they thought modernisation work would begin. So far nothing has happened and councillors fear that work may be postponed again because of the present financial crisis.* [CEN 30 November 1976] (Photograph: L. Cobbett)

Elsworth – Plough Inn, before 1927. The Plough Inn, Brook Street, is now a private house and the advertising signs have been removed. Not all villages had such amenities: *Application was made for a new full licence in respect of the former Three Horseshoes at Knapwell. It was discontinued as the former owner had extreme views on the temperance question and purposely shut the house up. The nearest public house was at Elsworth and if a man had to walk two miles to fetch his supper beer there was a great temptation for him to have more before he left. It was the wish of the inhabitants that they should have some means of obtaining drink in the village. Many lives were saved by the prompt administration of brandy during an illness; cases might frequently occur at Knapwell and lives be lost through there being no stimulant brandy.* [CDN 5 February 1903]. (Photograph: H. Moore)

Eltisley – Green, *c.*1920. Like all communities Eltisley suffered great losses in World War One; a Peace Tree was planted in March 1919 with a row of lime trees as a memorial to the 14 men killed. After the war the village had the opportunity of having on display a gun taken from the Germans but it was constantly being tipped onto its barrel. [M. Sawyer & M. Flinders, The Eltisley millennium book, 2000] Whilst John Cozens and his bus provided an important service for the village other traffic was less welcome, but in 1973 peace descended with the opening of a new bypass: *The rumble of continental juggernauts stopped and the danger from fast-moving cars almost disappeared. To celebrate the arrival of the by-pass one young married couple took a leisurely stroll down the middle of the old main road – something that would have been impossible during a normal Bank Holiday with a stream of traffic travelling at least 50 mph. But not all Eltisley welcomed the by-pass. The local garage owner said it could be a disaster as far as his business is concerned.* [CEN 30 May 1973]

Ely Cathedral from the river, *c.*1900. A classic photograph of Ely Cathedral on its island overlooking the surrounding fenland. The Cambridge Antiquarian Society's collections include dozens of boxes of glass negatives, many of which have never been printed, including a comprehensive survey of the cathedral building and precincts at the turn of the century.

Ely – Overfall windmill interior. The Overfall drainage mill at Ely was a giant structure that lifted water from Middle Fen Drain into the River Ouse. Such wind pumps needed constant attention or sudden squalls could cause damage, or blow them across the fen. The Cross family ran the mill for several generations and included amongst a batch of negatives donated to the Survey is a very rare interior view of the living area at the base of the mill taken sometime before its demolition in 1917. The negative is one of a large number of Ely, going back to the 1860s, which were donated to the Survey by Mrs F.L. Harlock in 1935.

Ely – October Fair on the Market Place. Fairs in Ely date back to the early days of the monastery. *The tradition of proclaiming the Fair was, until the 1930s, carried out by the Bailiff who, accompanied by the Town Crier with his bell and preceded by a fiddler, read the charter at Parnell Pits, St John's Road where a stock fair was held, on St Mary's Green for the horse fair, at the Market Place 'for the merry-making' and at Waterside for the cheese fair. The horse fair gradually died out and today the only fair is that held twice yearly at the end of May and October to provide entertainment and fun. As it is on Thursday, Friday and Saturday, the market traders are ousted from their usual position on the first day and moved to cramped quarters along the north side of High Street.* [P. Blakeman, The book of Ely, 1990] Following repaving of the Market Place the traditional fairs have been banished away from the city centre which no longer resounds to the sounds of Jollity Farms and hurdy gurdies.

Ely – St John's Farm, 1935. In 1934 Dr Louis Cobbett investigated remains of the hospitals of St John the Baptist and St Mary Magdalene at St John's Farm Ely, buildings that had not been researched for over a century. *St John's Farm is a curious building of Tudor appearance with 'crow-stepped' gables of brick which I believe to have been built on the site of the chapel of St Mary's Hospital and to contain parts of the original building. It is now used as a laundry and workshop. The substantial farm-house is alongside it, and a little farther away hidden among other farm buildings is a large barn which I identify with the chapel of the hospital of St John. The buildings on St John's Farm include, besides the two chapels, a third ancient structure made of Barnack stone which must belong to monastic days, though it now has a roof like an eighteenth-century dove-house, and is almost devoid of architectural features.* [L. Cobbett, The hospitals of St John and St Mary Magdalene at Ely, 1935 – PCAS vol.36] The buildings remain largely unknown to most visitors. (Photograph: L. Cobbett)

Eversden, Great – Banks' Farm, 1928. A mid-18th-century farmhouse, beside the High Street; two-storied with attics and a tiled roof the house was built of red brick with a distinctive projecting horizontal band of brickwork at first-floor level. When Dr Palmer photographed it the Banks family occupied the farm. *Bob Banks converted an old agricultural worker's cottage across the road into a billiard hut and this 'clubhouse' became a meeting place for the local farmers.* [L. Wood, Quiet lanes and orchard ends: a visual archive of Little & Great Eversden, 2000] Some of the farmer's produce ended up in the village shop as Enid Barraud discovered: *At the far end was the marble-topped counter with the scales at one end and the bacon slicer at the other and, on the shelves behind, a noble cheese (with wooden handled wire to cut it) and a great slab of golden butter and a smaller one of margarine and yet another of pallid lard. Whole sides of bacon were there, back and streaky, hocks and corners.* [E.M. Barraud, Tail corn, 1946] (Photograph: W.M. Palmer)

Eversden, Little – Buck's Lane Farm, *c.*1928. *A 'Titan' tractor, the first in the Eversdens, parked between a wheat stack and the 17th-century farm building known as the 'brewhouse' at Five Gables Farm, Lt Eversden. The brewhouse was also used as a granary. The building has since fallen down.* [L. Wood, Quiet lanes and orchard ends, 2000] Darren Tebbitt comments: *The tractor is an International Harvester Titan, one of about 3000*

shipped to Britain. When early tractors such as this first arrived on farms during World War One, farmers were sceptical of their abilities. Time proved their opinions right; designed for the vast, flat, and mostly dry American prairies, their long wheelbases and primitive steering systems soon showed their limitations in Britain's small fields, prompting typical comments of "needs 'alf an acre to turn round". However these early models were high in horsepower, and capable of towing a three-furrow plough to good effect. Another good point was their belt pulley performance which meant they could also serve as a substitute to replace the traction engine for threshing. I suspect it was going to power a drum to thresh the adjacent corn stack. Until better more versatile models came along, farmers chose the best power source for the job in hand with tractors used for ploughing, heavy cultivation, occasionally mowing, hauling, and threshing, milling etc in the yard & old faithful Dobbin retained for tilling, harrowing, drilling etc. When the majority of Titans arrived here in 1914 to 1918 most younger farm workers were otherwise occupied in World War One, so often older employees had to learn tractor operation. With only large farms able to afford and justify the expense of a tractor there was normally someone within the ranks who showed an interest in technology. But in peacetime, if a first tractor was acquired usually a younger worker was chosen as the operator – easier to teach a young dog new tricks! Few pre 1930 tractors exist today, universally outmoded by newer siblings in the nineteen thirties, defunct and unloved, most were melted down in WW II. [Darren Tebbitt personal communication, January 2003] (Photograph: J.H. Bullock)

Fen Ditton – High Ditch Road, *c.*1900. Manor House, formerly Manor Farm House, 18 High Ditch Road. The mounting block outside would have enabled the farmer to get on to his horse more easily, it remains, though the distinctive trees have been lost. The Leys School's Clapham Society surveyed the village in 1961: *Fen Ditton is becoming a dormitory suburb of Cambridge but still retains the flavour of an agricultural village. There is main water and most of the houses have electricity, but there is not much main drainage and much of the drainage is thought to go into the river. Hence the river is becoming a major problem because of the offensive odour and pollution.* [Leys School, A survey of Fen Ditton, 1961] Still people liked to live beside the water: *Cambridge Preservation Society object to the chalets and caravans at Grassy Corner, Fen Ditton. They say haphazard development of individually respectable shacks has seriously spoiled this length of river. The fifteen owners said they paid £14 a year rent for their plots and the land flooded in winter. The gypsy encampment and rubbish dump on the opposite side of the river made it difficult to understand the objections.* [CDN 20 June 1952]

Fen Drayton – Dutch house, *c.*1929. Charles Cudworth made a special study of the Dutch influence in East Anglian architecture in which he featured this cottage at Fen Drayton. *Near the church stands an unpretentious cottage, which upon close inspection reveals signs of a chequered career, visible in numerous patchings and repairs no less than in its inserted neo-Gothic windows. But its most interesting feature is the stone doorway which bears an inscription in Dutch, dated 1713. It reads: 'Niet zonder Arbyt' – 'Nothing without work'. The language and the sentiment have led to its being attributed to Cornelius Vermuyden, who strove so hard for the draining of the fens. But Vermuyden, who had a grown-up son fighting in the Civil War, could hardly have been erecting doorways in the next century!* [C.L. Cudworth, Dutch influence in East Anglian architecture, 1935 – PCAS vol.37] (Photograph: L. Cobbett)

Fen Drayton – Old Manor Farm, 1929. Youngsters photographed in front of old thatched cottages at Fen Drayton. Good behaviour was demanded, as V.K. Johnson recalled in 1931: *Robert Ding, a Waterloo veteran, was paid a shilling a week and armed with a stout stick to keep the boys of the village in order during church services. In 1851 there were five public-houses in the village, one alone remains. It once boasted two windmills: now they are no more. Moreover the village was more beautiful then. The population was about six hundred but there are now less than two hundred: in the last fifty years alone some forty cottages have been destroyed by fire or decay and neglect. Ill-health was pretty prevalent: even today there is no water laid on. There was a conflagration when five cottages were struck by lightning; many other cottages, alas, have collapsed in decay.* [V.K. Johnson, Fen Drayton: reminiscences of an octogenarian inhabitant – Christ's College Magazine, Lent 1931]. In 1935 the village agriculture was transformed when the Land Settlement Association bought Fen Drayton House, 15 cottages and 350 acres of land to provide smallholdings for unemployed industrial workers during a period of depression. (Photograph: L. Cobbett)

Fordham – windmill, 1931. Millers faced a multitude of problems: *The friction of the millstones is absorbed in grinding the corn, should corn run out the friction makes the stones very hot and many fires in mills have been caused. So most mills have a warning bell. A windmill with the sails burning at night is one of the most terrifying of all sights. Many Fordham people still remember the sight of their mill burning.* [H.C. Hughes Windmills, 1931 – PCAS vol.31] The mill on the Isleham Road was rebuilt after the fire in 1877 and survived until 1950. [VCH vol.10. 2002] The problem of fire was ever-present; Fordham was home to the Victorian poet, James Withers who in 1889 penned a verse dedicated to the newly formed village fire brigade: *Should some wild incendiary from deep revenge or spite, Crawl forth to do his fiendish work beneath the silent night; When all are sleeping peacefully, without a sense of fear, The thrilling cry of 'Fire', 'Fire', breaks on the startled ear … Forth rush the gallant band of men on deeds of mercy bent, To save the precious grain and stock that Providence had sent.* [J. Withers, Fairy revels, 1901] (Photograph: J.H. Bullock)

Fordham – houses opposite the church, 1926. Generally however village life was less dramatic: *Horticulture is the principal occupation and the large nurseries and seed-growing establishments absorb much local labour. The village is noted for the growth of scabias which has been developed over about 30 acres. During the season two lorry loads of these flowers leave Fordham daily for Covent Garden and the northern markets. In the last winter a system of street lighting has been introduced, incorporating the erection of 44 gas lamps. Nor is gas the only means of illumination for the village has had the electric light for five years. All the places of worship, the Victoria Hall and the British Legion Clubroom are lighted by electricity, the installation being carried out by Mrs J.W. Townsend as a practical memorial to her husband.* [*Cambridgeshire Times,* 19 June 1936] (Photograph: W.M. Palmer)

Fowlmere – dedication of war memorial, 1919. Village life changed forever with World War One; at Fowlmere the names of 12 victims are recorded on the War Memorial. *They are John Baker, Alfred Chamberlain. George Ingrey, Charles Knights, Arthur Sheldrick, Harry Smith, Mark Smith, Frank Ward, Septimus Ward, Albert Wilkinson, Wilfred Maulkin Nash, and George Payne. This last name was added in the year 2000, when the memorial was rededicated after renovation. His name had not originally been included as he died of his wounds after the Great War ended. The Rev. A.C. Yorke performed the original dedication of the War Memorial in 1919 at a special ceremony, attended by three trumpeters of the recently formed Royal Air Force, and a large crowd of villagers.* [L.W. Price, Bird lake village, 2002]

Fowlmere – milestone and airfield, 1917. Fowlmere airfield opened as a training establishment in 1918 and ended its days as a storehouse for planes until its hangars were demolished in 1923. A machine-gun firing range is shown in this photograph presented to the Survey in 1917. *When the war ended, a rather free and easy attitude prevailed at the airfield and joy rides were given to local people in aircraft such as the Avro 504.* [L.W. Price, Bird lake village, 2002] The milestone was one of a series erected in 1731 on the road from Cambridge to Barkway, believed to be the first true milestones set up since Roman times. They were originally paid for from a bequest of Dr W. Mowse, the Master of Trinity Hall and carry the college arms. (Photograph: W.M. Palmer)

Fowlmere – watercress beds, *c.*1880. Watercress beds on The Moor, Fowlmere. *The beds, some about the area of a football pitch, were of an even shallow depth and most were dug out with spades and the earth barrowed away. The beds were made flat using long rakes and wooden walkways, called trestles, were built to give access to the cress. In the late 1930's about ten men were employed full time with another three being taken on at busy periods. There were also six women who bunched up the cress. They were paid about sixpence for 144 bunches, each woman doing about a hundred gross a day. Lorries loaded with wicker baskets full of cress went to London's Covent Garden Market. Work was carried on all year, with separate Spring and Winter beds. One bed was always used as a stock bed and the plants were planted out by just putting them in the mud by hand. The beds full of cress looked just like a lawn and the grassy paths alongside were cut level and short, so that the picked cress could be laid down on them. After a bed was harvested, it was cleared and hand weeded under water, then 'stock' plants put out. The bunched cress was put in a washing hole to keep fresh and cool in spring water before it was packed and despatched to Covent Garden Market. The main cress beds ceased production after the 1950's although W Hailworth was still supplying the markets and the village in 1965.* [L.W. Price, Foulmire Moor and Fowlmere RSPB nature reserve, 1994] (Photograph: J. Bishop)

Foxton – pump, before 1926. Don Challis recalled: *As children there were opportunities to earn a copper or two after school. One of these involved the ubiquitous water cart with which my friend Dennis Redfern and I used to obtain Mr How's water supply. As the village did not boast mains water, unless you were the occupant of a Press cottage or lived in a couple of selected dwellings supplied by their private bore, the village pump was the only alternative. Since the sight of the Headmaster of the village school struggling along Station Road dragging a water cart, slopping water all over the road was a sight too painful to contemplate, other arrangements had to be made. Quite how Dennis and I came to be selected for this onerous task escapes me, I doubt if we were first choice, but selected we were and on two afternoons a week could be seen at the pump filling up our Head's cart.* [D. Challis, Schooldays in Foxton, 1998] (Photograph: R.H. Clark)

Friday Bridge – St Mark's Church. In the Friday Bridge area farmers planted hundreds of acres of fruit and at the peak season there was far more work than local pickers could handle. They were soon employing up to 1,300 people many imported from the East End of London. *It was usual for them to come for a month – men, women and children of all ages. They lived in 'bunks' – tin huts, old stables or converted railway carriages. It was not the farmer's duty to provide amusements for his workers and the only entertainment was in public houses. Mothers brought their children but there was nobody to look after them in the fields and the working conditions produced a host of minor ailments, but to go to Wisbech to the doctor would mean a day off work. In 1910 the Cambridge Fruiting Campaign was launched to cope with such problems and to preach the gospel to the poor, neglected by the churches in their industrial homes. Undergraduates and dons came to organise the canteen, play the organ, give recitations and sketches or teach boxing. The Campaigners were scattered around the area with their headquarters at Leverington and tents at Sutton Road for recreation, canteen, medical treatment and day nursery.* [Cambridge Fruiting Campaign report, 1925]

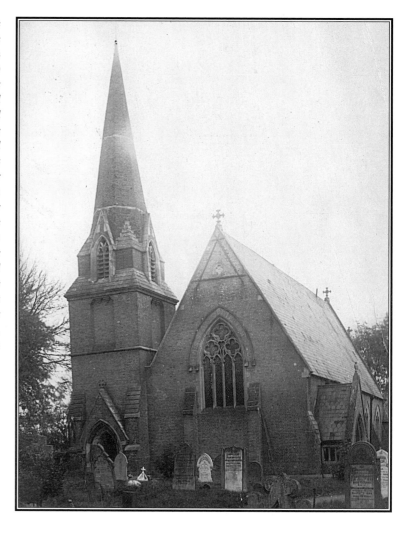

Fulbourn – High Street, 1925. The cottage on the left was destroyed by fire in the 1960s and cottages on the right have been converted into an antique shop. Fire was an ever-present worry and Dr Palmer would have been concerned about an accident that happened to the Fulbourn doctor. *His many friends throughout the county will learn with regret of the unfortunate mishap that befell Dr Nicholls. On Sunday afternoon he was filling a petrol lamp in his consulting room, when the lamp exploded. Miss D. Nicholls, who happened to be upstairs at the time, heard the noise of the explosion and a crash, and hurrying downstairs saw her father leaving the consulting room with his clothes well alight. Miss Nicholls snatched some coats from pegs in the hall, and wrapping them around her father extinguished the flames. On opening the consulting room door she found chairs, mats and one of the doors alight, and the place a mass of flames. Securing a Minimax, she turned it on, and so effective did this prove that in a few moments the fire was subdued. Dr Nicholls was burnt about the arms, chest and neck, and has been confined to bed suffering from shock.* [*Cambridge Chronicle* 22 January 1926] (Photograph: L. Cobbett)

Fulbourn – interior of smock mill *c*.1930. Photographs of the exterior and interior of Fulbourn mill were presented to the survey by the editor of The Master Builder. The mill was built in 1808 and later ground animal feed until it was damaged by a storm in 1933: *Fulbourn windmill has been struck by lightning and is in danger of demolition. In a recent storm the mill was split from top to bottom on one side. Its sails were also damaged and it is likely that it will have to be dismantled. The steps leading into the mill were shattered but a man standing only a foot away had a miraculous escape from injury. The mill was evidently struck twice, and heavy iron bolts were thrown 30 yards. It is one of the finest examples of Dutch work and with three sets of stones is one of the most powerful windmills in England. Mr Mapey has spent a considerable sum in keeping the mill in repair and the Cambridge Preservation Society has been anxious that it should be preserved.* [*Cambridge Chronicle* 5 July 1933] The sail shutters were removed and the stones driven using power provided by a tractor. The mill ceased to work in 1937 and remained derelict until restored by Fulbourn Windmill Society between 1974 and 1987. [VCH vol.10, 2002] (Photograph: Master Builder)

Gamlingay – garage, Pit Corner, *c*.1930. The growth of petrol filling stations gave cause for concern in the Cambridgeshire Regional Planning Report of 1934. The danger of fire was ever-present: *A fire broke out in premises at the back of the Chequers Inn and adjoining the large wood stores of Mr Thomas Cox, of Gamlingay. A large crowd soon assembled in the street and by the help of ladders, pails of water were thrown down the eaves of the house to keep the blaze from spreading. Meanwhile from the street the same work was carried on, and a large butt of water emptied of its contents. On the opposite side of the road the inhabitants poured water upon their thatched cottages to save them from flying sparks. A messenger was hurriedly dispatched for the Potton fire brigade, who arrived very promptly. One of the greatest constituencies that visiting fire brigades have to contend with, is a lack of water, and if a plan could be found whereby the large pond known as The Pits could be kept full, the first steps towards avoiding tremendous blazes would be made.* [CDN 16 March 1898] (Photograph: W.M. Palmer)

Girton – school, 1890s. Girton attracted little attention from the Society's photographers but the Photographic Record also includes a number of sketches by John S. Clarke that were published in the *Cambridge Express* between 1892 and 1896. Girton school suffered from a lack of drinking water: *Sir – there are many schools that have no water supply at all on their own premises, where the children have to depend on 'kind and motherly' neighbours who are good enough to attend to the children's wants in this respect. I do not know how many children attend Girton school but can only*

feel amazed at the task of the kind neighbour who was equal to the work of filtering and supplying the thirsty little throats of the village school children during such a drought as we experienced in 1898. She is undoubtedly well worthy of an honourable position in the annals of Girton – Rusticus. [CDN 19 January 1899] In June 1949 a tender of £34,887 was accepted for the erection of the first instalment of a new school for 300 children aged from five to eleven. It opened in 1951 and included a nursery class for the under-fives. (Engraving: J.S. Clarke)

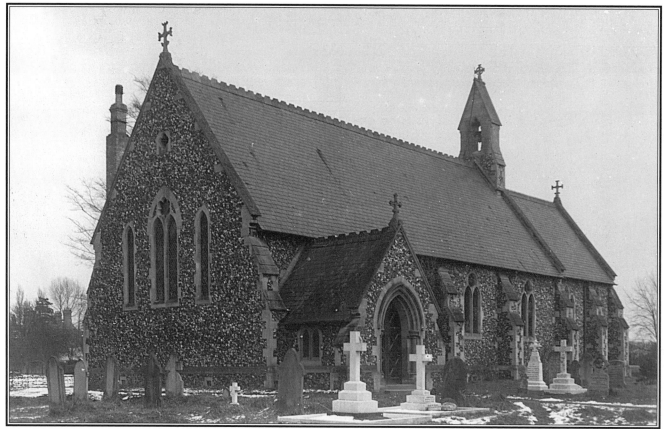

Gorefield – St Paul's Church, *c*.1900. Gorefield church was erected in 1870 and its exterior has changed little. Enid Troughton recorded her memories of life in the village: *"We would get into little groups for Sunday school when we were smaller, in the morning, again in the afternoon, and church with our mothers in the evening. Then for a walk afterwards. As we all grew up we were allowed to go to church in the evenings on our own as long as we were home by nine o'clock. The service was at six p.m. and we were out again by 7 p.m. We would come out and then walk arm in arm along the road looking for what we could find! The boys from Wisbech St Mary were always there. If we went dancing the boys from Parson Drove would also be there, although they didn't mix very well, they would get into fights. We had Sunday outfits, with new clothes on Easter Sunday every year. Just a dress or coat and hat and things like that. Chapel people had their new clothes for the anniversary, which we also attended. You were welcome anywhere in the village. It was like a large family, you know".* [L. Faulkner, The light of other days, 1998]

Gransden, Little – Brook Farm, 1924. The Revd James Musgrave, Rector of Little Gransden bequeathed land and property in the parish for the benefit of poor widows and widowers in 1744. *The income from the property was to be distributed annually at six o'clock in the morning to all those eligible who came to the Musgrave family vault in the churchyard, when each widow and widower, together with the bellringer, who was to toll the bell for an hour, would receive a shilling. Any money left over was to be given, still at the vault, to poor families. This charity was last distributed in 1961. During the eighty or so years preceding this attendance at the vault had not been required, the money being handed by the churchwardens to the recipients whose names were read out by the Rector. In modern times the former hour-long ceremony took only ten minutes.* [E. Porter, Cambridgeshire customs and folklore, 1969] (Photograph: W.M. Palmer)

Grantchester – watermill before 1928. During work to install a turbine at Grantchester Mill in April 1902 it was noticed that the brickwork to the wall supporting the public road was becoming unsafe: *The arch over the waterway appeared inadequate to bear any but the ordinary traffic and there was considerable risk if traction engines were allowed to pass. The tenant of the mill had put up a notice that the bridge was unfit for heavy vehicles. The bridge was a private one, although the Council had to make up the roads on either side and the matter was referred to the Highways Committee.* [CDN 24 April 1902] (Photograph: L. Cobbett)

Grantchester – watermill fire 1928. Grantchester mill was destroyed by fire on 30 October 1928: *A disastrous fire, resulting in the almost total demolition of the famous old mill broke out at about 4.30 p.m. Despite all efforts to save the building the flames spread with such rapidity that in about 30 minutes the position seemed hopeless. The outbreak was at its height just after 5.30 when the interior of the mill was like a flaming cauldron, presenting a fiery beacon. Crowds were gathered in large numbers, attracted by the blaze which could be seen for miles around. There was a stream of cars along the road from Trumpington well over a quarter of a mile long, while cyclists gathered in hundreds. At this time the fire was at its height and it was obvious the ancient building was doomed, but after a strenuous fight the cottage adjoining was saved. The wooden grain hoist on the front of the mill fell with a tremendous crash across the roadway, the roof was gradually falling in and about six o'clock a huge piece of the roof at the rear thundered down into the water. The mill was in the occupation of the Nutter family, by whose family it has been worked for nearly a century. The fire appears to have originated in the engine room, where there was an oil engine.* [CIP 2 November 1928] The report continues: *Though plenty of assistance was forthcoming, some undergraduates being prominent among the volunteer helpers, some were heard to lament because they had not their cameras with them.* Ted Mott, a photographer from Trumpington, issued a series of postcard views, some of which found their way into the survey. (Photograph: E. Mott)

Graveley – cottages near the church, 1939. Graveley is a small parish that belonged to Ramsey Abbey from the 10th to the 16th century after which it was sold by the Crown to Jesus College, Cambridge. By 1909 they owned 13 cottages in the village which were in poor condition: *The Rural Housing and Sanitation Association wrote to the Bursar of Jesus College saying that many of the cottages in Graveley were of a very low standard. Some were without back doors and windows so there was no through ventilation; some had one room only which had to serve for food storage and washing, as well as cooking and eating. Some labourers who would have married and lived in the village had left because there was no accommodation. So they asked the College to build more cottages. There was no reply to this letter, so a second was sent and the College finally replied that it was impossible for them to do anything, as the income from all their property in Graveley was only £10. At least the tenants were charged very low rents, and may not have been as dissatisfied with their housing as the Association was.* [A.M. Bishop, The short and simple annals of the poor – a history of Graveley, 1981] (Photograph: L. Cobbett)

Guilden Morden – stacks, 1936. Thatched stacks on the roadside from Guilden Morden to Wrestlingworth. Houses, outbuildings and sheds were also thatched until the introduction of corrugated iron roofing. In a paper to the Cambridge Antiquarian Society in 1938 L.F. Newman commented: *Even today the art of thatching stacks is a highly skilled one, as they have to be covered in quickly with the smallest amount of straw possible, and, at the same time, the thatch must be weatherproof. Straw is thrown into a heap, saturated with water to make it tough, and then drawn by hand into long wisps, known as 'yelms'. The work of securing the layers of straw to the sides and over the top of the stack roof demands considerable skill, or rainwater, instead of running down the straw, will penetrate through and soak into the stack underneath.* [L.F. Newman, The rural craftsman and his tools, 1938 – PCAS vol.39] (Photograph: C.F. Tebbutt)

Guilden Morden – Priory House, 1932. Back view of Priory House, Guilden Morden showing the continual work of repair and redecoration. In 1899 builders were called in for an unusual job: *The funeral of John Sanderson took place at Guilden Morden. Deceased was well known as in addition to being a carrier to Royston he was a familiar figure at the feasts held in the district. On the arrival of the corpse at his home, the window of the cottage had to be removed before the coffin could be placed in the house. It was made of stout elm, and measured 6ft 9 inches in length, 2ft 6 in width. The weight of the coffin and corpse was estimated at 40 stone. The new bier was brought into requisition and found to be only just wide enough to admit the coffin being placed upon it.* [CDN 8 February 1899] (Photograph: J.H. Bullock)

Guyhirn – Toll Gate House, Rings End, 1932. Tolls were collected to maintain the riverbanks, the charges being specified on the boards fitted to the tollhouse. These boards were unintelligible to many local residents. *When the present vicar came to reside in 1871 there was no Sunday Morning Service, the Sabbath appeared to be regarded as an idle holiday and spent by many in visiting their friends, in their worldly business or at the public house. Sin appears to have taken root and within the memory of the present generation the village has been noted for its immorality, Sunday revelling, want of education and drunkenness. Nothing but dame schools existed*

and the education of the young had been so neglected that many of the inhabitants cannot even read and out of fifty marriages solemnised in the place during the last seventy years, in twenty-five instances one or more of the parties could not sign their own names. [W. Carpenter, Our country parish, or, annals of Guyhirn-with-Ring's End, 1879] (Photograph: E.B. Haddon)

Haddenham – Aldreth Causeway. For many centuries the main route from Cambridge to Ely was via the Aldreth Causeway. In 1901 Haddenham Parish Council were urging the County Council to rebuild the bridge across the Old West River at as early a date as possible: *As the lack of accommodation is an inconvenience and loss to the parish. However it was not only a question of re-building the bridge but of making the roads on either side. They were in a very unsatisfactory state and unless these were repaired the bridge would be perfectly useless except in summer.* [CDN 14 February 1901] In April 1902 the paper reported: *The contractor for the erection of Aldreth bridge is making progress with the works. There have been great expectations of antiquarian finds but very little has been found. A square oak beam some thirty feet long, thought to have been used in the erection of a bridge previous to anything known, has been taken out in good preservation. Smaller things such as hammer heads and an old sword etc have been taken to Cambridge.* [CDN 19 April 1902] An alternative route, the Twentypence Road between Wilburton and Cottenham, was opened in the 1930s. (Photograph: D.G. Reid)

Haddenham – Earith Seven Holes Bridge, *c.*1930. A second causeway linked Haddenham with Earith, where the two Bedford Rivers join the Great Ouse. A Seven Holes Bridge was constructed across the Old Bedford River in 1824 but the fence on the top of the parapet was constructed at the expense of Mr Tom Benton of Earith. *A spirited horse that he was driving in a light cart shied at the bridge and jumped the parapet, taking the cart with it. There happened to be a boat moored nearby from which he was saved from drowning. As a result of the accident Mr Benton paid for the rails to be erected and caused a boat to be permanently moored there as long as he lived.* [C.F. Tebbutt, Bluntisham-cum-Earith, 1941] (Photograph: D.G. Reid)

Haddenham – Earith suspension bridge, *c.*1930. An iron suspension bridge was erected across the New Bedford River at Earith in 1865 replacing a wooden bridge which was badly damaged when a heavy steam threshing engine and tackle passed over it. *The driver, on hearing the crack, ran for safety, leaving the engine to cross by itself, which it did without mishap. The new bridge was tested through bearing the weight of the engine that had damaged its predecessor but it was discovered that it suffered from an excessive amount of sway and had to be anchored to prevent this.* [C.F. Tebbutt, Bluntisham-cum-Earith, 1941] It was replaced in the 1960s. (Photograph: D.G. Reid)

Haddenham – High Street, 1933. Mabel Demaine recalled: *"The village grocers delivered the goods, his grocer boy coming round to your door with a long pencil tucked behind his ear – his long white apron flapping between his legs and a big notebook in his pocket to take your order. I can remember Sid Carter doing the round for Doyley's, he would run over along list, sugar, tea, lard, salt, mustard, vinegar, pepper on and on he would go, chewing his pencil and jotting down the order, later in the week the goods would be delivered. Tebbutt's at the Top Shop, had a pony and cart to deliver their goods and the bakers also had a pony and cart. Tebbutt's shop is now an International*

Supermarket and Doyley's is a first class Drapery Shop well stocked with the latest fashions in ladies, children and men's wear, as well as wools, materials, wall paper, boots and shoes and fancy goods". [M. Demaine, Reflections of a country woman, 1989] (Photograph: J.H. Bullock)

Hardwick – St Mary's Church, *c*.1910. St Mary's Church spire, Hardwick under restoration; a photograph reproduced as a postcard by William Tams, one of the contributors to the survey. In 1925 there were arguments between the rector and his parishioners: *The rectory garden had been used since the rectory had been built 75 years ago. It was the nearest piece of arable land. It temporarily ceased to be used as a garden owing to a change of incumbents and the outbreak of war. The then rector went on war service and did not return to his duties in Hardwick. In 1920 the rectory garden was included in a demand for allotments and nothing was said to him when he was appointed. He had been pressing for its return since 1922. He was now buying for his house vegetables that should be grown on the rectory garden.* [CDN 25 January 1925] Matters turned ugly a few months later: *The rector of Hardwick was fined 10s. for assaulting a farm labourer. It was the outcome of considerable friction over the right-of-way of a roadway leading through the rectory grounds to a farm. The rector claims he had the right to turn back people whom he considers objectionable, whereas villagers declare the road to be public for everybody's use. Complainant said that when he was part way down the road the rector had rushed out of his garden with a four-tined fork and said: "You are not going this way". He was pushed into the hedge and the tines of the fork probed through his coat. The rector said he thought the man was going to make one of his flying rushes and raised the tool to defend himself.* [CDN 16 May 1925] (Photograph: W. Tams)

Hardwick – Jonah Randall's blacksmith's shop and the former village bakehouse, disused by 1928. That year the village was described as: *the poorest parish in the district.* [CDN 5 January 1928]. Then in 1935 philanthropist William Game bought land with the idea of it becoming a 'green dream' for Cockneys who wanted to quit London for the countryside. *His vision was for a one-acre plot and a cow for each owner & many people who bought land there reared chickens. But when the bottom fell out of the egg market in the mid 1950s most of the land fell into disuse. By May 1972 the 480 strong village was said by many to be 'dying' through lack of interest. A building firm bought 84 acres from 51 landowners for close on £1 million for a huge new Limes Estate, the first phase of which comprised 147 houses and 10 bungalows* [CEN 18 May 1972] (Photograph: J.H. Bullock)

Harlton – derelict cottage. In June 1901 Chesterton RDC reported: *Harlton was not badly supplied with water but a few houses were situated on the gault and could not obtain a supply except from the greensand at a considerable depth, from the spring at Butler's Spinney which would have to be raised by some motor, or from the church from which the greater part of the village is supplied. They should search for a disused well indicated as existing on Monk's land in the angle near Yew Tree Gate and make an experimental boring.* [CDN 20 June 1901] Water was still being debated 50 years later: *The question of whether to connect the hot water system or the water closets in the new council houses at Harlton was debated by Chesterton R.D.C. The Housing Committee recommended that a tap over the sink be provided and the WCs only connected because it is not yet certain whether the drainage is good enough to take the effluent from both. Coun F. Adams asked: "What is the use of building these bathrooms in these houses if we are not going to use them? It seems ludicrous". Another observed it was much better to have a flush lavatory than an unlimited supply of water to the bath.* [CDN 2 November 1950] But at least it seems to have been a peaceful place. In 1924 a resolution passed at Harlton annual parish meeting: *That in view of the high rates we pay we should have our local policeman's house coupled by telephone to the police station at Cambridge. The Chief Constable said he did not want the telephone at Harlton; it was a most expensive business. Harlton was one of the places where a telephone was least required.* [CDN 7 July 1924]

Harston – Dove Cottage, later the Dove House Tea House, behind the Three Horseshoes public house, now demolished. *Ours is a village of water springs. Everywhere flowing water from the deepest and purest artesian wells, never do our springs run dry. One hot dry summer we remember how the water carts came from many neighbouring villages to draw drinking water from us, for their shallow wells were dried up.* [M. Green, The village of flowers and springs – *Cambridge Chronicle*, 22 June 1927] An outbreak of scarlet fever caused concern in 1926: *A general feeling of dissatisfaction at Harston as to the supervision exercised in quite an epidemic of scarlet fever in the village led to some questioning at Chesterton Rural Council. A child had been sent home too early from the Isolation Hospital and infected other members of the family who were now suffering from scarlet fever. Provided there were no traces of peeling or discharges from the ears and nose after six weeks isolation it was considered safe to allow a patient to be discharged. The parent had kissed the child on the station platform when it was discharged from the Hospital and did not realise how dangerous that was.* [CDN 30 January 1926] (Photograph: J.H. Bullock)

Haslingfield – The Bushel and Strike public house, 1930. Nora Cannell recalled: *Of the six public houses in the village only two remain. Of the other four, three are now private dwellings and the other was demolished in 1958 for the self-service shop at the junction of Fountain Lane and the High Street. It was a picturesque thatched house with a curious sign, the Bushel and Strike, this representing a form of measuring corn. The bushel was filled and the strike, a piece of flat shaped wood, was drawn across to level the contents.* [N. Cannell, Memories of a Haslingfield childhood, 1983] One item of news discussed around the bar in 1923 was the adventures of the village shopkeeper: *William Hunt told the court he had a milk round and a general stores at Haslingfield. In September he was hard pressed for a pony and paid £10 to have one on trial and then pay so much a month. On the way to Cambridge he, his wife and children were nearly thrown out on two or three occasions on account of the pony stumbling. He concluded the pony was not fit. A vet said the horse had several old scars and he would describe it as broken-kneed. It was not well nourished and was liable to go down at any moment.* [CDN 19 December 1923] (Photograph: J.H. Bullock)

Hatley, East – church, *c*.1910. St Denys' Church comprised just a nave and chancel which was rebuilt in 1874. By 1959 the church was considered unsafe and closed. The graveyard is still in use and the church building has been designated a nature reserve for bats and owls. The Revd H.W.P. Stevens was minister for more than 50 years being appointed in December 1888 and still in place in 1938. One of the most significant events in the village occurred in July 1900 when the Castle was totally destroyed by fire. *The house is part of the estate of Sir Charles Hamilton, of Hatley Park and was rented as a summer residence. The fire originated when a small methylated spirit stove was overturned. Once the thatch caught the flames spread with marvellous rapidity. The walls were lightly built of match-boarding and corrugated iron after the style of an Indian bungalow and in a quarter of an hour the pretty building had collapsed like a house of cards. A more solidly built wing, separated by a conservatory was, with great effort, saved.* [CDN 9 July 1900]

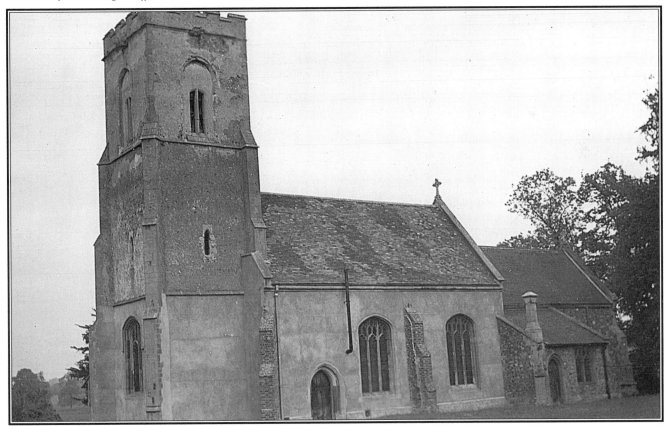

Hatley St George – church from south, 1956. St George's Church stands in the grounds of Hatley Park. In June 1947: *A report by the Bishop of Ely's Advisory Committee on the Care of Churches considered eight churches which were in danger of partial collapse. Typical examples are the fine medieval towers of Soham and Orwell, the interesting chancel of Hatley St George, the roof of Caxton and almost the whole church of Wicken, which is splitting in half. There were also a large number of churches where considerable repair was needed now to prevent serious decay later. Some of the failures could be attributed to soil subsidence or rough weather, but for the most part were due to the accumulation of repairs postponed because of the war.* [CDN 12 June 1947] The chancel had been rebuilt in 1892 but by 1967 was no longer in use and partitioned from the nave by a wall; it was demolished by 1993. (Photograph: F.J. Bywaters)

Hauxton – Manor Farm barns, 1930. In the 1930s a good many people lived off the land at Hauxton: *Albert Jackson (Poplar Farm), H.B. Hart (Manor Farm) and Bob Howard (Church Farm) all employed labour. John Jackson combined a little farming with small-scale building. Thurley Jackson and his father extracted gravel and sold it whilst also being coal merchants. Several men somehow made a living by selling produce from their gardens or eggs from backyard hens. Casual employment included the catching of frogs which were sold via an agent to a university department in Cambridge. In the 30's Hauxton had many ditches with grassy banks in which lived hundreds of frogs. Beating the grass with sticks caused the frogs to be caught and placed in containers of various sorts. The frog catchers then took the frogs home where they would be stored until Sunday in a metal drum sunk in the ground. The vast majority survived this ordeal before being sold for 1½d each to 'Froggy'. He visited, by cycle, each Sunday morning. Frogs were placed into canvas bags which were suspended from every conceivable point of the cycle. On a good week a frog catcher could have 60 – 80 frogs to sell.* [A. Elliott & I. Jordan, Hauxton in times past, 1994] (Photograph: J.H. Bullock)

Heydon – church, *c*.1956. *The little church of the Holy Trinity at Heydon stands in a tree-screened churchyard on the hills near Royston. It is a quiet and isolated spot but by freakish chance an odd enemy bomb fell on it during the 1940 raids and did considerable damage; the tower collapsed and tore down half the nave and part of the aisle. The five bells were blown out of the tower, one bounced across the road into the schoolyard, without cracking.* [CDN 18 December 1955]. Parishioners continued to worship in the rectory until the War Damage Commission agreed to meet the cost of re-building and the church was restored in 1956. (Photograph: F.J. Bywaters)

Hildersham – Rookery House, before 1868. The Revd Robert Goodwin and his family playing croquet in the grounds of Rookery House, with his curate in a Top Hat! Rookery House was pulled down in 1868; the story of its demolition was related by the Mayor of Cambridge, J.H. Conder, in a lecture at Hildersham in 1927: *"One of the earliest things I remember was a great fire which broke out in two places at once. The rectory farm buildings, tithe barn and the barn belonging to the Manor Farm were burnt down. After the fire a Mr Tom Webb, who held the Manor Farm wanted a new barn. At the time there was a large house called the 'Rookery' which was standing empty and Tom Webb went to the Squire and asked that it should be pulled down and the bricks taken to build the barn, and this was done. I thought it was a very great pity because the house was a very fine one. Anyhow, it was pulled down and a very big barn was built with the bricks. It was built with the idea of putting corn into it, as was the custom years ago, but I do not think it has ever been filled".* [J.H. Conder, Hildersham fifty years ago – CDN, 5 October 1927] The barn still stands. (Photograph: Scott & Wilkinson)

Hildersham – Post Office, 1891. Mr Conder's recollections continued: *"As I first remembered the village there was a gate at either end, one opposite the School and the other opposite the blacksmiths shop. At that time there was a parish herdsman as the cows belonging to various people all went into a common herd. With the ploughing up of the baulks a great many roadways and pathways disappeared. About that time also we only had one bell in the church and that one, from being continuously rung in the same way, cracked. New bells were provided by the rector and his sisters and I worked with the man who fixed them. After they were fixed a man named George Davey composed a wonderful peal which they used to ring nearly every night, causing the people from Linton and Abington to make fun at them. Anyway it was good exercise".* [CDN 5 October 1927]

Hinxton – fire engine house, 1927. Sarah Stutter, tenant of the Manor Farm, left £100 to the parish in 1830 to buy a fire engine which was shared with Ickleton. The pump was worked by two men on either side and when it was needed John Page, horsekeeper to Mr Robinson of Hinxton Hall, would fetch one of his horses to pull it. It was used at a disastrous fire on Mr J. Coxall's farm in 1921 which involved the whole of the summer's harvest. *It was supposed that a spark from a thrashing engine set fire to a stack. As the nearest water was about a quarter of a mile away the would-be-helpers were much handicapped. Fire Brigades from Duxford Aerodrome and Saffron Walden were called upon. These with the local firemen did their best but without avail, as the fire had such a strong hold. In addition to the many stacks, the drum, chaff cutter, straw pitcher etc were all demolished, as was also a tractor and straw stack in the neighbouring barn.* [*Cambridge Chronicle*, 12 October 1921] The hut still stands, but without the sign above the door. (Photograph: P.S. Palmer)

Hinxton – children playing in the ford on Duxford Road, 1936. The ford provides a playground for children but can prove hazardous following sudden rain. In May 1888 villagers were excited to hear that otters had been seen in the river. The response was to hunt them: *Alfred Bard captured a fine specimen 4ft. 6ins long and weighing about 15lb. Whitehead Andrews subsequently caught two of the otter's young. The mother otter died in captivity at Hinxton Hall and was stuffed by her captor.* [V. Walker, The life and times of Hinxton, 2000] (Photograph: L. Cobbett)

Histon – Cottenham Road before 1929. *Stone Corner Cottage was condemned in 1929 and demolished to improve the Cottenham Road when the Abbey Estate was being built. Beyond is the gable end of the 'Garden Gate' beerhouse. The distant white railings surround Dodd's Pond at the corner of Clay Street where Moses Carter, the Histon Giant, is reputed to have bathed and washed his clothes.* [E. Whitehead, Photographic memories of Histon and Impington, 1999] Other work continued a decade later: *An improvement that has been wanted for several years is being carried out by the County Council at the bad corner on Cottenham Road, generally known as Clonny's corner. The corner on the same road nearer the village is also to receive attention in the near future. With the new street lighting recently erected there by the Parish Council all danger should be removed.* [CIP 11 November 1938] (Photograph: O.H.H. Jermy)

Histon – strawberry pickers, 1890s. Strawberry picking on one of Chivers' farms: Histon was renowned for its fruit and Cambridge folk, both town and gown, would walk to the village to procure it. During a glut year in 1873 Chivers started making jam and this became an important part of the economy. In 1924 the newspaper commented: *The land problem has been one of the pressing anxieties of our country for many a long year, and to it has been added more recently the question of general unemployment. The jubilee presentation made by the employees of Messrs Chivers to the managing director, Mr John Chivers, is consequently of special interest, as being a tribute to one whose energy, enterprise and foresight have done so much for agriculture and manufacture. The firm now farms about 6,000 acres and gives employment to some 3,000 people in the factory and on the land. Where tens were employed, hundreds are now busy and happy and contented workers, many of them enjoying, and many of them qualifying for a stake in the business as co-partners.* [CDN 1 August 1924]

Horningsea – High Street, *c.*1890. Gingell's Cottage, High Street, Horningsea; by 1996 the thatch had been replaced by a corrugated-iron roof. In 1930 a Horningsea bachelor placed a notice on the front of his cottage. It read: '*S.O.S. Wanted a Wife. A real girl, not a church prude*'. *He described himself as a poet and farmer, born in County Cork. He went to sea and lived in the USA before coming to the village two years ago. He has published one volume of poems but complains that with working in his garden and preparing meals, he has no time to write. When he marries he will write a 'best seller'* [CDN 15 April 1930]. The notice worked: he was inundated with letters: *They have come from all parts of the country, including Jersey. Many have come from London, from Mayfair as well as Hampstead, from servant girls as well as from girls who run their own cars. One letter enclosed a photograph of a delicate, refined-looking blonde, whom he declares he will probably marry.* [CDN 30 April 1930]

Horningsea – churchyard, c.1865. Clay continued: *Adjoining the churchyard is a small residence house for the perpetual curate, with a garden. It is much to be regretted that some care is not taken, and some expense incurred, to render it more convenient and attractive than it now is, in order to induce the holder of what has at length become a benefice, to reside among his people, over whom he is permanently placed. The steep-pitched tile-covered roof of the church porch has been replaced.* In 1949 the Leys School Clapham Society undertook a survey of Horningsea. *The village comprised some 85 houses, only 36 of which had mains water, the rest depended on wells and pumps. Only three had main drainage, the rest relied on cesspools. 58 homes had connections to the electricity system, but two generated their own and 25 homes were without, relying on oil and paraffin for both lighting and cooking. Even those who had electric light did not generally cook with electric, preferring an open hearth or oil stove. Of the 93 men surveyed 46 worked in agriculture, the majority as farm workers. Two were employed as butchers with one each of grocer, furniture man and fishmonger in the village services whilst others were categorised as craftsmen – boot repairer, carpenter, potter, blacksmith's mate or builders.* [Leys School, Horningsea 1949–50, 1952] (Photograph: O.J. Jones)

Horseheath – Cardinal's Manor House, 1924. Cardinal's Manor House stood in two successive moated sites but was in a very poor condition and demolished in February 1924. Catherine Parsons recalled: *Several cottages have been demolished in my lifetime; five cottages in Roper's Yard have fallen down. John Pamenter, a general shopkeeper and carrier lived in the best of them. He was a sleepwalker and had a trapdoor put in the floor over the top of his staircase, fastened with heavy iron bars, to ensure he did not fall downstairs in the night, and to protect him from robbers. Cardinal's Farm is very old and I have a parish constable's staff marked with the initials A.F. and the date 1727 which were given me by a former tenant of the fine old timber and plaster house which stood within the moat until 1914.* [C.E. Parsons, Horseheath: some recollections, 1952] (Photograph: C.E. Parsons)

Horseheath – hauling oaks, 1928. A team of five horses hauling oak trees across the fields to the main road. Some believed such work could be disrupted by witchcraft, as Catherine Parsons told a meeting of the Cambridge Antiquarian Society in 1915. *In Horseheath today witchcraft is by no means a lost art; in this parish we have ghosts as real as ever they were, superstition is rife, we have our folklore, interesting customs and cures for almost every ill. The parishioners tell us there always were witches and there always will be – the witch is in league with the devil – she has the power to do evil. People believed they were safe provided the witch did not possess anything belonging to them but could you be sure she had not picked up a piece of your broken crockery, or taken a sprig from your garden hedge – that would be enough to give her power. Witches were extortioners and their craft remunerative: she could cast a spell on your coal so that it would not burn and influence animals. Horses would stop dead in their tracks and only move after she had spoken to them. She could send swarms of fleas to pester you and prevent cows giving milk.* [C. Parsons, Notes on Cambridgeshire witchcraft, 1915 – PCAS vol.19] (Photograph: Leslie Hancock)

Ickleton Church, 1937. Ickleton church from the south, looking down stream. Dr F.J. Allen told the Cambridge Antiquarian Society in 1911: *Ickleton church had the most perfect lead-covered wooden spire remaining in the county, and a quaint feature was the bell that hung out on the spire near its apex.* [F.J. Allen, Church spires of Cambridgeshire, 1911 – PCAS vol.16]. The bells were subject of controversy in 1927: *The Chancellor of the Diocese of Ely presided at a Consistory Court when the vicar of Ickleton asked for a petition for the casting of all the bells of the church. It had originally been decided that only one be re-cast but the bell-founders advised they should all be done and the work had been completed. This was rather serious. On account of their wrongful action the bells were lost forever and no order would restore them. The churchwardens were suspended from office and the vicar reported for acting in a most improper way.* [CDN 10 June 1927] The church suffered severe damage by fire in 1979 and photographs taken by the Antiquarian Society were consulted to aid the restoration. (Photograph: L. Cobbett)

Ickleton – Harlequin House under restoration, 1944. Captain Percy Mundy inherited Caldrees Manor, Ickleton in 1933. During the inter-war years much old property fell into decay including cottages known as 'Town Housen' in Abbey Street, dating back to the 1600s. Mundy purchased them from the village charities and undertook their reconstruction. His photograph shows the work in progress, clearly revealing the timber framework of the ancient structure. [P.C.D. Mundy, Memorials of Ickleton in the past, 1945] (Photograph: P.C. Mundy)

Impington Hall, *c.*1896. Impington Hall was sold in 1864 to a very rich undergraduate, Charles Bamford: *He spent a fortune remodelling the Tudor Mansion and emulating the lifestyle of his fellow student, the Prince of Wales. More changes were undertaken by the Macfarlane-Grieves family before the Chivers family bought the Hall and grounds in 1926. They presented land for the Impington Village College which was built between 1936 and 1939. The Hall became an educational centre for their employees until the war, when it was occupied by the Royal Engineers, with Italian prisoners of war housed in Nissen huts in the gardens. After a fire in 1953 it was demolished to within three feet of its foundations and a granary erected. Forty years later the site was cleared for the present Percheron Close* [E. Whitehead, Photographic memories or Histon and Impington, 1999] (Engraving: J.S. Clarke)

Isleham – clunch cottages in The Pits, *c.*1932. At Isleham a crowded settlement called the Pits grew up in an old chalk quarry, 20ft below street level. *Recurring epidemics of cholera together with a gradual demolition of the closely-set, gardenless, chalk-built cottages reduced the number of residents, though there were still 55 inhabited dwellings in 1910. By the 1960s most of the dilapidated cottages had been removed and the Pits were redeveloped with new brick houses.* [VCH vol.10] Arthur Houghton recalled: *There used to be the Maid's Head and a shop where they sold sweets and groceries. Then there was another shop in The Pits where they sold groceries and meat, kept by Mrs. Cooke. A man named Howe had a workshop down there. He used to do odd jobs, painting houses, etc. and carpentry. You could go to his workshop and purchase wood, putty, a pane of glass and laths which were in great demand in those days, and were used for ceilings. The houses were crowded together, no gardens or ground, not even enough for a linen line. Some of the houses (the Maid's Head is one) have entrances on the ground floor and on the top floor.* [A. Houghton, Memories of Isleham village, 1988] (Photograph: D.G. Reid)

Kennett – St Nicholas' Church, *c.*1920. St Nicholas' Church stands entirely on its own amongst trees, well away from roads. *Chiefly built by Benedictine monks in 1360 it was restored by the Rev William Godfrey in 1859. In 1996 masonry bees ate into the church walls and damaged the flints & the roof was repaired in 2002. Proposals to unite with the benefice of Chippenham in 1929 came to nothing owing to the opposition of the Squire.* [VCH vol.10. 2002]

Kingston – nonconformist chapel interior, 1932. Kingston Congregational meeting house dates from about 1839. *The first Sunday in June was recognised as the Chapel anniversary when the evening service was held in the large barn at Town Farm. There was usually a visiting Minister who used a portable manger for the pulpit. This anniversary used to be the occasion to wear some new clothes, especially if it was a fine sunny day.* [L. Jacklin, Kingston remembered, 1977]. Although in 1851 an evening service attracted 100 people, filling two-thirds of the available seats, by 1926 there was a congregation of 26 in the two chapels of Kingston and Great Eversden, a number that had dropped to 14 by 1954 and six in 1967. [VCH, vol.5. 1973]. But in 1961 there was concern that it was the entire village that was in danger of dying: *Twenty years ago the site of the village could be described as very small, but unlike most other villages which have grown almost beyond recognition, Kingston has decreased until the number of people is under 150. The villagers themselves are worried about what is happening and recognise that it is a 'pensioners village'. Few young people live there, merely because there are no houses for them. Since the few Council houses were built over 20 years ago there has been*

virtually no development and as the older properties have fallen down and become uninhabitable the problem of accommodation has become acute. [CIP 31 March 1961] (Photograph: P. Salmon)

Kirtling – Tower. Kirtling was dominated by its squire, Lord North, a Roman Catholic with a private chapel and chaplain at his home, Kirtling Tower, adjacent to the church. *The North Family had added a memorial chapel to the parish church in the sixteenth century in which several members of the family were interred. In 1905 his Lordship noticed that a communion table had been placed in what he considered the family's private chapel* and the new vicar had started conducting services there. He ordered him to stop. The vicar however was reluctant to surrender one third of his church and felt that this represented an attack on his ministry. Matters were exasperated when the Catholic chaplain objected to the inclusion of religious material in the parish magazine and supplied a list of 10 parishioners who did not wish to receive it – though the vicar claimed the right to deliver it to anyone who wanted them. The controversy came to a head in 1906 when the vicar resigned claiming North 'has made further demands which… he may be inclined to drop if I leave'. It may have been a clash of personalities, or had the resignation something to do with the poverty of the post – a mere £92 a year when even £200 was thought of as a 'starvation living'. [R. Kemsley, An avowedly hostile religion?: conflict in… Kirtling 1905–06, Liverpool University unpublished dissertation, 1996]

Kirtling – Post Office, 1930. James Bullock's caption to this photograph sums up the spirit of their survey: *Kirtling Post Office, showing the well-known antiquarian Dr W.M. Palmer FSA of Linton (Saffron Walden Museum annual report) on a chocolate raid.* There were six shops in the 1890s, falling back to two after 1918 but the shop at Upend closed about 1956 and by 2000 the one in Kirtling Street was open only two days a week. [VCH vol.10]. Enid Barraud's account of a village post office at Great Eversden is typical: *Inside the shop was warm with the heat of an oil stove and two hanging oil lamps. The light glinted cheerfully on jars and tins and packets and bottles and mingled with the smell of paraffin was the scent of everything else in the place. On the right the shelves held stocks of good cotton shirts, striped in patterns of blue and black, and stout fustian trousers and corduroys and cord breeches and boots hung up and wellingtons on the floor, towels and dusters and flannel nightdresses and school pinafores. On the other side were the dry groceries, with boiled sweets, lemonade crystals in giant glass jars. There were bottles of non-alcoholic wines, tins of biscuits, cartons of soap, torch batteries and lamps, cigarettes, plugs. Patent medicines were there too, a terrifying array of remedies for everything under the sun, and toilet requisites. Beyond the haberdashery was the post office with its own special flap in the counter and wire grill, and the usual bunch of curl-cornered leaflets about insurance, licences, permits, sheep dipping and all the other information available in such places... and the usual post office pens and blotting paper!* [E.M. Barraud, Tail corn, 1946] (Photograph: J.H. Bullock)

Knapwell – church, *c.*1956. The 14th-century tower still stands, but the main body of the church suffered from centuries of neglect and was ruinous by the 18th century. *In 1753 the chancel collapsed and the rector obtained permission to rebuild 'the great rambling old chancel to one of smaller and more useful size'. However the problems were far from solved. In 1785 parts of the nave also collapsed and the church became unusable. For the next eighty years services were held in a village barn. Worse was to come. In 1857 the rector vanished and was found in his night-shirt, totally insane. Eventually the tide turned when in 1861 Henry Brown was appointed curate, walking from Cambridge to take the morning and evening services. He set about raising money to rebuild the tumbledown church and a grant was made by the Incorporated Society for Building Churches. The most successful local architect, W.N. Fawcett, was employed to make the designs and the new church was completed in 1866. The unfortunate rector lingered on in an asylum until 1900 while a succession of curates carried out his duties and the church once again fell into a state of disrepair. His successors have sought to remedy the neglect but even today the church is badly in need of repairs and a Restoration Fund has been launched with the aim of raising money for a new roof.* [D. Longair, Knapwell village, 1978] (Photograph: F.J. Bywaters)

Kneesworth – High Street, *c*.1931. Peter Sell recalled in 1989: *"As a boy with a stout hazel stick and as a youth and a young man with a double-barrel twelve-bore, I walked many miles round and round the fields after the binder, waiting for rabbits to come out. Rabbits were abundant in the village, but not in every field. Sometimes there were none at all, usually there were a few, occasionally a very large number. On one never to be forgotten evening, in a field on the Whaddon boundary, I shot 46 rabbits with 48 shots, and more got away than I shot. The villagers in nearby Kneesworth came to see what all the banging was about and all went home with at least one rabbit. The rabbit was the poor man's pheasant and an important item in his diet".* [Bassingbourn-cum-Kneesworth Local History Group, A chronicle of two villages, 1994]

Landbeach timber cottage, photographed in 1928. Landbeach has a rich mix of buildings including a tithe barn that is over 400 years old. *Such barns were built in the days when all landowners, however small their holding, were required to deliver to the church a tenth of their crops (fish, fowl, timber etc were included in the tithing). The tithing requirement ceased with the Tithing Commutation Act of 1836. In recent times the barn became a repository for ageing farm implements and fell into disrepair. In 1975 the Landbeach Society raised the necessary funds to carry out restoration. The ownership of the barn continued to be vested in the Diocese of Ely until it was purchased by South Cambridgeshire District Council for use by the village under the auspices of the Landbeach Society.* [M.A. Lynn, Historical Landbeach, 1998]

Landbeach – wheelwright, 1928. Albert Abrahams, carpenter and wheelwright, Landbeach. In December 1899 a destructive fire destroyed the W.D. Greenhall's wheelwright's shop and stable and following March there was an auction of his furniture and outdoor effects. The carpenter was an important tradesman. In July 1901: *Cambridge Guardians agreed that a child who had expressed a wish to learn the trade of a carpenter should be boarded out for a year. If he was given a good trade there was very small likelihood he would come to the House again; if they made him an agricultural labourer he would probably be on the books again in later life.* [CDN 4 July 1901] (Photograph: L. Cobbett)

Landwade – church, 1937. Church restoration was a constant problem: *Landwade church is small & dates back to the 15th century but today there is only Lord St Davids and a few labourers in the congregation. Some wonderful old armorial glass which was taken away by the Cotton family has now been handed back. Its re-erection will enormously add to the interest of this unique old church but the stonework of the window is so much decayed that it will have to be restored. The summer services begin usually on Easter Sunday but this year, owing to the repairs, it will not be possible to open so early in the year.* [CDN 18 March 1927] Further restoration followed in 1933. (Photograph: L. Cobbett)

Leverington – church, 1861. Samuel Smith of Wisbech, one of the county's earliest photographers, took this photograph on the 21 June 1861. His negatives are housed in the Wisbech and Fenland Museum. *Leverington possesses one of the most beautiful churches in a district abounding with such edifices. It has a well-proportioned thirteenth century tower, capped by a Decorated spire, with good gable lights. The church was extensively restored by Canon Sparkes who had been presented to the living by his father, the Bishop of Ely, in 1827. During the 43 years he held the living he received £103,845, and in addition other preferments were conferred upon him by his father who did not, at all events, 'neglect those of his own household'. A slab in the church to Captain Anthony Lumpkin is said to be the Tony Lumpkin of Oliver Goldsmith's comedy, 'She Stoops to Conquer'. He wrote the play, it is alleged, under a mulberry tree, and in a house still existing in the village not far from the celebrated 'Crackskull Common'* [F.J. Gardiner, History of Wisbech, 1898] (Photograph: Samuel Smith)

Linton – Dr Palmer with Antiquarians outside 'Chandlers', 1938. Excursions form an important part of the programme of Antiquarian Societies. In June 1938 Dr Palmer led a group around Linton, pausing outside 'Chandlers', the oldest inhabited house in Cambridgeshire. *It was originally built for Adam the Chandler in the reign of Edward III. In Adam's time there was no chimneystack nor any of the present windows. The central portion was open from floor to rafters. The door opened to a passage which went right through the house & was separated from the hall by an oak screen, still in position. The two-storeyed portion on the right was the women's quarters and that on the left of the buttery, with men's quarters above. There were no stairs, only ladders.* (Photograph: R.N. Salaman)

Linton – Grip corner. The latter half of the 19th century saw little new building in the village and combined with depression and low rents the standard of housing fell. Linton Rural Sanitary District reported: *The cots are built in the majority of wattle and daub and many are thatched … a man and his wife and two grown-up daughters and three grandchildren slept together in one small bedroom without any screen or attempt at the presence of decency. Linton became one of the first districts to adopt powers to build new houses to help remedy the problem.* [F. & I. Jeffery, Housing in Linton in the 19th and 20th centuries, 2001] Until the 1920s most of the houses were contained within the High Street, the Grip and one or two of the lanes. 'Grip' is a word meaning a stream which is sometimes dry. The grip at Linton is usually dry, but sometimes floods the whole road in front of the house.

Linton – Grip corner. With inadequate maintenance old properties could literally fall apart, especially during inclement weather. During a blizzard in December 1927: *The thatched cottage at Melbourn occupied by Mrs Greig, collapsed about 7 o'clock on Sunday evening. The bedroom end of the house fell out, but happily Mrs Greig was in the bottom room and escaped injury. She would not move however until the policeman came on Monday morning.* Dr Palmer was on hand to record a similar incident at Linton about 1913, the two photographs demonstrating the importance of the photographic survey.

Linton – firehooks. Fire was another ever-present danger: *On the side of Chandlers hung two massive firehooks used for pulling the thatch off burning buildings. They were photographed standing alongside the Race Horse Inn, almost opposite, whose eaves have rings into which the hooks would have been inserted. An antique fire engine, bought second-hand in the early 1800s was in use about a century later and was kept in the church.* [W.M. Palmer, The antiquities of Linton, 1913]

Linton – Guildhall before restoration (left) Linton – Guildhall after restoration (right). Not all change was for the worst: *Linton Guildhall was built between 1510 and 1530 and served as the Town House until the 1660s after which it was used for housing the poor. A town record book which begins in 1577 shows that it was used for marriage feasts, by troupes of players and as a refuge for fellows of Pembroke Hall during times of plague. William Millicent left money in 1527 for pargetting the building. The timber frame has been exposed and careful examination shows where there were original window openings and a doorway on the south side.* [Linton Parish Council, Linton: the story of a market town, 1982]

Litlington – lock-up, 1923. Dr Palmer told members of an Antiquarian Society excursion in 1925: *Litlington lock-up or cage, now used as a pump house, is the descendant of the prison of the Honor of Clare. In ancient days the punishment for minor offences was often in the hands of the Lord of the Manor but in this part of the county there were so many Manors in each parish that the police courts or courts leet were under the control of powerful nobles.* [W.M. Palmer, Neighbourhood of Melbourn and Meldreth, 1925]. Albert Pell gives a description of a similar structure at Wilburton: *The Wilburton village cage was a square, brick building, small, and arched over with brick at the top. The door was narrow but stout, adorned with auctioneers' and other posters. A delinquent was apprehended, forced into the cage and locked in. A few children loitered about the door, indicating that the cage had a tenant.* [A. Pell, The reminiscences of Albert Pell, 1908] Litlington lock-up is largely unchanged, though the one at Wilburton has disappeared. (Photograph: W.M. Palmer)

Littleport – Old White Hart, 1934. The Old White Hart Inn, on the junction of City Road and White Hart Lane Littleport was surveyed by the Society in September 1934. *The doorway was found to be 15th century and the stones had been reused, obviously taken from an older, important building. By December 1936 it had become dilapidated, the roof had fallen in & it was cleared for road widening, the ancient stones being sold off for use in rockeries.* [Note on an old building at Littleport known as the Fisher's Cottage – PCAS vol.37 p72] In March 1925 another Littleport pub was the scene of a dramatic confrontation after two men booked into the Marquis of Granby Hotel. *They attempted to steal a cash box containing about £100 in notes, gold & silver & when discovered barricaded themselves in one of the bedrooms. Police Sergeant Newell had seen the strangers and, becoming suspicious, enlisted the services of various well-disposed people to surround the hotel, which was to all intents and purposes in a state of siege. He invited the men to come out of their room but the reply he got was, "If you attempt to force the door we shall shoot". In their endeavour to get away they had drawn the bedstead up to the window and knotted the sheets with a view to lowering themselves to the ground.* [CDN 9 April 1925] (Photograph: J.H. Bullock)

Littleport – Arber's mill on the Ten Mile Bank before 1929. From its situation on the bank of the Ouse it was one of the loveliest of mills and was run by the Arber family from 1861 to 1929 when miller Ben Arber retired. His brother James had in fact worked the windmill for him from about 1910. The shutters and fantail were removed by Hunt Brothers of Soham. [Peter Filby personal communication]

Lode – derelict watermill, 1930. The future of Lode watermill was in doubt until 1935: *Lode Mill has been restored from dilapidation at the direction of Lord Fairhaven. The weather-worn tiles of the roof remain but much of the exterior boarding has been replaced. Inside most of the old timbers are still stout and unrepaired. The machinery has long been in disuse, and so it will continue, but it is to receive attention to restore it as far as possible to its original appearance. In recent years the structure has housed plant for the manufacture of cement. Not far away are the remains of the kilns. A pit has been transformed by skilful landscape design into a pond quite pleasing to the eye. The machinery used in the manufacturing process will be removed and a lean-to cottage by the side of the mill and a small bakehouse have already been demolished. The pool below the sluice into which the lode discharges its sluggish flow is much overgrown with grasses and rubbish litters the bottom. Lord Fairhaven had offered to dam the channel below the pool so that a sufficient head of water would be obtained, and to clean the bed of the pool, providing a bathing place for the villagers.* [*Cambridge Standard* 6 September 1935] (Photograph: J.H. Bullock)

Lolworth – Main Street, 1929. Mrs Moore noted: *Main Street, Lolworth showing the crossroads & Middle Road, all of which are at present cul de sac; some time ago land was offered for road making taking one of these through to Childerley Gate.* In July 1938 the Lolworth Grange Estate including several cottages, barns and a blacksmith's shop was sold. But Hall Farm was older. *Legend has it that a former owner of Hall Farm used to ride around in a gig singing "Hey diddley, diddley dee, All Lollar belongs to me". Another story connected with this farm concerns a bell on one end of the house. This was used in the past either for signalling when the master wanted his horse, or else for the farm workers to come to lunch or stop work. The last time it was rung was on V.E. Day in 1945. The village has no really outstanding characters to boast, either in the past or present and no customs of any note. But in spite of this the inhabitants are entirely satisfied with their life.* [CIP 12 May 1961] (Photograph: K. Moore)

Longstanton – cottages, 1929. William Coles, a Methodist lay preacher recalled a visit to Longstanton: *Once on arriving on a bicycle, an old cushion tyred specimen (pneumatic cycles were seldom or never seen), a friend who was at the gate gave me anything but a warm welcome & said, when he recovered from the shock "You wouldn't see John Wesley riding a bike on a Sunday". "No", I replied," he would be riding his horse, my horse is resting in his stable". Then one evening a message was brought saying he wanted to see me. I made enquiries as to his whereabouts and at last found him in bed, very ill, in a room in a mud walled thatched cottage, but it was his home. After praying with him that mud walled cottage became very near to 'the gate of Heaven'. I never regretted that journey on a dark night to the distant village of Longstanton.* [W. Coles, Memoirs of W. Coles, 60 years a lay preacher in the Cottenham circuit, 1948] (Photograph: L. Cobbett)

Longstanton – cottages, 1929. Longstanton St Michael cottages dated 1759 which were demolished in 1935. They stood on the south side of a lane beside the thatched church of St Michael. The village has two churches: *There was general approval of a proposal to unite the parishes of Longstanton All Saints' and Longstanton St Michael at a public inquiry and the meeting also brought forth a suggestion that the name of the village should be changed. There was in effect only one village and few people knew where the boundary between the parishes was located. There was one school, one post office, one police station, one village institute and one recreation ground. All these were in the parish of All Saints' whose council administered the same public service for the benefit of both parishes. It was suggested the combined parishes should be called 'Stanton Green'.* [CDN 15 September 1951]. The union was agreed, but the suggested name was not adopted. (Photograph: L. Cobbett)

Longstowe – Middle Farm, 1928. Controversy raged in Longstowe in 1897: *Let no reader think that this is a pleasant story. It is not, for it is tainted by tyranny distasteful to free citizens. For the past two years education at Longstowe has not pursued its onward course quite smoothly, for during that time the rector and his daughter appear to regard the master of the Church Schools as their sport and plaything, to be bandied about 'from pillar to post' just as suits their autocratic fancy. Having made a schoolmaster in a Lincolnshire parish fairly uncomfortable the sire and his daughter came down to Longstowe rectory in 1895 and at once tried their hand on Mr & Mrs Rowland, who for several years had been training the young of the parish to the satisfaction of the manager, the parents and the inspectors. But they have now resigned their position rather than lackey to the new-comer who, with his 'I insist' made life anything but one of pleasurable liberty.* [CDN 17 September 1897] (Photograph: J.H. Bullock)

Madingley – The Three Horseshoes, 1929. The Three Horseshoes was the centre of activity at the village feast. Villages visited each other on these occasions – *Lolworth usually came over for a cricket match in the afternoon and in the evening the men of Girton visited the Inn. This was the time when all the children were chased indoors and the door locked. The curious went upstairs and watched from their bedroom windows while the gentlemen of Madingley and Girton enjoyed their annual battle after the Inn had closed – the men of Girton were great fighters in those days. Sometimes there was a 'Dancing Booth', a large tent where one could dance all the evening for one shilling – one dance cost twopence. Music was provided by a concertina and 'fiddle'. Until about 15 years ago there were still coconut shies, a few stalls and swingboats.* [C. Barlow, Memories of Madingley – Cambs Local History Council Bulletin, 1957] The village had a Squire who took an interest in the property: *Ambrose Harding keeps the charming thatched houses of Madingley in excellent repair, and lately rebuilt the inn,* commented the Cambridge Preservation Society; adding that Harding was one its first members. [Cambridge Preservation Society, Report, 1935–6] (Photograph: L. Cobbett)

Madingley – old windmill, 1904. The original Madingley windmill was last tenanted by Mr Charles French. *He was in bed one July night in 1909 when he heard the mill creaking ominously under the weight of the millstones and it collapsed. The great oak timbers were so shattered as to make restoration impossible.* [CIP 30 August 1935] (Photograph: E.C. Hoppett)

Madingley – new windmill, 1936. But in 1935 came the news that a new mill would be erected on the site: *The purchase of a post mill at Ellington, five miles from Huntingdon, completed a six years' search which has been conducted on behalf of Mr Ambrose Harding, Squire of Madingley. Workmen have been engaged in dismantling the mill, calling for great care, as it is essential that none of the timbers be harmed. On the site of the old mill at Madingley foundations are being dug and soon the process of reassembling Ellington mill will begin. This is not the first move which the mill has made. From its original site it was transported across several fields to a spot where its sails might better catch the wind. It is said to date from the sixteenth century.* [*Cambridge Standard* 16 August 1935] H.H. Brindley made a photographic record of the reconstruction of the Ellington mill between 3 November 1935 and 14 June 1936. (Photograph: H.H.Brindley)

Manea – Station Road, 1920s. The isolated fen village of Manea was to have been the site of a new town to be constructed by King Charles I after he had succeeded in draining the fens. It was an ambition never realised. But in the 1830s it became the base for a Hodsonian community; centrally-heated brick-built cottages were constructed and money was abolished. The scheme lasted for only a short time. Bicycles provided more than just a method of transport: *Favoured with ideal weather the annual sports meeting arranged by the Pymoor and Oxlode Committee attracted a large attendance. This event, which has the reputation of being one of the best in the district, was more than up to the standard of previous years, and some keen competition was provided for an enthusiastic crowd. This year the interest of the meeting was enhanced by the production of a Challenge cup for cycle racing, and A.F. Hawes, the well known Manea cyclist, was successful in securing the honour of being the first holder of the trophy. The Manea Silver Band rendered selections throughout the day and the proceedings were further enlightened by entertainments by the Magpie Concert Party from Cambridge.* [CDN 7 June 1923]

March – High Street, c.1920. Edna Stacey recalled: *At the beginning of the 20th century there were eleven public houses along the High Street, starting at St. Peter's Road: The White Lion, The Queen Adelaide, The King William, The Cock, The Sun, The Red Hart, The Windmill, The Griffin, The Golden Lion, The Red Lion, and The Royal Exchange. Today only five remain. Of the several large houses along the eastern side there is one which, in the middle of the 19th century, created interest among the residents. The 'Maze' situated next to the Cock Inn was once the residence of the curates of the chapelry. In 1836 it was purchased by Mr Firmin Fuller who was a veterinary surgeon. The house had 1½ acres of garden and at great expense and labour Mr Fuller set about creating an exotic garden. He bought choice flowers and evergreens, some of which came from America, and he made a rectangular lake with a Chinese pattern footbridge across the centre, connecting it with attractive walks along each side. There was a bandstand at one end and concerts took place regularly and on certain specified days the gardens were open free of charge to the general public. A notice board found in the stables a hundred years later said, 'Garden Open. All Welcome except dogs and policemen'.* [E. Stacey, Streetwise, 2000]

Melbourn – Elm tree and old parish cottage in the corner of the churchyard. Dr Palmer told Antiquarians in 1925: *In 1640 each English county was compelled to supply money for the building and upkeep of ships. Feeling spread against the tax & in Melbourn Benjamin Metcalfe addressed the villagers under the old elm tree and got together a small army of men to meet the collectors from Cambridge. These men of the village, armed with sticks, forks and other weapons awaited the King's men at the elm tree, and when they arrived set about them with the result that the collectors left the village very much quicker than they entered it, tattered and torn, wounded and bleeding. The agitation spread throughout the county and later throughout the whole country and Metcalfe was looked upon by the villagers as a hero. Parliament discussed the matter and the tax was abolished in June 1641.* [W.M. Palmer, The neighbourhood of Melbourn and Meldreth, 1923]

Melbourn – Little Lane cottage, made of clay lumps. *Locally made unbaked clay-lump bricks, known as clay bats, much bigger than baked bricks, were dug from pits in the neighbourhood. When dry this material is porous and requires sealing and so was plastered with a mixture of cow dung, horse hair and earth. Later some were tarred. It was not unusual for walls to collapse suddenly if water and frost had penetrated the plaster.* [Melbourn Village History Group, A glimpse into Melbourn's past. 2005]. *Recently a bungalow of clay lump was built in Cambridgeshire for £720. The clay lump bricks are made by first laying on the ground three or four inches of barley straw, then covering these with three or four inches of clay, dug close by, and pouring plenty of water over all. Then the whole is trodden into a paste by a horse which walks backwards and forwards, and round and round till all is well mixed. Wooden moulds are then filled with the mixture and smoothed over.* [CDN 6 August 1923]

Melbourn – rear of cottages at Cowslip Corner, near Sheene Mill, photographed by Percy Salmon in 1930.

Melbourn – Sheepshead Row after preservation by the Cambridge Preservation Society, 1938. The Cambridgeshire Regional Planning Report of 1934 stressed the importance of preserving old cottages and in 1938 Cambridge Preservation Society started work on these cottages at Sheepshead Row, Melbourn. The centre section appeared to have been an old farmhouse of perhaps the sixteenth century, built round a great central chimney. It had for many years been divided into two cottages, while the rest were originally constructed out of the old barns and out-buildings. But their scheme for reconditioning did not quite work out as hoped; financial problems during the run-up to World War Two meant that not all the cottages could be brought up to the sanitary conditions of the day. By 1953 they were home to several families. Some people had lived there continually for many years, others were newer tenants soon to move on as bigger and better council housing became available. By 1963 many of the cottages were not considered suitable for habitation and as families moved out they were left empty. The Cambridge Preservation Society could no longer afford the required renovation costs and Peter King of Bourn Hall took on responsibility for their upkeep and preservation. But he discovered that it would cost far more to upgrade the property than any rent would bring in. He maintained the essential structure and fought to prevent their demolition and replacement by a modern housing development. Then in 2003 builders moved in once more, thatchers ensured the roof was sound, old timbers were treated, walls replastered and, almost unnoticed, central heating, showers, baths and all the accoutrements of 21st-century life incorporated. (Photograph P. Salmon)

Melbourn – the White Lion, 1927. Traffic became an issue: *The White Lion pub, dating from the time of King Edward IV, was damaged when Mr Elbourn's steam lorry, driven by John Pateman, crashed into it. Crowds gathered to inspect the scene. Later the recovery operation was carried out with the aid of his traction engine. It was next door to a fish shop owned by 'Fessor' Hinkins who was also the chimney sweep and sold ice-cream. A small door next to the White Lion was used as a lavatory by the men; in summertime it became very smelly and people turned their heads as they passed by. It was one of several old taverns including The Old Elm Tree, Tailor's Arms, Locomotive, Hoops, and Spotted Dog.* [Melbourn Village History Group, A glimpse into Melbourn's past, 2005]

Meldreth – stocks, *c.*1929. *One of the too few reminders of olden days are the village stocks at Meldreth. Standing under a monster chestnut tree, they are a valuable asset to the village. They are specially mentioned in English and foreign guidebooks and are often visited by parties of tourists. A few days ago a motor coach containing about twenty sightseers on their way from London to Cambridge, left the main road at Melbourn and took the loop route via Meldreth and Shepreth, to see the old stocks. Some of the natives found very interesting the story the party's guide had to tell the visitors. He said the last legitimate occupant of the stocks was a drunken man in the year 1864. He told his party of the old yarn, current in the village, of how the stocked man's pals, hearing of his predicament, took him some beer, also some beer for themselves, and sat with him for company. When the village constable arrived to set the man free he was even more tipsy than before, and all his companions had qualified for the stocks! But what the guide did not tell the visitors – as old inhabitants are prone to relate – was that the day was a wet one and that the revellers borrowed a tarpaulin and pole and built a tent over the stocks to keep the man and themselves dry.* [CIP 26 June 1936] A somewhat more serious story of imprisonment was related in October 1936: *One of the last men to be sent to Botany Bay lived in an old cottage at Dolphin Lane, Melbourn, now due for demolition. In the Botany Bay days (1787-1868), a wagonload of convicts, manacled and in chains, passed through Melbourn on their way from an East Anglian prison to the London docks. One of the prisoners was a Melbourn man. The driver managed to take his wagon and charges past his former home and on hearing some shouting the old couple came to the door and were able to bid their son a tearful and last goodbye.* [CIP 30 October 1936] (Photograph: F.G. Turner)

Meldreth – Sheen Farm, 7am August 1903. Mowers sharpening their blades, Sheen Farm – left to right, Jack King, Walter Harup, Fred Sell, J. Sell, Bob King, Gus Harper, Alf Negus, W. Jacklin. P.H. Emerson described the harvesting process as if told in dialect by one of the harvest-men: *We went to the blacksmiths and bought our scythes – three & six each – and they weren't good neither, I slit too that harvest. I got a pair of gauntlets and a big straw hat from the shop. We went back to the blacksmiths to grind our scythes. All the gang were there – lord and all – some of them fitting new sticks to the scythes and some of them putting in tacks and some of them making grass nails and fitting them. Next morning we begun in earnest. Five o'clock. We started in and cut the corner round with the scythe. "That cut none too fit", says Joe. "That's rather ripe – that might have been cut a'fore", say another. "I think I'll have the first spell, mine's a new scythe, I want to get her an edge". "How does she do it" I asked as I was taking off after him. "I think she'll come to an edge. I think you'd better have a whet". And so we'd turn up and sharp, then start on again a little bit further. Then I say "Let me have a try to see how she hang and I'd take her and mow a stroke or two – "Bor that hangs like a fiddle, I think though she's ligging at the point a little. Where are our other chummies". "There they be, they're holding up their hands – beer-o. We'll go and get some cocoa".* [P.H. Emerson, A son of the fens, 1891] (Photograph: P. Salmon)

Meldreth – hovel. Elmcroft, an old wheat hovel or storehouse at Meldreth. This picture meant a great deal to Dr Palmer as he would tell his audiences: *It shows, in the background, the chimney of the house in which he was born and when a boy he used to hunt for hens' eggs under the hovel.* [W.M. Palmer, Peeps at old Cambridgeshire – CDN 9 March 1927] Sara Butler recalled her memories of Meldreth: *A carrier used to go to London with eggs and produce each Thursday returning on Saturday evening. Meldreth was a fruit-growing district. We children had to go 'cherry keeping' rattling tins and clappers to keep away the birds. The men used the old powder and shot guns and the blackbirds which were killed were usually eaten in a pie. Fruit was sent to market in the half bushel and bushel baskets. In the season, additional lorries were used by the railway to collect the fruit up. On Mondays, the streets were full of cattle being taken to the station for loading for Cambridge Market, and the same applied in the evening when cattle which had been bought was brought home.* [S. Butler, Memories 1895–1920 – Cambridgeshire Local History Society Bulletin, 1967]

Mepal – bridge, *c.*1930. Ireton's Way, linking Mepal and Chatteris, was constructed during the Civil War. By 1900 it was a private road which attracted the attention of the Isle of Ely highways committee because of its dilapidated condition. *On one occasion their steam roller got stuck in the road and was with difficulty extricated. There was no other way to get to this part of the Isle. A very heavy toll was charged upon it but there would be no complaint if it were properly repaired. They did not know the peculiar circumstances of the owner of the road. The best plan would be to obtain control of it, otherwise it might only be half repaired.* [CDN 15 February 1900] The road was taken over in 1902 and the tolls removed. But problems continued with the bridges across the New Bedford River. In 1922 the Ouse Drainage Board, owners of the bridge, advised that it was not sufficient to bear the modern traffic. *The bridge was originally built for tenants and servants of the Bedford Level Corporation, and they were under no obligation to build a new bridge suitable for modern traffic. The Board desired to know whether the County Council would be prepared to discuss terms for the erection of a new bridge, and for the future maintenance of such bridge.* [CDN 4 August 1922] The 17th-century wooden bridge over the New Bedford River, believed to be the last wooden Dutch bridge of its type in England, was replaced by a new concrete structure shown in the background of the photograph. (Photograph: D.G. Reid)

Mepal – Fortrey Hall, 1930. Fortrey's Hall stands in 'Byall Fen', a mile or so up a track alongside the Old Bedford River at Mepal. It was erected by Samuel Fortrey, one of the original Adventurers involved in the drainage of the fens and subsequently enlarged with a fine garden making it 'the admiration of the time'. In 1930 when James Bullock photographed it the plaster was beginning to crack, by 1984 it was *crumbling and derelict, virtually propped up by the trees and undergrowth surrounding it. Very little of the building is now visible. A lovely old roof of local tile projects through the trees and once elegant and formal windows stare blankly through the elder bushes.* [CEN 6 October 1984] It was bought by a builder and renovated; the chimney, which was said to be too heavy for the house and dragging it down, was greatly reduced in size. (Photograph: J.H. Bullock)

Milton – William Cole's house, 1932. The Revd William Cole was one of the country's leading antiquarians; he was appointed curate at Waterbeach but 'not being a water rat, I moved to higher ground at Milton' in 1769. By that time he had already filled over 50 folio volumes and during the next 13 years he was to compile nearly as many again. *The house was altered into its present shape by the Rev William Cole, the Antiquary and here he lived until his death in 1782. Although some modern additions have been made by the present owner, all the rooms used by Cole have been carefully preserved, and, inside and out, can be identified by his descriptions. The original house ended on the west with the two small windows. The part containing the two dormer windows was added during the tenancy of Mr Dunn.* [W.M. Palmer, William Cole of Milton, 1935] (Photograph: W.M. Palmer)

Milton – Queen Anne Lodge, 1938. Queen Anne Lodge, a 16th-century house at Milton which Cole always passed on his way to Cambridge. *The medallions on the right hand portion of the house are ancient. Those on the portion standing at right angles to the road were added by the collector and vendor of antiques who lives in it.* [W.M. Palmer note] The house was nearly burnt in 1938: *Fire destroyed a considerable amount of property at Milton and the action of the Cambridge Borough Fire Brigade was instrumental in saving the centuries-old Queen Anne Lodge from possible destruction. The fire broke out at the premises of Mr William Constable, smallholder and market gardener of High Street, who had retired to bed and was knocked up about 11 o'clock and told his sheds were on fire. The property concerned in the blaze was an open shed, a cart shed, pigsties, a packing shed and a big open shed where the flames had gained so strong a hold that the sheds were burnt to the ground. Their contents including a pig float, motor cycle and several bicycles were destroyed and a sow, a dog and about 50 head of poultry perished in the flames. The flames spread to within a few feet of two neighbouring thatched properties, one of them Queen Anne Lodge which bears the date 1703, and some outbuildings in one of the gardens was caught.* [Cambridge Independent Press, 25 March 1938] (Photograph: W.M. Palmer)

Newton – cottages on the London Road, 1930. A steam roller at Newton; such machines were essential in maintaining the roads, but were expensive, in 1899 *Caxton rural district council considered whether it would not be a financial gain to purchase a steam roller to combine the rolling of the roads and the haulage of the granite. A great outlay in carting by means of horses would be avoided. The Surveyor thought the council should hire a roller when they wanted it, as beyond the first cost there would be the continual expense of upkeep. He thought the roller belonging to the Chesterton council cost about £200 a year.* [CDN 27 July 1899] It would break down as Chesterton Rural District Council heard in 1922: *The steam roller had been in their possession for 21 years. It required considerable repairs. Messrs Aveling and Porter had been consulted and had reported that it would cost £500 to repair the old roller. A new roller would cost £811 and the old roller would sell for £200* [CDN 22 July 1922] (Photograph: J.H. Bullock)

Newton – the Queen's Head, 1930. Newton was always a small village where most of the men were employed on the land at very low wages: *Within living memory it was sometimes the case that farm workers could only go and stand outside the Queen's Head, lacking the money to enter and buy drinks. A small cottage in the yard housed the village library, the books given by the Hurrell family in connection with their Evening School.* [J. Hall, About Newton – the five went ways, 1987]. *During the 1920s Councillor H.W. Hurrell of Newton Manor established a Technical school affiliated to the Home Industries Association for instruction in metal work. Boys produced beautiful works of art in copper, brass, silver and pewter which were sent all over the country as well as to America and India. "It is one of the finest things the village ever had", said a resident.* [CDN 25 September 1926] (Photograph: J.H. Bullock)

Newton-in-the-Isle – the White Lion, 1932. There are two Newtons in Cambridgeshire; this one is four miles north of Wisbech, near the old Roman sea bank, but was still reached by a member of the Photographic Survey team. Unlike its southern namesake, the pub in Church Lane has closed, but the house looked much the same, although the fence and hedges had gone by 1996. (Photograph: E.B. Haddon)

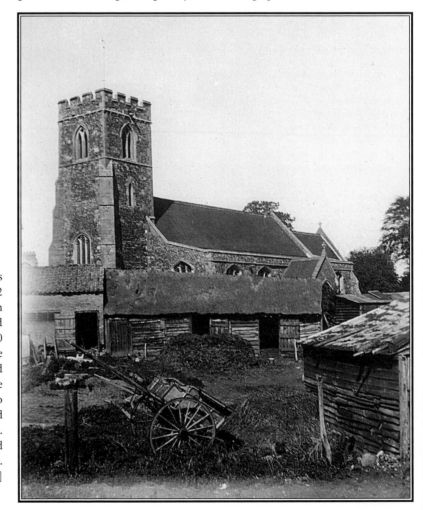

Oakington – church, 1942. St Andrew's Church was almost too prominent a feature of the village in 1942 when it was shaken by bombers taking off from Oakington airfield. Building of the airfield had started in 1939, but flying in the village dated back 30 years earlier when a newspaper reporter visited the aircraft works of Messrs Grose and Feary. He found them in a barn at Mr Cook's farm. As the time for the first flight neared there was debate between the two designers as to who should not be the pilot – one had a family, the other a widowed mother to support. The plane eventually careered across a field, but did not become airborne – except when it struck a bump. [*Cambridge Chronicle*, 17 September 1909] (Photograph: K.M. Murray)

Oakington – dove house, 1938. Pigeon houses were constructed mostly of local materials: *Clunch block or rubble in chalk areas; timber frame from the wooded areas; brick, and to the north of the county in the limestone belt are the durable Barnack stone structures, with locally quarried Colleyweston tiles. Most are of a square design, having either a saddle-back roof or a pyramidal roof rising to a cupola or 'lantern'. Circular pigeon houses had a special mobile ladder called a 'potence' for squab collecting. A king post was erected from the floor centre to the roof: from this two arms supported the mobile ladder just a few inches from the walls. The dovekeeper was thus able to propel himself from nest to nest without descending to the floor.* Peter Jeever found only three circular dovecotes surviving in Cambridgeshire. [P. Jeevar, Dovecots of Cambridgeshire, 1977]. This one did not: it was destroyed when hit by a British bomber attempting to take off from Oakington airfield during World War Two. (Photograph: L. Cobbett)

Orwell – Town Green Road, 1928. Dr Palmer described these cottages as being in Lotfield Road, behind the village shop; by 1995 the cottage in the background had been replaced by a modern house. *Here you may see another cage or lock-up. In later days used for thieves and drunkards it was in earlier days used for different kinds of lawbreakers, the fanatic preacher and his listeners known as Muggletonians. Ludovick Muggleton, the founder of the sect, was at Orwell in 1666 and the vicar and constable laid a trap for him, but the prophet was a shrewd man and escaped the fate of imprisonment in the cage. A little further on is the Mare Way and site of the Maypole, which stood until 1870 on the highest point of the road.* [W.M. Palmer, The neighbourhood of Melbourn and Meldreth, 1923] (Photograph: W.M. Palmer)

Over – thatched cottages opposite the church, 1926. The photograph is brought to life in the writing of the late Ernest Papworth whose father lived near the church: *Having finished his tea, Old Frank decided a short walk to the church seats would do him good. Locking the back-door and putting the key 'in the spout' he was forced to leave it protruding for if it fell flat in the guttering he was not tall enough to reach it. The fact that it was also visible to any caller did not occur to him, nobody would rob Frank's old cottage, not that there was much to rob. Although he liked to think of himself mainly as a vegetable man, he like most of the farm labourers in the village, grew flowers in their cottage gardens and commercially on their allotments in Mill Field, Webster's and Soldier's End. Not only were they essential to back-up their meagre agricultural wages, but provided the colour and charm to their simple homes. His particular love were pinks and carnations and naturally the three rose trees grafted on to the wild dog rose stocks which he had dug and collected from Mill Pits. All these were assisted in their growth by any horse droppings which were frequently deposited on the road that passed the front of the cottage. As a horsekeeper, even they indicated how much and with what the animal had been fed, and consequently how much good it would do his roses. A green pile always annoyed him, as it indicated the poor old horse had been fed literally on grass only. This brought forth the comment "How the devil does he (the owner) expect it to pull on that". This did not, however, stop him collecting it with a small hand shovel and pail from the coal-shed, stored there especially for that purpose.* [E.G. Papworth. Old Frank. 1993] (Photograph: Miss Johnson)

Pampisford – leather mill, 1930. Pampisford water mill was originally used for grinding corn and seeds for oil. It was bought in 1893 by the Eastern Counties Leather Company. *£500 was raised to convert the water mill into a power-source for the leather works. An eight horse power steam engine was installed for this purpose. After this time the mill was used for processing and became known locally as the 'oily mill' which referred to the cod oil used in tanning the leather. Heavy wooden stocks were driven by the mill and rather like large hammers, they literally punched the oil into the leather. The 'oily mill' eventually closed and was put up for sale in 1941. Eventually, when the mill's function fell into disuse, its tall chimney was demolished and in 1960 the mill became converted for residential use.* [O. Mayo, Pampisford places, 1985] (Photograph: J.H. Bullock)

Papworth Everard – St Peter's Church, *c.*1910. Papworth church was constructed in 1851, with a tower added 20 years later and topped off by a spire in 1875. In 1963 the spire was deemed to be in a dangerous condition and was removed. [J.D. Collens, Papworth in 1933, 1989] A millionaire speculator, Ernest Hooley, bought Papworth Hall in 1896 and spent some of his fortune on refurbishing it before he went bankrupt and was gaoled for fraud. After World War One the Hall became home to a settlement for people suffering from tuberculosis with a nurses home, two new hostels and new cottages formally opened by Sir Alfred Mond, the Minister of Health: *The hostels are admirably equipped in every respect and will bring joy to the hearts of the single men whose happy lot it will be to lodge in them. The cottages are for married men who wish to bring their wives and families to live with them.* [CDN 22 July 1922] As Papworth Hospital it has pioneered treatment for heart, chest and lung diseases. The Settlement had an impact on other areas of the community: *Crowds of people thronged to Papworth Everard on the occasion of the opening of the new Wesleyan Chapel, which is up-to-date in every respect. Mr Inskip offered a word of warning: In small congregations quarrelling could be a cause of trouble. They should work together to make this venture a success. Many people come to Papworth on account of their health and will come to the chapel with hearts full of thanksgiving.* [CDN 29 April 1927]

Papworth St Agnes – Manor House, *c.*1900. The Manor House, Papworth St Agnes was enlarged in brick in the 17th century and retains an ornate plaster ceiling of about 1600. Dora Tack visited it in 1943: *The front door was ajar and inside we saw the iron fire-dogs holding up the remains of a huge half-burnt tree. The floor of the entrance hall was of square, worn flagstones. We were invited in and offered a conducted tour of the old Elizabethan Manor House. The house had been in a bad state of repair when Mrs Butler moved in. One of the downstairs rooms had been partitioned off and used as a milking parlour for cows, so the walls had to be repaired and the plasterwork restored. On our way up the wide stairs we were told about the Priest's Hole, hidden behind the panelling right at the top, above the doorway leading to her bedroom. When the priest came down from the hole he did so by rope ladder; when he returned, he pulled it up after him and closed the panel, leaving no sign of the entrance from below. A little chapel had been found many years ago in a sealed-off room in the roof, with drawings on the walls.* [D. Tack, From bombs to buckets, 1989] (Photograph: W.M. Palmer)

Papworth St Agnes – cottages and village bakehouse, 1936. Dora Tack was a London girl who fled the wartime bombing and met and married a farm worker. They needed a home: *We did not know when there would be another empty house in Papworth St. Agnes if we were not lucky enough to get this one, so if we were offered Miss Poole's cottage, we intended to accept it. The inside of the cottage was, as yet, unseen, but from the outside, although the steep sloping path was muddy, the thatch appeared to be in fairly good condition, and we hoped it was watertight. At last a letter came from Mr Sperling giving us the tenancy and asking Frank to go and see him to discuss the rent and date of moving. He came home full of enthusiasm, carrying a large key, and the news that our future home was, in fact, two cottages made into one by the use of a connecting door upstairs and down. The rent would be only four shillings a week, not as much as we expected to pay for so much living space and such a large garden. We went at once to look at our new home. Two planks rested across a fairly deep ditch between the road and a slippery, muddy, cinder-strewn path which badly needed attention. Behind the cottage was a large wooden barn with a tiled roof, divided into equal parts by a wooden partition, with a door each end. In the corner through another door with a latch was the lavatory. Such luxury! It had a modern bakelite seat and lid and an inner container using Elsan Chemical Liquid. This lavatory had been installed by Mrs Poole and she had left behind a whole tin of chemical for our use, giving a fresh tarry-smelling aroma to this white painted little room. It was a big improvement on the little wooden hut we had used up to now!* [D. Tack, From bombs to buckets, 1989] The House and much of the estate village became derelict in the 1970s but has now been restored. (Photograph: J.H. Bullock)

Parson Drove – woad mill, c.1900. At Parson Drove some ancient buildings attracted the attention of a correspondent for the *Daily Mail*: *The atmosphere of this little pile of primitive and weather-beaten buildings suggests something distinctly apart from modern agriculture; and, indeed, it might well do so. For the place is the only woad mill in this country where the woad is pulped and prepared for the dyers in the fashion of centuries ago. At Parson Drove the power employed is that of the plodding horse. During recent seasons ten acres of woad have been sufficient to keep the Parson Drove mill working at a profit. The present mill has been in existence for fifty-three years although some of its plant is obviously a great deal older than this.* [Percy Izzard, The Woad-makers of Wisbech – *Daily Mail*, c.1900]. Professor Sir R. Biffen who presented a series of photographs to the survey, noted: *The conically thatched building at the end contains the mill proper; the low building in the centre is the 'couching house' in which the fermentation process is carried on. The low walls built of turf and the thick thatch tend to keep the temperature more or less constant. In the foreground are the remains of a 'drying range'.* (Photograph: J. Palmer Clarke)

Parson Drove – woad cutters. *Parson Drove woad mill showing three cutting rollers. The freshly gathered woad leaves are placed on the stone floor of the mill and pound to a paste by means of the horse drawn rollers. Each of these is about six feet diameter on its outer surface – the cutting bars of iron being about ½ inch thick.* [R. Biffen notes] The mill was pulled down in 1914. (Photograph: J. Palmer Clarke)

Prickwillow – cottage at Burnt Fen, *c.*1890. Revd Claude Kingdon wrote of his parish of Prickwillow in 1893. He described the houses dotted all over the fens, often miles apart. *Many of the wooden dwellings are mere hovels, and with them, as with the more substantially built ones, there is an almost entire absence of straight lines owing to the quaking ground on which they are built, cracks being visible everywhere, and chimney pots so precariously crooked as to seriously threaten the inmates on gusty nights. These houses are terribly overcrowded, many of them having only two rooms, and containing as many as a dozen occupants.* [C. Kingdon, Prickwillow in the fens – Home Mission Field, May 1893] (Photograph: F.L. Harlock)

Pymoor – windmill, *c.*1930. Pymoor mill was heightened in 1898 and worked into the 1930s, when it was visited by members of the Photographic Survey in their motor car. Two of its sails survived in 1960, but by 1995 the sails and cap had been removed and it was being used as a community post office. In 1906 H. Rider Haggard published his account of a visit to the area: *Driving down a 75-foot wide 'drove' of black peat we came to the dwellings of some of the Downham small-holders. Certain of the houses were smart and new, while others were tumbledown-looking shanties, sunk at one end or other owing to the shrinkage of their peat foundations, with out-buildings of rough board or tin. Canon Thornton said that the cottages were distinctly bad, as many of them were owned by small people who could not afford to keep them up. Often they contained two rooms and no more.* [H.R. Haggard, Social researches 1901–1902, 1906] (Photograph: R. Wailes)

Quy – tiled house by road, 1927. The quiet village of Quy has one day of excitement – the day that the Mayor of Cambridge journeys to proclaim Reach Fair, and scatters coins en route. In 1904: *Their drive was triumphal in nature and their distribution of coppers a source of much rejoicing. All along the route commencing with the Barnwell end of the town, continuing through Quy, past Lode, through the two Swaffhams to Reach, Rogation Monday is remembered as the day when a smart cavalcade of gentlemen, wearing robes with dignity, silk hats, and benignant smiles, distribute largesse as they sweep by. The distribution commenced before the Borough boundaries were past. Then there was a lull of a few miles broken only by the respectful salutations of the workmen in the new cemetery on Ditton Corner. The village of Quy showed however a scene of eager expectation. Here young and middle-aged matrons joined in the jubilant scramble for copper. One good lady who spoke gleefully of the 'tu'pence' she seized last year improvised a step dance not yet seen on the stage as a special inducement for coin to come her way, meanwhile holding out her capacious white apron as a receptacle for freewill offerings. At the school the children packed themselves along the wall which borders the road and raised simultaneous shouts of welcome and entreaties for spending money. The Lode scholars, who had the advantage of a holiday for the occasion, went one better. They almost encroached on the Quy preserves for they wandered far up the road to meet the procession, which they welcomed with a shrill chant of "Please – sir – pray – sir" and after picking up the money which fell to their lot, scuttled after the last carriage as fast as their small limbs would allow them in hopes of more. So the comedy continued, with slight variations to the formula of entreaty until the scene of action was reached.* [Cambridge Express, 13 May 1904] (Photograph: R.T. Bellamy)

Rampton – church interior before restoration, 1910. This postcard was presented to the survey by the rector, the Revd C.H. Evelyn White who undertook considerable restoration during the 1920s: *Thanks to the efforts of the rector, restoration and repair work has been going on at Rampton church. The rector has held the living for thirty years and has devoted himself to beautifying the church during the whole of that time. The Lord Bishop of Ely dedicated the new east window erected in memory of the men of the village who fell in the war. Other work includes the re-roofing of the south aisle and the re-building of the east wall, during which many interesting relics were found.* [CDN 1 December 1924] He did not however succeed in replacing the church's roof, which was rethatched in 1934.

Rampton – Black Horse pub, 1938. The Revd Evelyn-White also left an impression on Reg Young: *There used to be a grave inside an inclosure, with railings. There was a rhyme printed on the railings in gold lettering. His mother told him that a gypsy boy named Emmanuel Buttress was buried there. As a boy he remember jumping over these rails and playing around inside the churchyard. The rector, C. Evelyn-White came out looking very angry and shouted 'desecration' to him and his friends. They didn't know what 'desecration' meant but got the message and didn't play there again.* [R. Young Rampton reminiscences with Cambridgeshire Local History Society survey] By 1995 the trees had gone and the buildings on the right beyond the pub replaced. (Photograph: W.M. Palmer)

Reach – Devil's Dyke. The Devil's Dyke is the longest of the man-made defences, running across open countryside between the previously heavily forested Wood Ditton and the fens at Reach. It is an important botanical as well as archaeological feature but was ravaged by fire in 1899: *The grass which grows in luxuriance on the banks of the Devils ditch at Burwell caught fire about 1½ miles from the main road from Cambridge to Newmarket. Very quickly the undergrowth on the side farthest from Newmarket in both the ditch and on the bank was ablaze. Portions of the Heath became ignited. Assistance was quickly forthcoming from the farm and houses in the vicinity, but the fire had extended about a mile before it could be got under control. It is believed that a lighted match was dropped by someone passing.* [CDN 13 March 1899] (Photograph: D.G. Reid)

Reach – Devil's Dyke wartime excavations, May 1940. Excavations on the Dyke have been carefully monitored, but during the Second World War an underground storage shelter was dug into the bank of the dyke, an excavation not reported at the time for security reasons. *It was constructed as a Home Guard lookout point opposite the track leading to the cemetery and enabled them to see down the railway line and up the Burwell Road to the church and railway station.* [Bob Smith personal communication, December 2004] (Photograph: M. Brindley)

Reach – church, *c.*1938. The village pump stands in front of the church, which was severely damaged after being struck by lightning in 1958. *Behind it are the ruins of a chapel dedicated to St Etheldreda the Virgin, founded in 1378. The building to the right became the latest in a line of pubs that included the Black Eyed Susie, The Ship and the Black Swan. Bill King kept the White Horse until his death in 1954 and remembered times when he had as many as 36 customers at the bar and two standing on the doorstep. A new pub, the Dykes End, opened alongside the church in 1975 but closed shortly afterwards. A committee of villagers was formed and secured its reopening.* [G. Miller, Reach. 2000] (Photograph: L. Cobbett)

Reach – fair, 1930. The final section of the Dyke terminated at Reach where it was flattened to provide an open area on which a trading fair had been established by 1201. It continues to be held and is proclaimed by the Mayor of Cambridge: *At Reach fair, in accordance with custom, the mayor and members of the corporation forsook their dignity and became boys (and one girl) again. Following the official proclamation the mayor (H.B. Bailey) performed the opening ceremony of the new village pump. His worship pumped the first jug of water and quaffed off, or rather sipped suspiciously the first glass of it. Following luncheon the mayor repaired to the field and commenced an onslaught on the coconuts. First blood in this respect was drawn by the Chief Constable but the Borough Coroner contrived to 'wangle' three with one throw. The more sedate members of the corporation contented themselves with the roundabouts.* [CDN 27 May 1924] (Photograph: W.M. Palmer)

Royston – fair, before 1900. Most communities looked forward to a visit from a travelling fair with amusements such as A.J. Harris' 'Park Swings to let for fetes and school treats'. Albert Sheldrick described the scene at Ashwell: *After morning Sunday school it was important to be at the recreation ground in time to see the first caravans arrive from Melbourn where the fair had ended the previous night. Then came the big steam engine, Lord Kitchener, towing a huge wagon loaded with all the bits and pieces which made up James Harris and Sons flying horses, soon followed by Viscount Lascelles, a slightly smaller engine towing more of the fair equipment. By midday most of the fair had arrived, the water tap near the Cricketers pub had been connected to supply water for the horses, the engines and the caravan people. It was only a small fair. The Harris's came from Biggleswade and Jim's brother drove the Lord Kitchener which provided power for most of the fair's lighting, powered the flying horses, and the organ with its figures automatically banging drums and playing flutes and other instruments, blasting out such popular tunes as 'Valencia' and 'I'm one of the nuts from Barcelona'. Every now and then, just to hurry patrons along, there was an almighty shriek on the whistle, which could be, heard all over the village. The Harris girls, blonde and smartly dressed, attracted the customers to the dart stalls and a shooting gallery where you fired corks at packets of Woodbine cigarettes, boxes of Swan Vesta matches and other two-penny items. Young Jim Harris was usually the caller at a set of large faces with open mouths and clay pipes instead of teeth. You threw three wooden balls for two pence in an attempt to smash the 'teeth'.* [CEN 10 October 2001, K.Page, The story of Harris's fun fairs, 2001] (Photograph: F.R. Hinkin)

Royston – contact sheets. The Cambridge Antiquarian Society Photographic Survey includes a large number of small contact prints of Royston scenes, photographed by F.R. Hinkins about 1900. (Photograph: F.R. Hinkin)

Sawston – High Street, 1929. The Rural Community Council stressed the importance of county planning in 1927 and H.C. Hughes visited Sawston: *South of the cross the village is charming: the old plastered inn and cottages ranged on the curve of the road very prettily, but it is the sort of curve that does make a dangerous high street. Yet it would be a thousand pities to pull down these houses; it might be wise to make a by-pass. North of the cross the street is too narrow for the traffic, and the houses are right on it. There is nowhere for children to play without being in danger of their lives. Most of the houses in this part of Sawston have been refronted in a dirty brick and look rather depressing, but behind the brook there is much of interest, including an old Manorial dovecote. There are some wonderful tumble-down deserted cottages down Mill Lane. The piggeries are hardly among the amenities of the High Street, and railway carriages are perhaps only temporary homes. But on the whole Sawston is a likeable place with a great future, if it will stick to good planning principles and protect to the death the trees, meadows, walks, views, and all that group of buildings which short-sighted traffic control might easily destroy.* [H.C. Hughes, Sawston and regional planning – *Cambridge Chronicle*, 16 February 1927] (Photograph: F. Robinson)

Sawston – pea-picking, *c.*1901. The Sawston pea-picking custom dated back to 1554 when John Huntingdon established a charity which obliged the owners of Huntingdon's Manor to sow two acres of peas 'for the relief of the poor people'. *It is said that when he was young he had seen a poor woman punished for stealing peas from the fields. Peasants made soup and a kind of porridge from crushed peas, and their bread often included a proportion of pea meal in the flour. In 1862 the vicar, the Rev E.S. Daniel, wanted to abolish the custom, but with more than 200 inhabitants benefiting from the scheme, local opinion was against him and won the day. The Town Peas continued & when Huntingdon's Farm was sold in 1922 the obligation to grow the peas was a condition of sale. But as time passed, anomalies grew. The prosperous as well as the poor turned up to pick the peas until eventually the unfortunate farmer was paying out good money for seed and losing crop income from two acres to enable his neighbours to stock their freezers free of charge. Subsequently efforts were made to keep the tradition alive by planting some peas somewhere in the parish for the common use.* [J. Patrick, John Huntingdon's charity, 1999]

Shelford, Great – watermill, *c*.1895. Mill House, Great Shelford was built in 1814, though a mill was mentioned in the Domesday Book. Philippa Pearce, the author, recalled: *In 1876 Alexander Pearce moved to the King's Mill & in 1929, his son, Ernest (my father) followed him as miller. The modernisation of the Mill began in 1890, when a roller-mill was built in brick at one end. A few years later part of the old timbered mill was pulled down to build a wheat-cleaning section in brick and corrugated iron. The remaining part of the ancient timber-clad mill (in which the miller's family had originally lived) was now used only for the grinding and storage of flour and for a workshop and office. A single-cylinder producer-gas engine, with a magnificent flywheel some seven feet across, was installed to supplement the water-power. Electricity was generated for use not only in the Mill but in the Mill House. This was such a novelty that people used to stroll down on winter evenings to see the illumination. Country mills were usually small, this one employing no more than a dozen men. My father conducted business in his office, helped out in the Mill, did his book-keeping at home in the evenings and spent several mornings a week on his rounds. He took orders from customers ranging from small village bakeries (there were two in Great Shelford) to the big confectioner's and bakery, Hawkins, in Cambridge. After the War there seemed no future for country milling; my father had already worked well beyond retiring age, and no one wanted to buy the Mill as a going concern. In 1957 he sold it to Sir Leslie Martin, Professor of Architecture at Cambridge, who converted it into dwellings. The Mill House was sold separately, and for the first time became a mill house only in name.* [Great Shelford remembered, 1894–1994, 1994] (Photograph: L. Cobbett)

Shelford, Little – Manor Farm barns, 1930. Barns inevitably attract rodents: *The County Agricultural Organiser gave an interesting lecture on the destruction of rats at Lt Shelford village hall. People did not pay enough attention to the rat menace. There were far too many rats about Cambridge for his liking and if they held a Little Shelford Rat Week it would do a world of good. Everybody should kill rats whenever they got the chance. If each person killed one a week it would be doing some good.* [CDN 20 November 1926] Despite wholesale conversions of barns into houses the main barn was still standing in 1993, though its double-pitched roof had been replaced and the front wall heightened. The shed in the foreground had gone. One of the treasures of the Cambridge Antiquarian Society is an illustrated manuscript history of Lt Shelford compiled by Fanny Lucretia Wale between 1907 and 1927 in which she describes the village and its people. [F.L. Wale, Shelford parva, 1927] (Photograph: J.H. Bullock)

Shepreth – Upper Mill before 1927. The upper watermill at Shepreth was probably used as a paper mill, a new waterwheel was put up in 1924 but an oil lamp set the building ablaze in January 1927 and reduced the mill to not much more than a wheel which was later used to generate electricity. The weatherboarded timber building is gone but the wheel is roofed-over roughly in wood and corrugated iron. *A large trout used to come every year for ten years and nestle down close to where the water ran down to the mill wheel.* [*Cambridge Chronicle*, 23 November 1929] (Photograph: W.M. Palmer)

Shepreth – Baron's Farm, 1929. Horses and carts beside a thatched barn at Baron's Farm – now demolished. Life in Shepreth was far from tranquil. In 1925 employees at the East Anglia Cement Company's works in the village went on strike for more pay: *They marched in procession to Parker's Piece where a platform was in readiness for a mass meeting organised by the Cambridge Trades Council. On the arrival of the strikers a very large crowd quickly gathered. The speaker protested against the idea that because the wages of agricultural labourers were low, those of cement workers should also be low.* [CDN 13 April 1925] The vicar however was not supportive: *The vicar's action in placing upon his church door a notice drawing attention to a pamphlet entitled 'Work or Starve' was severely criticised at a meeting of the strikers in the East Anglian Cement Company dispute at the village hall. Mr Watering, the men's organiser, gave an account of a somewhat stormy interview with the vicar and announced his intention of writing to the Bishop over the use of the church door as an advertising medium to divide the strikers. It seemed hardly possible that the dispute had been in progress thirty-five weeks. Only when Colonel Tebbutt was willing to meet the men's representatives and agreed to the approved rate of wages would the strike come to an end.* [CDN 4 November 1925] The strike dragged on into 1926: *It is with great pleasure that we are able to announce the arrival of what is hoped will be a satisfactory and lasting settlement of the long-drawn-out dispute between the men at the East Anglian Cement Works at Shepreth and their employers. Yesterday, a day after the anniversary of the beginning of the strike the men agreed to accept terms for the resumption of work offered by the Company. The Company cannot employ all the men immediately but the manager will be instructed to start as many as possible.* [CDN 9 March 1926] (Photograph: J.H. Bullock)

Shingay – Shingay Gate farmhouse, 1936. The Revd H.H. McNeice guided a visit of the Cambridge Antiquarian Society in June 1925: *The way to Shingay is over open fields more or less. On the way we pass Shingay Gate Farm, which occurs as early as 1260. Although the fields of each village were without hedges or gates, they seem sometimes to have been divided by a large balk or ditch, and a gate, from the neighbouring parish, and this represented the division between Abington and Shingay. This village is now represented by a farm and two cottages but here over 400 years lived a band of Knights Hospitallers; you can see where their preceptory stood in the meadow on the same side of the road as the farm, an avenue from which leads up to it. The bodies of criminals and suicides, which could not be buried in ordinary consecrated ground, could be buried here and in 1640 John Layer says that a fairy cart or bier used to be kept here to fetch the corpses of condemned criminals for burial.* [W.M. Palmer & H.H. McNeice, Melbourn, 1925] (Photograph: J.H. Bullock)

Shudy Camps – Manor, 1923. In 1935 the Cambridge Standard featured Hanchetts Manor: *At the head of a richly wooded slope of parkland stands the fair mansion of Shudy Camps, the seat for these last thirty years of the Rev Canon Frederick Thornton, J.P., a leading administrator of local government, and an extensive land owner. The red brick edifice, part Elizabethan and part Georgian commands a fine view over the valley of the Bourne River to the Hadstock Hills. Here the Cambridgeshire countryside is at its best. Sweeping pastures which link knolls bearing oak, beech and fir in profusion, give no hint of the monotony of the fens to the north. In the house is a hidden room, but its whereabouts is Canon Thornton's secret. It is, he thinks, a relic of the Marian persecutions. It was discovered by accident when the estate carpenter was at work in the house. He never shows the room to anyone.* [Cambridge Standard, 26 April 1935] (Photograph: W.M. Palmer)

Shudy Camps – cottage, Mill Green, 1924. Conditions in rural parishes could be grim: *An inquest was held at Cardinal's Green, Shudy Camps, touching the death of a child of seven years. Her mother said the child had complained of sickness. For dinner she had beef, pudding and potatoes and drank water fetched from a pond in the garden. It was the only water supply for drinking purposes in that part of the parish. There was no pump, well, or other supply of water. Doctor Jones said that the water was most dangerous, full of injurious microbes, and ought never to be used, even for washing domestic utensils, without being first boiled. Linton District Council were told they should take immediate steps to cause a good supply of water to be effected.* [CDN 21 September 1898] (Photograph: W.M. Palmer)

Six Mile Bottom – windmill, *c.*1956. Six Mile Bottom mill on Bungalow Hill was in a good state of preservation, with the exception of the sails when photographed in about 1956. *The mill was most probably built on Mill Moor in Burrough Green and was moved to Westley Bottom in Westley Waterless sometime between 1796 and 1810. When the Great Chesterford to Newmarket railway was built in 1846, the mill was moved to its present position because it stood in the path of the railway. In 1879 the mill was damaged by lightning. It ceased to work in the 1920's and steadily deteriorated until restoration work commenced in 1983. New clockwise sails have been fitted, the buck re-clad, and the round-house roof repaired.* [R.D. Stevens, Cambridgeshire windmills and watermills, 1985] (Photograph: F.J. Bywaters)

Snailwell – church, *c*.1920. St Peter's Church Snailwell is one of two in Cambridgeshire with a round tower. In 1791 The Topographer described it as picturesque, being surrounded and nearly hidden by a grove of trees. But by 1820 it had fallen into disrepair with the windows offering limited protection from the weather. In 1878 a new rector started a thorough restoration which included rebuilding the south aisle and porch, repairing the chancel walls and roof. [VCH vol.10. 2002] (Photograph: Louis Cobbett)

Snailwell – mill and mill cottage, 1930. Ruins of Snailwell watermill, which was gutted during World War One. *Three mills were recorded in the Domesday Book and a new corn mill was erected about 1805 with a house occupied by the family of the miller. By 1910 there were only 31 dwellings in the village, most of them farmworkers' cottages. The Chippenham Park Estate Company was formed about 1931 and was the principal property owner in the village, though its control of village housing was reduced and the village layout altered in 1951-2 when Newmarket Rural District Council built 16 council houses.* [VCH, vol.10. 2002] (Photograph: J.H. Bullock)

Soham – millwrights at work. Cambridgeshire had one of the best remaining firms of millwrights in the country in Messrs Hunt of Soham and D.G. Reid photographed the firm in action. *Successive generations of Hunts worked as millwrights from the 1820s up to 1952. The master millwrights had their own yards in a town, or one of the larger villages. Sizes of workforce varied – often the immediate family, and one or two regular hands. They would often take on journeymen for a specific job, or perhaps hire them for a longer period if work were available. Drainage Boards usually put their work out to tender. A mill might be ordered in June, to be ready by November. Much of the work of building a mill was at the yard, where parts were prefabricated. The mill or materials would then be transported to the site for assembly. Most yards were situated near a navigable waterway; some millwrights owned a lighter, but these, as with horses, wagons and labour, would often be hired by the day.* [P. Filby, The fen millwrights, 1998] (Photograph: D.G. Reid)

Soham – drainage mills, 1914. Drainage mills were a common sight in the fens in the 19th century, lifting water from low dykes up into the rivers; but as the fens dried so the level of the land shrank and one mill could not push the water high enough. So another mill was built alongside the first, to lift the water into a reservoir. In 1914 Bullock photographed these mills in Middle Fen Drove, Soham. Soon wind pumps were being replaced by diesel engines. (Photograph: J.H. Bullock)

Soham – drainage mill, 1929. By 1928 there were few large wind drainage mills left; one, which belonged to Cambridgeshire County Council, stood at Soham Mere and still had the old type of tail beam and sail. It had been built by Hunt's in 1867. But by 1948 the mill was thought to be dangerous and the Council arranged for demolition men to pull it over with a tractor. They failed. Undaunted they returned with gunpowder. They failed. So in the end eight charges of gelignite had to be used to topple the 'dangerous' structure. Ironically just eight years later another Hunt's mill, much younger, much less impressive and in a much worse state, was re-built and erected just next door, at Wicken Fen, where it is lauded as the last of the fenland wind drainage mills. (Photograph: D.G. Reid)

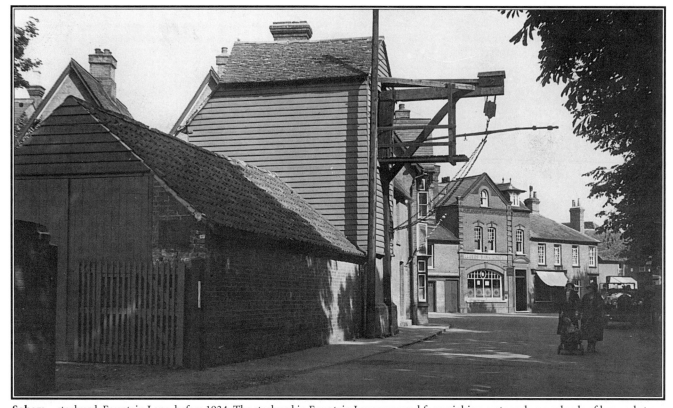

Soham – steelyard, Fountain Lane, before 1934. The steelyard in Fountain Lane was used for weighing carts and wagonloads of hay and straw until 1879 when the Ely to Newmarket railway opened their weighbridge at Newmarket. It is one of two surviving in the country. The surrounding area was swept by fire in 1900: *A most disastrous fire broke out in the centre of Soham which has reduced to a mass of blackened ruins an ancient hostelry, with its contents and outbuildings, a tradesman's shop and houses, & rendered homeless a dozen persons. The old hostelry The Fountain, with its rooms panelled with oak, and interesting alike to the antiquarian and lover of old-style architecture, stood at the corner of Churchgate Street. It was built mostly of timber and had plaster walls, with lath and reeds between. The firemen succeeded in preventing the fire involving a tall building, used in years gone by as a steelyard, hay and straw weighing apparatus.* [CDN 5 May 1900] The pub was rebuilt, incorporating one bar which survived the fire. (Photograph: D.G. Reid)

Stapleford – windmill, 1927. Stapleford corn mill was erected on the southern slope of the Gog Magog Hills in 1804 and worked until 1905. It subsequently fell into decay, and was photographed for the Survey in 1927. *During the early years of the Second World War it served as a look-out for the Home Guard. It deteriorated rapidly and the superstructure collapsed. By 1959 the brick base remained together with some of the old wheels and larger timbers, overgrown by bushes and weeds.* [G.T. Hall, A few notes on Stapleford windmill – Cambs. Local History Council Bulletin, 1959]. The village had a sad claim to fame: *Stapleford boasts of having been more frequently visited by outbreaks of fire than almost any other village in the county, and to enumerate those of a more or less disastrous nature that have taken place in the near vicinity during the last half century would be a tedious task. During that time over half a dozen farmsteads have been completely burnt down, innumerable stack fires have expanded their short-lived vigour, and several cottages have ascended to the clouds in smoke. And few of the present inhabitants do not remember the conflagration at Galls rope factory when the amount of damage was assessed at thousands. Yet they have no fire engine, nor have they fear for the morrow, what it may bring forth* [CDN 30 April 1898]. (Photograph: H.C. Hughes)

Steeple Morden – houses opposite churchyard, before 1928. In January 1901 other cottages had an unexpected visitor: *The visit of a 'ghost' to the cottages of Steeple Morden, known as 'Moco' and occupied by a gamekeeper and his wife and a shepherd, has caused a great sensation in the village. A fortnight ago the gamekeeper heard strange noises, as from a person in agony, emanate from the party wall. He then heard a thud and the firing of a gun in one corner of their room. It is stated that one if not two murders were perpetrated at this place many years ago.* [CDN 3 January 1901] (Photograph: R.H. Clark)

Stetchworth – May tree, 1927. The old elm at the junction of Church Lane and Main Street was decorated on May Day formed the centre for May games and festivities. Many villages had their own forms of the celebration. A Waterbeach res recorded in 1820: *Our May Day was our grandest holiday. Preparatory to its celebration the young men collected materials to a garland; they consisted of ribands, flowers and silver spoons, with a silver tankard to suspend in the centre. Then woe betide th of loose habits, the slattern and the scold; for while the young woman who had been foremost in the dance, and whose amiable ma had entitled her to our esteem, had a large branch or tree of whitethorn planted by her cottage door, the girl of loose manners h blackthorn planted by hers. The slattern had an elder tree planted by hers and the scold a bunch of nettles tied to the latch of her co door.* [W.K. Clay, History of Waterbeach, 1859 – CAS Octavo publication] (Photograph: L. Cobbett)

Stretham – Ferry Bridge, *c.*1922. Although a Roman road, Akeman Street, formerly connected Cambridge and Ely this had fallen into disuse by the 11th century and the main route between Cambridge and Ely was via the Aldreth Causeway. *The present road from Ely to Cambridge was started in 1754 by Bishop Mawson & completed by 1783. A bridge was constructed, replacing the former ferry. It was single width with alcoves and was very steep, farmers needed to put extra horses on their carts to pull them over. It was replaced by a new bridge in 1925 which carried increasing traffic until it was itself superseded and the road realigned in 1976.* [Cambridge Heritage Associates, Stretham millennium history, 2000]

Stretham – Cross and church, 1926. Road improvements continued at Stretham with a new road running between new council houses opening in 1928. In the centre of the village the churchyard wall was set back in 1926 and again in 1928 when the road was straightened to remove a bend that caused difficulty for increasing motor traffic. The 15th-century cross had a flight of stone steps when sketched by William Cole in 1748 but these were replaced, probably to allow more room for stagecoaches to turn. The top of the cross was removed for restoration in 1909. (Photograph: O.H.H. Jermy)

Stretham – the Malt and Hops, 1928. Beatrice Stevens recalled: *The Malt and Hops was one of fourteen pubs in Stretham, one of them also being a brewery, and the village boasted another brewery, whose trade was selling its beer in bulk to farmhouses and the like. Isaac Nicholas and his wife kept the "Malt and Hops". Like most landlords Isaac had a regular job elsewhere, so it was left to his wife to serve any customer who might call during the day: maybe a drover moving animals from one farm to another or taking bullocks to market. It might be a man returning home early from work for one reason or another, although never for pleasure. Although the Malt and Hops was an old building it was a popular pub because of its situation, which was convenient for those who worked at the Gravel or at the Wooden Bridge, both riverside spots which gave their names to areas where there were several farms. After the Nicholas' moved from the Malt and Hops it was taken over by Tom Stubbins. Tom was tall, and he was a blunt man, given to calling a spade a spade, but with adjectives which were descriptive if not entirely acceptable in mixed company!* [B.C. Stevens, Stretham: a feast of memories, 1989] The pub is now a private house and the adjacent thatched barn has been replaced by houses. (Photograph: J.H. Bullock)

Stuntney – church notices, 1937. On a visit in 1937 Louis Cobbett found his eye caught by a notice requesting women to remove their pattens – wooden overshoes with a metal sole – when entering the church. Not everybody could afford shoes: *A man and his wife were charged with neglecting to keep their children in a proper manner. The Inspector of Nuisances said he found the room in a most filthy state. There were only a few things in the room, besides a heap of old rags in a corner which seemed to make a bed for the children, and the stench was most terrible. He saw three or four children without shoe or stocking on; the youngest was outside the front door with only a torn shirt on. He only found a small portion of bread, a little piece of butter, and a little sugar in the house. This was all they had.* [CDN 16 June 1897] (Photograph: L. Cobbett)

Stuntney – Anchor Inn, 1933. Dr Palmer took this snap of the Anchor Inn at Stuntney being photographed for the Survey by J.H. Bullock in June 1933. Over 600 of Bullock's photographs and negatives are the backbone of the collection. The Anchor closed in 1966: *Stuntney – adult population about 150 and once the possessor of two public houses – has become a village without a pub. When Mr Victor McGee, licensee of the Anchor Inn, shut the doors last night, he was doing so for the last time. The tenancy has been in his family for 50 years. The owners, Steward and Patteson Ltd of Ely, have decided that it would not pay to repair a 'very old property that has outlived its time'. Last week a petition signed by over*

60 villagers headed by the vicar, Canon John R Pelloe and Mr David Morbey, a farm company director, urged the brewery to reconsider their decision. Yesterday one of the directors, Major B.E. Dillon said the board had considered the petition sympathetically but could not in the present economic circumstances, change their policy. "What is happening is that more and more people, particularly the younger, go into the towns. Such money as is available is spent on modernising the larger houses in the bigger centres, such as Ely. It is sad, but there it is". [CEN 28 September 1966] (Photograph: W.H. Palmer)

Stuntney – Anchor Inn notice, 1933. J.H. Bullock's attention had been caught by this notice on the pub wall. Vagrants had problems finding a bed in 1926: *Ely Guardians heard a complaint from a vagrant of a shortage of accommodation in the casual ward of the workhouse which was full up with Beet Sugar Factory employees who paid 1s per night. There was no registered common lodging house in Ely but the workhouse was for destitute people and not for those with money in their pockets. But some of them concealed what money they had. If they filled the casual wards with people with money what were they going to do with the poor chaps who really were down and out? Some of the casuals were looking for work. If the Beet Factory did not take them on they would only go on the land and take jobs from agricultural labourers. Last year there were 60 or 70 living at the Jam Factory. The matter was left to the discretion of the Master.* [CDN 3 December 1926]

Stuntney – Hall, 1927. Stuntney Hall, a picturesque brick house was the birthplace of Elizabeth Steward, mother of Oliver Cromwell. In the 1920s it was home to Cole Ambrose who, it was said, could lie on his back in bed and see the stars through the hole in the roof. He built a new house in the village and the Hall fell into disrepair. In December 1976 permission was given for its partial demolition. By 2002 work was underway to rebuild the property. (Photograph: L. Cobbett)

Sutton – Guildhall, 1908. Ruins of Sutton Guildhall. *There were religious or social gilds in almost every town and village. The Gilds almost everywhere placed themselves under the patronage of a Saint, and in honour of their patron placed wax candles on the altar of the chapel and before the image. On one day at least in the year the brethren and sisters being assembled, clad in their hoods or livery, and bearing lights in their hands, marched in procession to the church, and placed lights on the Altar and before the Patron Saint, and made the prayers enjoined by their rules, thus consecrating that brotherly love and peace they were sworn to cherish. Having made their offering they went their way to the Gild Hall to transact business, and enjoy a festive meal, and afterwards to indulge in open-air sports. Vestiges of these Gild Halls remain, I believe, in many villages, and after an examination of the ancient house opposite the south side of the church, I incline to the opinion that it is the original Hall of the Gild of the Virgin Mary, of Sutton.* [M. Sheard, St Andrew's Church, Sutton, 1908, CHAS Trans.vol.2]

Swaffham Bulbeck – Commercial End, 1926. Mr A. Harding recalled his childhood in the area about 1866: *It was not known to me then as Commercial End. It was known to us in that part of the village as 'Down' Street, and the other end, where is Stock's Hill and the church as 'Up' Street. Something like 100 years back a great flow of merchandise came up to Swaffham Lode by barges and small boats drawn by horse, and some sails, and a few by steam power and unloaded their various consignments at the merchant's yard which I went into many times. It had large sheds and warehouses, now no more, where coal, turf, timber, fossils, corn etc were stored until claimed. The barges were reloaded and took things away. Commercial End has not for many years had very much that is outstanding, but I have never forgotten the goodwill that existed among the folk. It is a very healthy place as many of my relatives lived to see 90 years and over.* [CDN 14 May 1938] (Photograph: R.T. Bellamy)

Swaffham Bulbeck – Benedictine nunnery, 1930. The story of the Benedictine nunnery at Swaffham Bulbeck is complicated involving two Isabels de Bolbec, both of whom married Earls of Oxford and the annals of the nunnery are meagre. *It was the smallest nunnery in the country, consisting of a Prioress and six nuns and eked out its income by taking paying guests. At one time it was alleged that the Prioress had given a benefice to a Friar whom people said she loved well. In early 1536 the Prioress voluntarily surrendered her house into the hands of the King and she and her nuns each received a small pension.* [W.M. Palmer, The Benedictine nunnery of Swaffham Bulbeck, 1929 – PCAS vol.31]. When Bullock visited in 1930 the vaulted undercroft was being used for agricultural purposes. It is now a private house. (Photograph: J.H. Bullock)

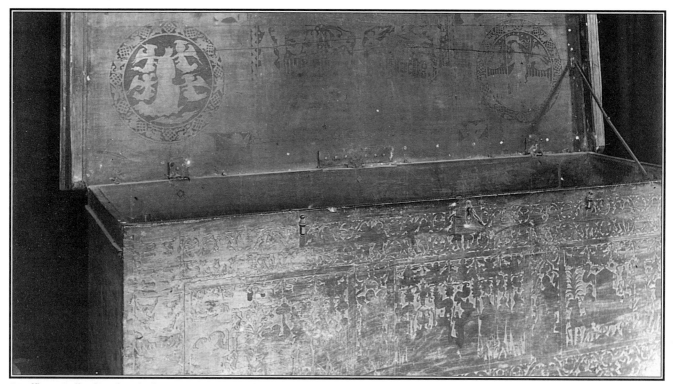

Swaffham Bulbeck – church chest, *c*.1910. In 1936 the church hit the headlines: *The delightful old church of St Mary, Swaffham Bulbeck, was the scene of a disastrous fire. Thankful the vicar and his parishioners must be that the fire, which badly damaged the organ, belfry and tower, did not spread beyond. Only recently the sum of £400 was spent in putting the tower in repair. A special feature is the old open benches which bear traces of handsome carvings, and there is a cedar chest of the 15th century with fine carvings of the Conception of the Blessed Virgin Mary, the Crucifixion and the Resurrection. During the fire Mrs Stearn, the wife of the vicar, together with her daughter and several villagers, worked valiantly to save valuable articles and amongst the ornaments so rescued was a vestment box of Italian workmanship and made of Cypress wood which dates back to the time of King Richard I.* [CIP 25 December 1936] (Photograph: C.H. Evelyn-White)

Swaffham Prior – churches, *c*.1890. Swaffham Prior is unique in that it possesses two churches in one churchyard. Restoration of St Mary's, on the right, began in 1878 when the chancel and vestry were rebuilt. By October 1902 the work was complete: *St Mary's church, Swaffham Prior, having been for years the ruinous companion in the same churchyard, of the parish church of St Cyriac is now open once more for public worship. The work of restoration had been proceeding for a considerable time. It is now probably one of the most unique looking sacred buildings in all England. The old and new parts form a bizarre combination. Above a new roof are the remains of what has been a magnificent Norman tower. About half of it is left and is still extremely picturesque. Before a large congregation the Bishop conducted the re-opening service after which St Cyriac's ceased to be, and St Mary's became the parish church.* [CDN 23 October 1902] (Photograph: Scott & Wilkinson)

Swaffham Prior – windmills, 1928. Swaffham Prior also has two mills; in 1928 Rex Wailes noted: *This mill out of action and rapidly decaying. The other still working but seldom repaired. Wonderful view from the mill garden across the fens to Ely. Mr Foster miller.* The second mill finally ceased work in 1946. By the 1960s they were both derelict and without sails but were restored shortly afterwards and their sails renewed. One was brought back into use and the other converted into a house. [VCH vol.10. 2002] (Photograph: R. Wailes)

Swavesey – fire engine house, 1933. Swavesey fire engine was in the news in September 1899: *Sir – Swavesey has a fire engine which today after a few years of peaceful repose, with a great ceremony and clatter, but with no wild haste, was taken to the scene of a fire. By almost superhuman efforts it was placed in position by a pond and then hose and suction pipes were attached. One gallant fireman in a white hat screwed on the nozzle, the pumps were manned but sad to say all that this parish relic of antiquity pumped was air. In vain the white-hatted hero pointed his nozzle and scorched his clothes. The fire burned on merrily while the engine stood useless by the pond – Q.* [CDN 4 September 1899] (Photograph: P. Salmon)

Swavesey – Swan Pond, before 1912. The fire engine was needed again in 1913 when Swavesey was devastated by a fire which destroyed every house shown, except the last two at the back: *The fire fiend reigned supreme at Swavesey and enormous damage was done to cottage property and workers' tenements in the Church End. Dozens of families were rendered homeless and in many cases the poorer inhabitants lost the little all which they possessed. Swavesey presents a sorry picture: blackened walls and charred debris are the relics of what were originally 29 thatched cottages, barns, buildings and so forth. The suddenness of the outbreak and rapid succession of events practically put the entire village in a panic. At one time 20 houses were burning! The Swavesey Parish Council has an excellent manual engine for a village of 900 people but the arrangements are totally inadequate. A Captain is appointed but he has no power to remove the engine from its shed unless the owner of a burning building has requested him to do so. He has no brigade to work the engine or direct the hoses. He must be dependent on volunteers and as these volunteer pumpers have had some difficulties in receiving remuneration from the Parish Council for their past services it is sufficient to say that they are not exceptionally enthusiastic volunteer firemen!* [*Cambridge Chronicle*, 7 March 1913] (Photograph: P. Salmon)

Swavesey – Boxworth End, 1930. Ruined cottage at Boxworth End. Old properties reach the end of their life, as do people; but one widow caused a stir when she remarried in June 1898: *Swavesey had a first class sensation on Monday night. It is not used to such novelties. It appears Swavesey has a widow. Nothing strange about that. But this was a fascinating widow. Nothing remarkable even about that. Her husband is scarcely cold in his newly-made grave before he is superseded. This is the story which bought out the inhabitants in hundreds into the main street to celebrate the widow on Monday evening. From eight o'clock until eleven the rattle of tin cans, the whistling and shouting, hooting and yelling, and a tuning of various other musical and unmusical instruments, filled the air in this usually quiet village. Whether these noisy attentions of the neighbours will do any real good is open to question.* [CDN 10 June 1898] (Photograph: J.H. Bullock)

Tadlow – granary, 1930. The granary at Tower Farm, Tadlow has moved to Wandlebury: *Originally built circa 1415, the granary had been part of a group of farm buildings at Tadlow Towers, Royston. In 1967 it seemed just a tumbledown barn, of no special interest. A request for planning permission to demolish the granary immediately aroused the interest of the Cambridge Preservation Society. Historians believe that originally the granary was thatched and stood upon staddle stones. At a later date the fabric was moved, repaired, peg-tiled and placed upon Tudor brick piers. As there was only one other known granary of a similar construction in Britain, it was considered essential to preserve the building and keep it in Cambridgeshire. The Cambridge Preservation Society agreed to pay the costs incurred by The Avoncroft Museum of Buildings in numbering and dismantling the timbers, and transporting them to Wandlebury where it was reassembled.* [W. Clark. Once around Wandlebury, 1985] (Photograph: J.H. Bullock)

Teversham – cottage, 1929. Cottage on the south side of the road between Manor Farm and Cherry Hinton Road, no longer standing by 1956. Teversham was birth place to Corney Grain, an entertainer, who in 1888 recalled his home village: *Picture to yourself a by-road turning off the road to Newmarket – a flat county, some farm buildings and cottages; on the opposite side of the way the remains of the village stocks, the Rose and Crown kept by one Muggleton (good name I always thought, for a publican); then more cottages, a farm with orchard containing an excellent mulberry tree, the blacksmith's; then a cottage tenanted by old Mrs Oliver, who prepared feathers for feather beds, then Hancock's the carpenter's house; and then in some meadows or, as we call them, closes, our house! A farmhouse covered with ivy, with pretty lawns and gardens, and a moat running round three-quarters of the grounds. There were no amusements for the people of the Parish – only the Village Feast once a year which began and ended with beer. The church services were bald, meagre, and altogether disgraceful, but the crowning point of the service was the music. The clerk (one Gilson who soled and heeled shoes in the world) left his desk and went up in a little gallery, in which sat certain gentlemen, viz: Mr. Pomfret, Mr. Muggleton and Mr. Lane. The two former played clarinets, the latter the violincello. As a trio the combination of instruments is odd, but not so odd as the sounds produced by the executants. There was no attempt at harmony, or even melody, in unison. Each individual went his*

own ways, or rather the way his instrument chose to take him. The clarinets were particularly erratic in their ways, and produced 'alarums and excursions' at the most unexpected moments. The clerk gave out one line of the hymn, and then proceeded to sing it as a solo, while the clarinets and the violincello grumbled round the melody – not quite there, or thereabouts. We never joined in, but stood respectfully listening to this nasal-voiced shoemaker snuffling forth some dreary tune, while discord reigned triumphant round and round about him. [C. Grain, Corney Grain, by himself, 1888] (Photograph: J.H. Bullock)

Thetford – roundhouse, 1937. The original use of this structure, used as cottages in 1937, has been the cause of debate. *A round house is not a common building in England. The one at Little Thetford consists of two tenements, inhabited by two separate families, and was probably, some centuries back, either a dove-cote or something similar. It will be noticed that the walls are far from upright, and seem to indicate that it might have been part of an old windmill, many of which are to be found in Cambridgeshire.* [Church Monthly, 1901] Louis Cobbett thought it the base of an old windmill but research by Bob Young of Lt Thetford confirms it was a dovecote. During World War Two it was the village's designated First Aid centre. It was restored in 1971. (Photograph: L. Cobbett)

Thorney – Church Street, *c.*1930. Delha Stebbings was born at Lodge Farm, Thorney. She recalled: *In our family there were five boys and five girls and two that died. There was no social life in the village then, but we didn't need it because there was enough of us to provide our own amusements. We had a radio but in the evenings mum used to knit and do her mending and dad used to play with us at the table. Cards, we could play cards, and all manner of games until it was bedtime. Dad always went to the Rose and Crown in Thorney on a Saturday night.* [L. Faulkner, The light of other days, 1998] But he might not have been drinking beer: *Another public house has been handed over to the management of the People's Refreshment House Association Limited. The latest acquisition is the new Rose and Crown Hotel which has just been erected by the Duke of Bedford at Thorney. It will be managed more as a house of general refreshment than as a mere drinking bar and food and non in-toxicants will be given prominence.* [CDN 6 April 1899]

Thriplow – Crouchmans, Middle Street, 1938. Sheila Andrews recalled: *Crouchmans was divided into three cottages. In the first one lived David Wade who was a roadman with his daughter Florrie. In later years that cottage was taken down and rebuilt in the meadow opposite Townsend Springs. In the second cottage lived a Mrs Neeves with her daughters, and in the third cottage lived three bachelors known by the names of Bullock, Skatey and Fee Gambie. Bullock would ride a bicycle without pedals when he went to Fowlmere. Skatey worked on the land and Fee walked with two sticks and stayed at home.* [S. Andrews, Steps back in time, 1997]. By 1994 the thatched roof had been replaced with tiles and dormer windows added. (Photograph: L. Cobbett)

Thriplow – smithy, 1937. The blacksmith was a busy man, as Fred Gambie remembered: *Before the days of the farm tractor there were 85 to 100 horses in the village, including the young ones in training. It was an interesting sight to see the farm men taking the horses out in the fields to plough etc., sometimes as many as 20, two or three to each man. A Mr Fordham farmed Cochrane's Farm, Thriplow and Duxford Grange Farm, and lived and farmed at Shelford; he had all his horses (85) on one big field at Thriplow at the same time as he wanted it done quick.* [F. Gambie, Thriplow in my young days – Cambs Local History Council Bulletin, 1974] By 1994 the roof had been repaired and the building restored, but it was largely unchanged. (Photograph: L. Cobbett)

Thriplow – refuse dump behind Thriplow Place, 1938. Fred Gambie continued: *When I started work first, crow scaring, they gave me an old muzzle-loading gun, the type used before cartridges were made, you put a measure of gunpowder in, then rammed brown paper in, and the harder you rammed the more noise it made when fired. Fancy giving a boy of 13 that to be out in the fields alone all day. If a long way from home you had to take your food with you and two sheep hurdles stuffed with straw for shelter, and get some wood and have a fire if it was chilly. We learned to light a fire with a thick glass in the hot sun. One day we was having our lunch, the men were sitting down, one old fellow in an old bowler hat. We stood behind with the sun focussed on the glass and burnt a small hole in his hat. He snatched his hat off quick and didn't know what caused the pain. And them old bowler hats used to last for years until they were green with age.* [F. Gambie, Thriplow in my young days – Cambs Local History Council Bulletin, 1974] (Photograph: L. Cobbett)

Toft – Brookside, 1927. Cottage in Brookside, Toft, showing Harold Constable with bike and a corn, offal and flour merchant's van. The area suffered a fire in October 1947: *A family who had been bombed out four times in London, yesterday evening lost their home at Toft when it was gutted by fire. The cottage was one of three completely destroyed at Brookside and was occupied by Mr Thomas White, his wife and daughter. Most of the furniture was saved. In another cottage occupied by Mr Owen Braysher practically everything was destroyed, although the animals at the rear of the property were rescued. A German prisoner of war did great work in helping to save furniture. Fire brigades from Cambridge and Whittlesford attended the fire and two major pumps were used.* [CDN 7 October 1947] (Photograph: R.T. Bellamy)

Trumpington – war memorial, 1973. Trumpington war memorial, designed and carved by Eric Gill, is considered one of the best in the land. *When excavations for the site of the war memorial on Cross Hill were in progress in October 1921 the base of an old stone cross was uncovered, the top being about three inches below the level of the road. An inscription read: 'Pray for the soul of John Stocton and Agnes his wife'. It may have been destroyed by order of Dowsing or was perhaps secretly hidden. The old base was placed under the church tower and the War Memorial substituted.* [S. Brown, Trumpington in old picture postcards, 1986] This photograph is one of the last to have been added to the collection.

Trumpington windmill, from Long Road, *c.*1880. Tower mill at Long Road, Trumpington. In 1928 A.C. Moule interviewed Miss Moore, the daughter of the last miller who told him: *The mill was built in 1812, part of the works coming from an old mill which had then recently been pulled down near Barrington. It stopped working in the spring of 1887 and a year later was sold to John Peile, the Master of Christ's College. He tried to let it but failing to do so had it pulled down that same year. She does not remember there was ever any difficulty in stopping the machinery in the highest winds, but great difficulty in dealing with sudden changes of wind. The miller would always go into the mill in a thunderstorm to be ready for such changes, when he would turn the fan-sail with a winch. Several times she remembers all hands being called up in the night because the fan-sail was going so fast that its machinery could not act and then it had to be unshipped and the mill turned into the wind with all available man-power on the hand-winch.* [A.C. Moule letter in the survey] (Photograph: R.C. Hopper)

Tydd St Giles – Church Lane, 1932. The corner by the church, showing the premises of Herbert Taylor, shopkeeper and cycle agent. By 1995 the little cottage on the left had been replaced by a large house. Bicycles were important, as John Parrin from Bunkers Hill recalled: *Nearly everyone had a bike usually made up of oddments picked up from the salvage heap, often the wheels were of different sizes. The frames could be male or female, but they certainly never had brakes.* Enid Troughton from Wisbech St Mary remembered: *I cycled to school, every day & came home in the dark. If it was really very rough my father used to pay the garage man to take me very occasionally.* [L. Faulkner, The light of other days, 1998] (Photograph: E.B. Haddon)

Upware – the 'No Hurry' inn, 1928. The Lord Nelson, Upware originally served the river trade. *It became the No Hurry – Five Miles from Anywhere from the 1860s, so dubbed by Richard Ramsey Fielder, a rumbustious graduate and poet of Cambridge who loved to join the steady drinkers here. A ferry plied across the Cam between 1901 and 1918 charging a person on foot one penny; with a bicycle, twopence; with pony and trap, fourpence; with horse and cart, sixpence and with cattle, twopence a head. Originally under thatch, the hugely popular Five Miles caught fire in 1956 and was demolished in 1957. The site stood empty for a long time before the new inn was placed on the site, carrying the old name.* [A. Day Wicken, a fen village, 1996] (Photograph: E.F. Watson)

Upware – Lock and fen pumping engine, *c*.1930. From the 1820s steam power took over the draining of the fens. *The tall-chimneyed, coal-fired pumping stations proliferated beside the rivers, although the windmills remained to lift the water from the smaller drains. Swaffham Engine at Upware, at the head of the Swaffham Fen Drain pumped the water up to the Cam level. This engine was installed in 1850, replacing another in a different shed built in 1821. It was demolished in 1939. An electrical installation stands on the site today with the replacement diesel shed, built in 1927, still standing. Another pumping station, the Burwell Engine, operated close by at the head of Commissioners' Drain and the building still stands.* [A. Day, Times of flood, 1997] (Photograph: L. Cobbett)

Upwell – Town Street, *c*.1930. In 1925 Christopher Marlowe published an account of a bicycle trip through the fen country: *At Upwell you cross the boundary from Norfolk into Cambridgeshire and exchange the cheery dialect of the East Anglian farmer for the soft 'burr' of the Cambridgeshire yokel. The chief attraction is the quaint old steam tram, which still carries passengers and goods from Wisbech, to the tinkle of a bell. The line runs by the side of the road until it diverges just before reaching Wisbech to enter the Great Eastern station there as a terminus. The scent of strawberries was strong in the air; the procession of carts with their gay baskets wound in a steady stream along every road towards the tram terminus as I proceeded into Upwell. The church here contains some interesting small relics, notably the old pews with doors and pews for one person, all up the middle aisle. There is a side gallery and a magnificent carved angel roof, comparable to the superb gem of architecture at March. A brass records the terrible cholera visitation of 1852, when over sixty-seven people died.* [C. Marlowe, The fen country, 1925] (Photograph: Coates postcard)

Waterbeach – Public baptism in the Cam at Bottisham Locks: *The ordinance of baptism was administered to six persons on Sunday afternoon in the river Cam, near the sluice, by Mr G. Williams. The candidates were five females and one youth. The greatest decorum was manifested on the occasion, and many hundreds on the river banks were witnesses.* [*Cambridge Chronicle*, 24 September 1886] The famous preacher, Charles Haddon Spurgeon was appointed minister of Waterbeach Baptist Chapel in 1851, when only 17 years old. He had been baptised in the River Lark at Isleham where the tradition continues.

Wendy – church. Wendy is a village that has been unfortunate with its churches. *The original medieval church, having got into a most ruinous condition was in 1737 replaced by a small plain building without a chancel, which on account of the badness of the foundations served for little more than a century. By 1863 the gable was a long way out of perpendicular and the congregation could look out into the churchyard through the huge cracks in the walls, and in its turn it gave place to the present Early English Church built by public subscription.* [W. Jones, A history of Wendy, 1902] But history repeated itself, the foundations were inadequate and the church was pulled down in 1950. (Photograph: W.M. Palmer)

Wendy – church roof, *c.*1950. Although Wendy church was only built in 1867 it contained a much older fine double hammer beam roof brought there from the old church of All Saints, Cambridge which had been demolished in 1865. In 1950 it was acquired by Mr N.A. Huddleston: *I have just bought the main timbers of the fine carved oak roof of Wendy church. They are extremely massive and are said to date from the 16th century. They were offered to me as firewood for £6. It is being demolished because failure in the foundations has made it unsafe.* [CDN 8 April 1950] (Photograph: F.J. Bywaters)

Wentworth – the Fish & Duck, 1930. The Fish & Duck at Wentworth, near Ely was owned by A. & B. Hall's Ely brewery in 1906 when the licensee was William Seymour who combined being a landlord and a farmer. The pub had two beds for the family and two beds for lodgers together with stabling for two horses and two vehicles. It has been demolished and replaced by a house. The hamlet had two public houses in the 1950s, the other being the Red Lion. (Photograph: J.H. Bullock)

West Wickham – public house, 1926. The White Hart public house on the edge of the green at West Wickham. In 1865 John De Fraine described the scene at fair time: *The village fair commenced on Saturday. In a little paddock, adjoining the White Hart, the stalls are built, and the great booth pitched, and the fun, and din, and roar goes on as in a town. The village fair is much like other fairs with gilded gingerbread, and wheels of fortune, and an infinite variety of toys. There is a collection of waxwork figures, a wonderful pony dancing 'Pop goes the Weasel' & a faded and tattered show, from the stage of which a dirty woman was perpetually beating a gong, and a wheezy clown constantly announcing a variety of 'comic and sentimental' performances within & ballad singers warning the young men not to 'kiss the girls at Wickham Fair'. Photographic 'artists' guaranteeing a perfect likeness in five minutes for sixpence; skittle players, full of noise and drink; the great dancing booth crowded. It was a glad sight to see the young merry and joyous; made happy with a few pence – running here and there, full of life and glee – buying a doll, or a whistle, or a penny trumpet. But he did not approve of all his fellow villagers: Men whose mouths are foul with low language, who cannot see beyond a quart pot, and whose lives seem so often given up to drink, and their own degradation. They will spend pounds, and not enjoy themselves in the end like those who don't spend a penny. We could scarcely see one face that indicated refinement or intelligence. There was hardly a man with any inner sources of enjoyment. Will it always be so? Will the day never come when they shall have better amusements presented to them. Will they never be lifted above the slavery of beer, and the companionship of the tap-room?* [J. De Fraine, The autobiography, 1900] By 1995 the pub was a private house called White Gables. (Photograph: W.M. Palmer)

West Wickham – church interior, 1898. The interior of West Wickham church before restoration showing the southern respond of the chancel arch and adjoining part of the nave walls leaning at a dangerous angle. A note on the back of the photograph reads: *Taken in 1898 before the restoration which was completed in 1900 at a cost of £1,236.13.6, when nearly another £100 was spent by friends in church furniture. The church was reopened for worship on 22 February 1900. 5/- was raised by the sale of this photograph.*

DWARFED BY THE GIANT OF WEST WRATTING HILL, players rehearse for Midsummer night's production. The story of how the open-air theatre came into being is told below. Inset: Mr. Gordon Macleod, the producer, and Miss Burrell, the author of the play.—"Standard" Pictures.

West Wratting – mill, 1935. In 1932 Philippa Burrell bought the windmill for £600 – including a cottage, granary and 20 acres of good farming land. *High & isolated she found it a little paradise – and promptly left to study in Paris! She returned in 1934 when she wrote plays and learned about planting and pruning – and all the while the windmill was watching her with its broken sails, cap all out, windows rotten and rain going in. It was an unwelcoming part of the property, and one she used to hide in when the bailiffs called. A millwright gave her an estimate of £100 for repair and to raise the money she studied cookery books and made date cakes which she sold from an old pram on Cambridge market, a picture of the mill fixed to the side. It was an immediate sensation and soon she was selling teas to the hundreds of people who journeyed to see the mill, sitting contentedly on rustic tables in the orchard. After two seasons however she closed the business as the mill was restored. It was not the end of the story; she wrote a play 'The wind and the mill' which was performed by the Festival Theatre Company in the fields around the windmill.* [*Cambridge Standard*, 14 June 1935] The survey contains a few such newspaper cuttings. (Photograph: *Cambridge Standard*)

Westley Waterless – cottages and 'White Horse', 1929. Westley Waterless school was erected in 1873 to accommodate 55 children, but by 1904 Mrs Emma Hands, the schoolmistress, had an average attendance of just 29. A house came with the job: *Alderman Few asked a question as to the condition of a teacher's house at Westley Waterless. The rent appeared to be fixed at £6 per annum. Was the place fit to live in? Mr Fordham said it was a very small house, let to an uncertificated teacher. One woman lived there by herself. There were two living rooms, two bedrooms, a scullery, and an entrance through the schoolroom.* [CDN 6 January 1926] Villagers had their traditional beliefs: *The howling of dogs, the hooting of owls, the flying of a robin into a house, the bringing of certain plants and flowers indoors, the refusal of cats to stay in a sick person's home – all these were thought to be omens of death in a family. The sudden stopping of a watch or clock in a house where one member of the household is seriously ill still means, to some Cambridgeshire people, that the patient will surely die. "Open a grave for one and you'll open it for two", quoted a Westley Waterless woman of 70 in 1960. "I still believe that because it so often comes true".* [E. Porter, Cambridgeshire customs and folklore, 1969] (Photograph: J.H. Bullock)

Weston Colville – back view of cottages, 1929. Weston Colville was the birthplace of the Victorian poet, James Withers. In 'My native village' he described one cottage:

Here in this cot once lived an ancient dame,
Whose pastry through the village spread her fame:
How have I stood and looked with longing eyes
When she displayed her prunes, her cakes, and pies

[J. Withers, Poems upon various subjects, vol.1. 1856] (Photograph: J.H. Bullock)

Weston Green – former inn, 1929. Cottage, formerly an inn at Weston Green; Withers described one such inn:

Here met the village youths on pleasure bent,
And the long-hoarded halfpence freely spent:
In the old kitchen by the chimney wide,
With foaming ale in good stone mugs supplied,
The old folk talked of times when they were young,
And the same songs, year after year, were sung.

[J. Withers, Fairy revels, 1901] (Photograph: J.H. Bullock)

Whaddon – Serf's House, 1921. This house was behind cottages facing the vicarage and had been demolished by 1926. Although the thatch was damaged in 1921 it was still inhabited, as the photograph shows washing on the line. Knee stockings, breeches and ribbons similar to those of Morris Dancers were part of the dress of the Whaddon Whitsun singers whose song was recorded by the BBC in 1956. Some of the words bemoan the behaviour of the young – as every generation has done:

Come all those little children
All in the streets we do meet
All in their playtimes so even and complete.
For how you may hear them lie both curse and swear
Before they do know one word of prayer.

Both young and old both rich and poor give ear
Don't allow your children to lie both curse nor swear.
Pray do not allow them to keep ill company
For that will surely bring them to shame and misery
[K.M. Lambeth, Whaddon WI scrapbook, 1958]

Whittlesey – Market Place, 1934. In 1931 Whittlesey council faced a dilemma: *On the left hand side of the entrance to the old Town Hall is a door studded with nails. At one time it answered the purpose of a town lock-up, but later it was used as a magazine by the old Whittlesey Company of the Cambridgeshire Regiment. In 1914, when they mobilised, they withdrew some thousands of rounds of ammunition, locked up the door and went to the war. The key was lost and the door remained locked from that time until a few weeks ago, when those in authority decided to open it. When they did so all that was found inside was a large bag of blank Martini cartridges from which the bullets had been extracted. The problem of the moment is: What to do with the ammunition now they have found it.* [CDN 26 September 1931] (Photograph: W.M. Palmer)

Whittlesford – Guildhall, 1903. The Guildhall was built early in the 16th century by a village guild, and was for many years the centre of life in the village. *Chimneys were added when it served as a workhouse and the building was later used to house poor people in receipt of a parish allowance. The plaster was removed in 1938 and concrete substituted between the studs. The tenements alongside were removed.* [F.A. Reeve, Victorian and Edwardian Cambridgeshire, 1976] Amongst the village characters was 'Doughy' Ward who *gave away hot cross buns on Maundy Thursday to children who came with their mothers' washing baskets to collect buns for themselves and their neighbours. This same Doughy once made a Yorkshire pudding with his own ingredients and with his own hands (literally) to save a small child, who had spilt the jug of batter on the way to the bakery for communal baking, from getting into trouble.* [Whittlesford Society, Whittlesford recalled, 1977] (Photograph: F.J. Allen)

Whittlesford – electrical cables, 1926. Cables of the Bedfordshire, Cambridgeshire and Huntingdon Electricity Company being erected between Little Shelford and Whittlesford in 1926. Electricity slowly spread to rural villages. In 1946 Miss E.M. Barraud from Little Eversden mused: *Once again we have been told we shall have electricity in the village by the end of the year. The promise has by now become a hardy perennial but so far it has borne no flower. First it was the war, since then it has been labour or materials that nipped it in the bud, but the pylons are marching steadily towards us: if not this year, then next year, sometime. There are times when I would give anything for electricity. Clean safe lighting at the turn of a switch with no danger of a flare up and smoked glass and sooted mantle and a major operation to put things to rights again. A fire for half an hour, and no grate to clean up afterwards, on chilly spring or autumn mornings and evenings. No one in their right mind could fail to appreciate all these things, to say nothing of being rid once and for all of the infinite permeability of paraffin where food is concerned. And yet it will not be all gain when the lamps and stoves are put up on the top shelf and then relegated to the tool shed. I shall miss the not unpleasant faint aroma of burning paraffin wafted through the place while the early morning tea kettle boils, and the soft glow of an oil lamp adds warmth as well as light to the scene.* [E.M. Barraud, Tail Corn, 1946] (Photograph: J.H. Bullock)

Wicken – green, 1929. Wicken village pump: *There has long been a good supply of excellent water in this parish. A time-honoured fountain in the centre of the village seemed almost inexhaustible, but being a long distance from many cottage homes the Parish Council caused to be erected two fresh pumps, east and west of the old one, which have proved a boon most acceptable and available to many of those who had borne the yoke so far before. In an article a few years ago on the Isle of Ely Fenland, Rev. S. Baring-Gould describes the natives as being very morose, and in consequence of the lack of good drinking water, he says people are driven to the public-houses for other beverages. This is news indeed to the writer, whose knowledge of the Fens has extended from the twenties to the nineties, and who has never heard such an imputation cast upon its waters before.* [M. Knowles, History of Wicken, 1902] (Photograph: L. Cobbett)

Wicken Fen. Douglas Reid described Wicken Fen in June 1931: *Sedge Fen lies, as it were, in a wilderness of cultivation, and we can well understand the dread ill the hearts of many at the very suggestion of its possible reclamation. Proposals to drain the fen were actually set afoot over thirty years ago! Let us be thankful that the late Mr. G. H. Verrall, of Newmarket and the National Trust, came to the rescue. There are several reed-fringed pits or pools – old gault and brick pits-that make a pleasant picture, especially when they are bedecked with the white lily and are the resort of moorhen, mallard and teal. Wandering heedlessly in the fen is dangerous. There are those who have fallen into a deep hole and would have been drowned – sunk in the 'moor' – save for a helping hand. Although the surface peat has a thickness in many places of some three feet, there is yielding turf, bog it may be, that descends to reach the gault as much as 16 feet down.* [D.G. Reid, Wicken fen: notes and memories – Cambridge Public Library Record, June 1931] (Photograph: D.G. Reid)

Wicken Fen. Fire ravaged the fen in August 1929; Reid recalled: *I visited the fen immediately after the fire of August 15, 1929. The fire, beaten out by many helpers, some attracted from the Cambridge road by clouds of smoke, was confined to the fen east of the Drainers' Ditch, which it failed to reach. The fire involved 70 to 100 acres of the fen, and much old and rough 'stuff' was destroyed. It brought very clearly to light many regular parallel furrows, and we have little doubt that these are indicative of old peat or turf digging. But let us wander down Sedge Fen Drove to the now large open space that marks the position of the fire. Its effects are still shown by the blackened branches of the bushes – carr – and of a lonely birch tree. But the sedge has made a splendid recovery, and the removal of the burnt carr has appreciably and beneficially widened out what was previously really only a drove. By good chance this unapproved 'cutting' has actually improved the fen.* [D.G. Reid, Wicken fen, June 1931] (Photograph: D.G. Reid)

Wicken Fen – peat industry *c.*1909. Peat was used for fuel. In 1909 there were some 300 men and boys, plus a few women, engaged in the turf industry in Wicken, Burwell and Reach and the turbaries continued until the 1940s. Boys wheeled barrows loaded with peat along planks over drains. *They were compelled to accustom themselves to this balancing act and it took time. To steel them in this enterprise the turf men gave them to understand that should they topple into the drain, barrow, turves and all, they would be compelled to buy a gallon of beer for their workmates. It happened quite often and caused fun more than anger.* [A. Day, Fuel from the fens, 1999] (Photograph: Scott & Wilkinson)

Wicken Fen – peat cutter, *c*.1909. The turves were not only used for burning. *Crude dwellings were once made of them bound in withers with roofs of osiers and reeds. The outer walls would receive a facing of clay to keep the weather out. A cottage pulled down in Lode Lane, Wicken some forty years ago revealed a layer of turves under the roof, each harder than bark. Fred 'Stubby' Bailey had one such shelter at Lapwing. Stubby and his wife Clara produced a big family, but he liked nothing better than to work in solitude. He spent his working life in the turf trade.* [A. Day, Fuel from the fens, 1999] (Photograph: Scott & Wilkinson)

Wilbraham, Great – London Road, 1929. Village life was not always dull: *An article in the London 'Daily News' gives an impression of Great and Little Wilbraham. After a thrilling account of the pursuit of poachers by the squire's foreman, the schoolmaster and ex-Police constable Walls, now a blacksmith, the reporter tells of his experiences in the village bakery. The squire's shepherd, turned 70, can sing 'something wunnerful'. "I can begin singing at six in the morning and finish at ten at night, and never sing the same song twice", he said. "They be old songs and some of 'em ud take a time. 'The Old Cow Shed' takes 20 minutes".* [CDN 9 September 1921] The scene was little altered by 1993. (Photograph: J.H. Bullock)

Wilbraham, Great – windmill, *c*.1894. In his survey of windmills H.C. Hughes commented: *Some mills such as that at Lt Wilbraham are on farms and used only for grinding required on the farm itself. Windmillers are very fond of their mills and often keep them for affection rather than profit. The strain comes when some repairs are necessary which the miller cannot himself cope with. Oakington and Willingham have stopped recently.* [H.C. Hughes, Windmills, 1931 – PCAS vol.31] Great Wilbraham mill was demolished in 1928 and the bricks used to build a bungalow. The figure in the foreground is Harry Sale who was the miller in 1894. [D.Hawkins, The Wilbrahams 1894-1994, 1994] This old photograph was lent by Mr A. Croot of Hinxton watermill and copied by James Bullock in 1930. (Photograph: J.H. Bullock)

Wilbraham, Little – Hawk Mill. Hawk Mill was run together with the windmill and last used in 1937. *The machinery from the old watermill, disused for more than 40 years, was discovered by Chris Hereward during a survey by the Cambridge Society for Industrial Archaeology in 1976. The farmer agreed to donate it to the Cambridge Museum of Technology where is was restored and re-assembled. Chris Hereward managed to transport many of the parts in his Mini van – although the ton-and-a-half main drive shaft had to go by trailer.* [CEN 12 February 1977] (Engraving: J.S. Clarke)

Wilburton – Twentypence Ferry, *c.*1900. A grassy drove linked Wilburton with Cottenham. *Until about 1907 the Old West River was crossed by a type of ferry known as a drawbridge which was attached by chains on either side of the river. After this was removed travellers had to shout for the bargeman, Albert Savige who lived in the cottage across the road from the public house. The punt was almost always on the other side of the river!* [L. Milway, Cottenham in focus. 2002]. There were similar ferries at Lt Thetford, Upware, Overcote & Mepal where floods attracted sightseers in 1903: *Many people travelled to Mepal, some on foot, some on bicycle and others by horse and trap to witness the great expanse of water lying on the Washes. Many hundreds passed over the road by the ferryboat for the novelty as well as from necessity, amongst the passengers being two motor bicycles with trailers. We understand Mr Charles Waters who manages the boat, was able to demand a handsome fee for taking such a modern conveyance across the water* [unidentified cutting, June 1903]. (Photograph: J.H. Bullock)

Wilburton – Twentypence Bridge, 1931. As traffic increased between Cambridge and Ely councillors debated improving the old Aldreth Causeway; but an alternative scheme was preferred: *Chesterton Rural District Council considered the proposed erection of a bridge at Twenty-man's Ferry, near Cottenham. An application was received from Wilburton parish council that the bridge should be erected and the road be put in good repair. It would relieve the traffic from the Ely main road and relieve the congestion which was very acute on that road. They ought to get the feelings of the Cottenham people; the bridge would be a bigger benefit to them more than anybody else.* [CDN 28 October 1927] The scheme was agreed and a new bridge was constructed in place of the ferry in 1931. (Photograph: D.G. Reid)

Wilburton – Burystead, 1926. The Buystead stands largely unchanged, but in 1908 Albert Pell recalled its place in the life of the parish: *We paid our visits to my father's principal tenant at the fine old Burystead House, and a court leet or court baron would then be held there by my father, who was Lord of the Manor, for the admission of copyhold tenants, the receipt of fines, and the adjustment of disputes about encroachment on the ways on which the commoners' cattle grazed. Breaches of the customs of the manor were also brought under notice and stopped, and the appointment made of a very important officer of the manor, the pindar.* [A. Pell, The reminiscences of Albert Pell, 1908] (Photograph: O.H. Jermy)

Willingham – Rod peeling, Cole's Yard. Canon F.J. Bywaters, vicar of Willingham donated a series of early photographs to the Photographic Survey. Rod peeling, usually involving women and children started in April and lasted about one month. The work was done in a rod-peeling yard, such as Cole's Yard, Willingham. *When cut and tied in bundles the rods were brought to the yard and put into a big clamp where they were watered at night. To peel the rods you drew them through a clave and then separated them into different sizes. The rods, as they were peeled, were dropped by the peeler in stacks of small, medium and large lengths. Family parties often divided the work between them. After being dried they went to the basket maker.* [H. Painter, Sutton in the Isle, 1980]

Willingham – kitchen at Ivy House. George Barton of Willingham celebrated his 100th birthday in August 1937; he had lived in the village all his life. *"When I began work at twelve we were treated worse than slaves. I was 'let out' by my parents to a farmer and my wages were a pound a year. It wasn't enough money to buy my clothes with. During the second year I was paid 30s. for the year's work. I had to get up between four and five in the morning and didn't finish till late. I married at 24 on a wage of 9s a week and on that we brought up a family of eight children. Seven on them I've buried: only one's alive now. We used to grow our own vegetables – I had ten poles of land when we were married. And we used to get corn. Then from the flour the womenfolk used to make bread – three loaves out of a stone of flour. But it was a hard struggle. I've known men who have had to steal to live. I worked till I was over 80".* [CDN 13 August 1937]

Wimblington – derelict cottage, 1932. Wimblington has a few houses of distinction, including Manor House and Addison House but it was these cottages at Triangle Corner that caught the attention of the Society's photographer. *At one time the village had many tradesmen and was self sufficient – cobbler, carpenters, butcher, baker, grocer, greengrocer, milkman, blacksmith and dressmaker. There was a post office and cycle repair shop, an undertaker and Mr E. Bradshaw, a carpenter who made the coffins for people buried by the parish. There was always a lady to attend births and deaths, the best remembered being Granny Bradshaw and Mrs Cornish. Now we have lost most of these and the railway but there is still a post office, two general stores, a butcher and a newsagent.* [Cambridgeshire Federation of Women's Institutes, The Cambridgeshire village book, 1989] More recently members of the Antiquarian Society have been following the discoveries across the fields at Stonea where a major archaeological excavation has taken place on the site of a Roman camp. (Photograph: E.B. Haddon)

Wimpole – Hall, *c.*1900. Wimpole Hall was begun *c.*1640 for Sir Thomas Chicheley and subsequently remodelled. The extensions to the East and West wings in the Italianate style, added in expectation of a visit by Queen Victoria, were removed in 1952. The Revd H.H. McNeice recalled: *The last Earl who lived at Wimpole was a great sporting gentleman, with mutton-chop whiskers. It was during his life that much of the property was dissipated. Once, many years ago I drove to the kitchen entrance of Wimpole Hall with old Isaac Waldock who was selling cherries. The only thing I remember about it is the number of domestics, grooms and pedlars hanging about with nothing to do. But the Earl was not altogether unmindful of the waste which was going on. One day he passed a large swill tub and, poking his stick into it he found a large lump. This turned out to be salt beef, which smelt all right, so the Earl said to a servant "Just wash that meat with hot water and I will have some of that for my lunch".* [H.H. McNeice, The neighbourhood of Melbourn, 1925] During World War Two the park grounds housed an American military hospital and in May 1947 the Wimpole Park Teachers Training College was established. In 1976 the Hall was left to the National Trust.

Wisbech – boats, 1856. The Cambridge Antiquarian Society did not cover Wisbech in any detail, but they did acquire a number of photographs taken by Samuel Smith who pioneered the use of photography to record the streets and scenes of the fenland capital between 1852 and 1864. He often set up his camera on its tripod in the same place to obtain 'before and after' views of a particular area that was undergoing redevelopment. Because of the long exposure needed people who passed in front of his lens would not appear on the negative. But the river on which the town depended for its prosperity presented other problems: The tall-masted ships would sway on the tide – so Samuel achieved his clear images of a bustling port by waiting for low water. *In this view of the Nene at Horseshoe Corner on 30 August 1856 the boats are the Amelia which had arrived from Quebec with a cargo of timber, the Cragger and Vigilant.* [M. Millward & B. Coe, Victorian townscape, 1974] (Photograph: S. Smith)

Wisbech St Mary – pound and lock up, Tholomas Drove, 1931. Tholomas Drove is a hamlet of Wisbech St Mary; its facilities included a Mission Chapel, Primitive Methodist Chapel, a lock-up and pound. It was not only the pindar who profited from recalcitrant animals as John Parrin recalled: *"My father was a bit of a dealer. He would buy and sell anything if he thought he could earn from it. He also would do the work for other people who had land as most land workers also had land – about half an acre to about four or five acres – which they worked after they had completed their day's work for their bosses. He would also school dodgy horses – those that were prone to shying or running away which never made the market value. He would have them working. Someone might see and want to by it. He would sell it, but probably have it back in a fortnight because they could not work it (it would be for less money of course)".* [L. Faulkner, The light of other days, 1998] (Photograph: J.H. Bullock)

Witcham – street, 1929. Like all villages, Witcham men played their part in World War One: *At a special service held in Witcham Parish Church the Bishop of Ely dedicated a handsome brass memorial tablet, upon which was inscribed the names of the fifteen men of Witcham who gave their lives in the Great War. The Bishop asked that the memories of those who had fallen should always be revered, and that their sacrifices should not be in vain. It was our duty to keep the villages pure, sober, and Christian, and so be worthy of the lives which had been given.* [CDN 9 June 1922]

Witchford church – *c.*1907. Witchford church was restored between 1851 and 1887 and additional repairs to the roof and tower were completed in 1923 at a cost of £1,100. The chancel and nave were re-roofed in 1989 as part of a major restoration project that also saw floodlighting installed. In 1943 the peace of the quiet village was shattered when it was invaded by over 2,500 Irish labourers who started to demolish four farms and six farm cottages to construct a new airfield. *Lorries by the hundred moved through the village, while draglines and excavators were used to clear the site. Stretham station played a key role during construction, carrying up to 500 tons of brick rubble from London at a time. This hardcore was then rolled out and used as the base for the runways, making them at least 8 inches (20 cm.) thick. A water supply was constructed from the main Ely water works to a tower on the airfield site. Most of the messes, quarters and communal sites were constructed just north of the village. They included shops, among them grocers, barbers, tailors and shoemakers. The huts that the Irish workmen had lived in were then converted to airmen's quarters. The biggest problem of all for the villagers, especially during the winter of 1943, was mud. Lorries continued trundling through the village, turning the main street into a mud bath, in some places up to six inches deep! But when everything dried out in March, dust storms became the issue!* [M. Chorlton, Airfield focus: Mepal and Witchford, 2001] After the war the bombers departed and the airfield was released back for civilian use. It has become an industrial park and includes a museum dedicated to Witchford and Mepal airfields.

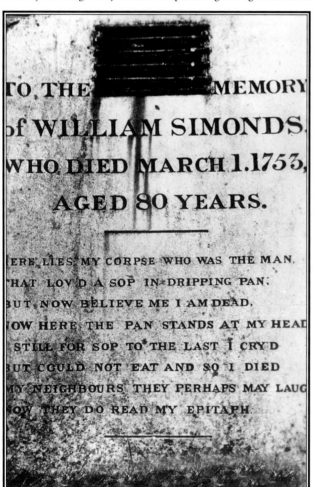

Wood Ditton – tombstone, 1929. Considerable interest was aroused in medical circles by details of a trance at Wood Ditton in 1899: *After the young lady had lain for 40 hours the doctors decided to try the effect of sudden shocks. She was taken from her bed and placed across some chairs over a bath. So rigid was her body that nothing was required to support the space between the chairs. A large can of ice-cold water was procured and one of the doctors, standing on a chair, directed a stream of water on to her face. The douches of water continued until she had apparently been fully aroused.* [CDN 14 September 1899] But no medical skill could save William Simonds, whose fate in 1753 is a warning to all:

Here lies my corpse who was the man
That loved a sop in a dripping pan:
But now believe me I am dead,
Now here the pan stands at my head.
Still for sop to the last I cry'd
But could not eat and so I died.
My neighbours they perhaps may laugh
Now they do read my epitaph

The men and women who compiled the Cambridge Antiquarian Society's photographic record have also passed away, but the photographs they took remain a lasting memorial to them and their project to record a county that was vanishing before their lenses. (Photograph: W.M. Palmer)

THE FENLAND PHOTOGRAPHS OF
DOUGLAS GAVIN REID

OUGLAS GAVIN REID undertook an important photographic survey of the fens, including 128 lantern slides and over 500 negatives. These were presented to Cambridge Antiquarian Society by his widow and are now split between the Cambridgeshire County Record Office and the Cambridgeshire Collection.

During the interwar years the drainage system was in crisis as the lack of maintenance during wartime hit home. In 1919 the combination of a rapid thaw of snow and rain combined to produce the worst flood within the memory of the oldest inhabitant. Other floods in 1924 and 1928 prompted fears that the fens could return to primeval conditions. They were followed by more serious breaches in 1936, 1937 and 1939. Denver Sluice was enlarged in 1925, the 10-Mile river was dredged and new diesel pumps were installed but coal supplies for the steam pumping engines were hit by railway strikes. In 1930 the Land Drainage Act established Catchment Boards. All this was expensive. Farmers resented the drainage rates necessary for improvements and refused to pay.

Agricultural workers joined a general wave of discontent, striking for better wages. By 1925 farmers were warning that 50 percent of arable farming would be ruined in 12 months. The area under agriculture shrank, farms became impoverished and equipment rusted in the fields. By 1933 it was described as the worst agricultural depression in living memory.

Some redress came in the form of a new crop: sugar beet. A factory opened at Ely in 1925 to process 1200 tons of beet a day brought by 30 barges unloading at the quayside. Gordon Fowler was transport manager for the Ely Sugar Beet factory and knew the area intimately. He inspected items dredged up from the rivers and read papers to the Cambridge Antiquarian Society describing ancient watercourses now only visible as roddons. His work cast entire new light on the fenland landscape. He was also a keen archaeologist and became part of the Fenland Research Committee, a pioneering group of Cambridge University academics who undertook major archaeological excavations throughout the fens.

Aldreth excavation, Old West River wash, 1930. The causeway from Rampton to Haddenham (page 120), was believed to have been the site of a major battle between William the Conqueror and Hereward the Wake. In August 1930 T.C. Lethbridge led an archaeological excavation seeking for evidence of weapons lost in the fen. Trenches were cut around the bridge and on the line of the causeway. Nothing whatever was found to suggest this was the battlefield though scraps of pottery, animal bones and a quantity of coal was discovered, suggesting that sea-coal had been landed at the hithe. [T.C. Lethbridge. An attempt to discover the site of the battle of Aldreth – PCAS vol.31]

Holme Fen pole, 1929. Some man-made artefacts actually rose from the ground. When Whittlesey Mere was drained John Lawrence took a cast-iron column removed from the Crystal Palace during its dismantling in Hyde Park and drove it into the underlying clay, leaving the top flush with the ground level as it was in 1851. As the peat dried it shrank, revealing more and more of the column. In June 1929 Reid photographed it using his wife as a guide to its height. By 1955 the soil had dropped 12 feet.

Fossil trees by Monks Lode looking towards Ramsey St Mary's, June 1929. Other natural artefacts also surfaced. His wife poses on fossilised remains of the forests that formerly covered the fenland basin which were exposed as the fen peat wasted away. Monks Lode was dug at the end of the 12th century to convey blocks of stone from the quarry at Barnack to build Ramsey Abbey.

Burwell waterside. The original Burwell Lode was improved as part of the drainage system along the chalk ridge about 1685. *The building of the new lode permitted a marked change in trade and prospects for North Street and Newnham, where the existing common hythe was probably extended. All along North Street small basins and canals were built from The Weirs and Catchwater drains up to the properties aligning the western side of the street By the nineteenth century trade was sufficient for the establishment of a toll collector's office in the hythe. Fen products were exempt from toll but coal charged at four pence per ton. Clunch and timber were also carried.* [W. Franklin, Burwell: the history of a fen-edge village, 2005]

Welches Dam, 5 June 1929. The Forty Foot Drain was constructed in 1651 from near Ramsey to the Old Bedford River at Welches Dam. During the floods of 1937 water began seeping through the bank of the Old Bedford between Welches Dam and Welney. Sack cloths were staked to the top and allowed to sink into the river to reinforce the earth banks. Boys from Letchworth School were amongst the volunteers, though they had to be sent away by policemen who were worried that they would be overcome with fatigue and exhaustion. Major work on a new pumping station started in 1946 but was badly damaged in the 1947 floods and had to be reconstructed.

Bedford washes at Welney, 1929. At Welches Dam one can cross onto the Hundred Foot Washes. This vast area of land between the two Bedford Rivers provides a rich grazing area for cattle and horses when not flooded. It is a peaceful, lonely place, with wildfowl reserves at Purls Bridge and Welney.

Borough Fen duck decoy. Borough Fen decoy near Peakirk is also a noiseless retreat, no gun can be fired within a mile of the place. But it was not a safe place for wildfowl. *It comprises a pool from which several ditches or pipes curve away, narrowing as they get further out with the far end covered in nets. About forty tame ducks were kept on the open water which attracted other wild fowl to this peaceful place. Their attention was caught by a dog which appeared on the side of a pipe and the wild ducks swam over to investigate. Then the dog appeared again a bit farther down – and the ducks followed. This was repeated several times until the birds were well down the ditch, where it got narrower and was covered by the nets. Then the decoyman jumped out behind them; the frightened birds tried to take off but flew into the nets and were trapped. Duck could be taken anytime between June and October and teal and widgeon between then and March. 200 dozen duck could be taken in a week and sent down to Leadenhall Market.* [Fenland Notes and Queries volume 4, 1898–1900]

Salters Lode & Denver Sluice, 15 May 1929. Denver Sluice is the lynchpin of the drainage scheme executed by Cornelius Vermuyden in the mid-1600s. It is here that the Great Ouse and New Bedford combine. They are joined by the Old Bedford River further downstream, from which this picture is taken. The sluice was built across the Great Ouse and is opened at low tide to allow the pent-up river waters to reach the sea but closed to divert the incoming tide down the New Bedford river.

Brownshill staunch. The tide flows up the New Bedford as far as Brownshill Staunch on the Great Ouse midway between Earith and Overcote. This was constructed in the 1830s in order to raise the level of the river sufficiently to enable boats to pass over the shoals which were an impediment to navigation. By 1948 constant flooding had resulted in the decay of the foundations of the Boat Inn and the building was breaking up. It was demolished and replaced with a hut for the use of the sluice-keeper. The old manually-operated sluice gates have now been replaced by new electric guillotine sluices which are less picturesque but essential to allow free passage of floodwater.

Old West dredging, June 1929. The silting up of river beds presents a major problem. Draglines such as this Rushton working on the Old West River in June 1929 were essential in removing mud from the bottom of the channels and deepening ditches. Such dredging often threw out pottery, sword blades and other archaeological evidence that enabled Major Gordon Fowler to produce his assessment of the dates of the fenland rivers which he read in papers to the Cambridge Antiquarian Society in 1932 and 1933. [G. Fowler, Fenland Waterways, past and present – PCAS vols 33 & 34]

Roding the New South Eau, 15 May 1929. Constant work is also needed to keep channels such as the New South Eau, south of Crowland, clear. 'Roding' is the cutting back of the reeds growing on the bank while 'snickelling' involved pairs of men on either side of the drain using scythe blades fixed together on chains to cut down the underwater weeds that can restrict the flow of water. Such work demanded skilled workers: *They had to know how to use quite a number of tools. A good toolman was expected to turn his hand to almost any kind of work. A gang of men worked together as one unit with one leading man called the ganger who negotiated the price for the work to be done. If he was roding ditches he would need a roding scythe, stick and rake – which would cost him about three day's wages – and perhaps a two-tined fork and hatchet – three more day's work. After the First World War machinery came in and did a lot of the work that had been done by hand. The days of the toolmen were past. A lot of them were crippled or maimed for life. Some tried to carry on with croaky chests but modern machinery soon took their place. They were soon forgotten and so passed out a noble hardworking set of men.* [E. Wells, The fens as I saw them, 1976]

Ely – Roswell pits. Maintaining or 'puddling' the river banks requires a sticky Kimmeridge clay. *Puddling consists of opening the tops of the bank three or four feet deep and inserting strong clay or gault; the heavy particles sink to the base of the bank, making the seal or bottom firm and solid and preventing the soakage of water through the bank, which the porous nature of the fen soil had previously rendered almost unavoidable.* [S. Wells, The history of the drainage of… Bedford Level, 1830]. The Bedford Level Corporation had five places for obtaining this: two at Whittlesey, one near Chatteris, Branghill Pits near Sutton and the Roswell Pits near Ely.

Bardney beet factory, Lincolnshire. Sugar beet factories were constructed alongside rivers. The growth of the sugar beet industry owed much to Cambridge University Department of Agriculture whose experiments established that the crop could be exploited commercially. A processing factory was built in Norfolk in 1912 and others were constructed elsewhere. One of the first was at Ely where it was officially opened by the Minister of Agriculture in October 1925. It marked an important milestone in the development of agriculture at a time of depression. More than two acres of buildings were constructed on the 66-acre site. Once the factory was up and running it employed about 500 men, providing comparatively well-paid work for local people at a time of hardship.

Towing barges of sugar beet. The beet factory had its own railway sidings together with a riverside frontage with unloading berths provided for 30 factory-owned barges collecting the beet from riverside fields and towed by tug to the quayside. However, this caused problems: farmers erected a number of shoots on the banks of the Ten Mile River and the Wissey for loading sugar beet into the barges. But in so doing they weakened the banks, adding to the flood dangers. Then when the beet was loaded an amount of mud fell into the rivers clogging them up. This problem was not confined to fen fields: by December 1928 so much mud and refuse from Ely Sugar Beet Factory was clogging up the river that tugs could not get through even with no boats in tow, except on a channel ploughed day after day. The water was being held up towards Cambridge causing a serious danger of flooding while the whole of the river between Ely and Denver Sluice had a thin coating of slime all over it and was the consistency of a mud-pie. [CDN, 21 December 1928]

Stretham engine. The continual struggle to maintain the efficiency of the fenland pumping engines saw the substitution of diesel pumps for the steam pumping engines that had been installed in the 1830s. In many cases the old technology was scrapped, but at Stretham the steam beam engine was retained and is now preserved.

Nordelph old drainage mill. A few reminders of the previous generation of wind-powered drainage pumps are to be seen throughout the fenland; this former mill at Nordelph has been converted into a house. Reid photographed a number of drainage mills before they were destroyed. They include those at Barway*, Benwick*, Ely* and Soham* where he recorded the last of the great drainage mills, demolished in 1948 and a group of mills in Middle Fen Drove.

Soham Shade Mill. Another drainage mill was moved in the 1830s and converted to grind corn. The Soham Shade mill, a small hexagonal structure with a yellow brick base, was working when photographed by Rex Wailes in 1925. It went out of use a few years later, then stood derelict for 50 years but has now been repaired and still remains. [R.D. Stevens. Cambridgeshire windmills and watermills, 1985]

THE CAMBRIDGESHIRE WINDMILLS SURVEY, 1926–1933

'WINDMILLS ARE disappearing so fast that in many parts of the country they are a forgotten race. Some day antiquarians will be examining and digging in mounds, having quite forgotten that they were the mounds of old windmills made to raise them a little above the surrounding land', reported Henry Castree Hughes in a paper presented to the Cambridge Antiquarian Society in November 1928. [H.C. Hughes, Windmills in Cambridgeshire and the Isle of Ely – PCAS vol.31]

Together with J.H. Bullock, C.W. Smith and Rex Wailes he set about making a record of the windmills then existing throughout Cambridgeshire and the Isle of Ely. The survey was concluded, still incomplete, in October 1933 and the pictures are kept together in a separate collection now housed in the Cambridgeshire Collection.

The oldest mill at Bourn had been out of commission for some six years, its sails having been smashed in a gale in 1925, finishing its working life. But fears that it would be lost were dispelled when it was acquired by the Cambridge Preservation Society who have continued to preserve it. Many others were derelict.

The number of mills actually working was growing less every year. The long irregular hours needed to make the most of windy weather and the long spells of enforced idleness were a great difficulty without some auxiliary power. Some millers, however, were still making wheat flour including Mr Lawrence of Stretham, who then kept quite a good business going.

Hughes' paper identified the various types of mill. Those already illustrated in the main village sequence are indicated by asterisks.

Post mills

The earliest was the post mill where the whole structure was pivoted on the top of a big central post. A long tail beam projected from the mill to the ground so it could be turned to face the wind. This type of mill survived with very little change from the 13th to the 19th centuries.

Among the post mills surveyed were those at Bourn*, Chishill*, Fenstanton, Great Gransden, Madingley* and Six Mile Bottom*.

The mill at **Great Gransden** was photographed in 1914 when it was derelict but cared for. The date of 1674 is carved on one of the beams. It ceased working regularly in the early 1900s though William Webb operated it intermittently until his death in 1911. It was subsequently owned for a while by the exiled Queen of Yugoslavia and her son, King Peter. In 1950 it was offered to Huntingdonshire County Council, who accepted it reluctantly, and in 1962 repairs were carried out. It transferred to Cambridgeshire County Council at local government reorganisation in 1974 when it was again in need of restoration estimated to cost £26,000. With the aid of various grants the council employed an Essex millwright to repair it, straightening out the badly contorted buck and adding new boarding. It is now open to the public. [Robert Hardwick, Gransden windmill – Cambridgeshire Family History Society Journal, February 1975] (Photograph: J.H. Bullock)

The mill at **Fenstanton** was also in a derelict state when photographed in 1925. This one did not survive. Ralph Warboys was given the opportunity of rescuing the central post but it proved too heavy an object and, like the rest of the structure, it was demolished. (Photograph: L. Cobbett)

Smock Mills

In smock mills only the top of the mill turns to the wind, the lower part being usually built of brick or stone with three or four floors of working space. Among those in Cambridgeshire were Ashley, Bluntisham, Fordham*, Fulbourn*, Soham Hardfield and Shade mills, Stapleford*, Swaffham Prior*, West Wratting* and Willingham.

Ashley mill, standing high on a hill near Dalham, was still working when photographed in 1928. (Photograph: J.H. Bullock)

Woodend Mill, **Bluntisham.** The first mention of a windmill in **Bluntisham** was in 1277 when William the miller was tenant. The village was devastated by a hurricane in September 1741. *It began exactly at 12 o'clock and lasted about 13 minutes. All the barns in the parish except those that were full of corn quite up to the top were blown flat upon the ground; the dwelling houses escaped by a miracle; there were not above a dozen blown down out of near a hundred. The Alehouse was levelled to the ground but by good luck not a soul in it. One poor miller, who went in to his mill to secure it against the storm, was blown over and crushed to death betwixt the stones and one of the large beams. All the mills in the county were blown down.* Bluntisham Town Mill was also damaged in a later gale: *the sails were wrenched from their bearings and left swinging, so they were considered to be unsafe. Men were sent with saw, axe and rope to pull the sails down.* It was said to be haunted and on certain nights the miller would not stop there alone. After standing derelict for some years it was pulled down in 1899. From its site one could see 20 other windmills. One of these was the Woodend Mill which was built between 1824 and 1835. It had an early form of brick tower and a boat shaped cap. It was disused by 1899 and pulled down in 1926 [C.F. Tebbutt, Bluntisham-cum-Earith. 1941] (Photograph: C.W Smith)

Cattell's mill at **Willingham** is the largest smock mill in the county. It has an octagonal base of vertically built brick with a date of 1828 carved in stone over the door. It ceased working after World War Two and was badly damaged in May 1979: *Lightning struck Willingham windmill and started a fire in straw round the base of the 150-year-old mill. It came during a sudden thunderstorm and one terrific thunderclap shook doors and windows all around the village. But it was not until two hours later than a passer-by noticed the charred and smouldering wood of the sail and raised the alarm. Mr Ray Cattell, aged 73, who owns the mill which has been in his family for generations, managed to douse most of the fire at the base but it took firemen with a turntable ladder to tackle the still smouldering sail about 60 feet above the ground. They had to remove about a third of the sail because it had been weakened by the lightning. [CEN 23 May 1979].* It has been restored and is still in working order. (Photograph: C.W.Smith)

Tower Mills
Among the brick-built tower mills photographed were those at Arrington, Barrington, Haddenham, Manea, Pymoor*, Swaffham Prior*, Thorney, Trumpington* and Whittlesey.

Arrington was an elegant mill with arched windows and an ogee cap painted in red, white and blue segments. Sadly this was blown off in 1926 and it was then roofed over and used as a store. (Photograph: C.W. Smith)

Barrington had a windmill erected by William Totnam about 1600 but the existing mill was finished on 17 September 1822, the date being inscribed on its first floor. It was built of clunch ashlar and had four floors. The mill was the scene of a riotous disturbance in 1883; Edmund Cross had been directed to secure the mill and prevent removal of stock: *I drove to the windmill… Albert Prime then came up with about 30 or 40 more men, all more or less the worse for drink. I had some conversation as to a horse and cart laden with grist coming out of the mill-yard and asked him to stop the riot that was going on. I shut the gate and made gestures to some of the men and they at once came and seized my trap and tried to put it in the ditch. I got out and was truck with a long pole… a heavy piece of iron struck me on the chest and there was a general threatening of 'Kill the…'* The men were fined. [Cambridge Chronicle 6 January 1883]. It was derelict when photographed in 1928, lost its machinery during World War Two and was converted into domestic accommodation in the 1960s when a bungalow was built adjoining it. (Photograph: Rex Wailes)

Manea mill had six sails when it was photographed in 1914. One blew off in a gale but this was not disastrous since the opposite sail could also be removed and the mill continue but with less power. A six-sailed mill could be balanced with four, three or even two sails and became quite popular after the 1850s. The Manea mill was later badly damaged by fire and reduced to only two storeys with a corrugated iron roof. It had disappeared entirely by 1930. (Photograph: J.H. Bullock)

Another six-sailed mill was that on the east side of the Crowland Road at **Thorney**. It carries the inscription HFG 1787 but was probably heightened sometime afterwards. It had six sails probably fixed to an iron cross on the windshaft, an ogee cap with a gallery, a tall finial and an eight-bladed fantail. Inside its six storeys were three pairs of over-driven stones. George Kidd of Wisbech repaired a serious crack in the tower about 1900 but it was soon out of use. It was ruined when photographed on 2 May 1931. [R.D. Stevens, Cambridgeshire windmills and watermills.1985] (Photograph: J.H.Bullock)

Whittlesey had 13 windmills in operation in the late 1800s. Until 1870 nearly all the inhabitants fed on their own home-grown grain which was converted into flour by the local windmills. G.H. Fletcher, a Whittlesey miller wrote to H.C. Hughes on 9 December 1929, *My mill is the only one left in the parish. It was rebuilt about 70 years ago. We bought it in October 1924 and had it repaired at a cost of £135, which made it a very fine mill. Unfortunately yesterday the fan was struck off by a violent thunderstorm. Had this not happened it would probably have lasted about 20 to 30 years. Tourists are often seen photographing the mill and sometimes ask to be shown over.* Mr Fletcher wrote again in April 1931, *The mill struck by lightning was repaired and working again by the middle of January 1930, the cost was about £75. It is a very good mill and the only one left.* (Photograph: J.H. Bullock, May 1931)

Since the survey was concluded many mills have vanished but others, then derelict, have been restored and attract photographers today just as they did the enthusiasts of the Cambridge Antiquarian Society over 70 years ago.